George R.R. Martin

story

William

e

Daniel Abraham

sequential adaptation

Mark Seifert

creative director

Mike Wolfer

artwork & covers

Jim Kuhoric

managing editor

Digikore Studios

colors

David Marks

director of events

Kurt Hathaway

letters

Ariana Osborne

production assistant

Skin Trade Volume 1. June 2014. Published by Avatar Press, Inc., 515 N. Century Blvd. Rantoul, IL 61866. ©2014 Avatar Press, Inc. Skin Trade and all related properties TM & ©2014 George R.R. Martin. All characters as depicted in this story are over the age of 18. The stories, characters, and institutions mentioned in this magazine are entirely fictional. Printed in Canada.

www.avatarpress.com   twitter @avatarpress   facebook.com/avatarpresscomics

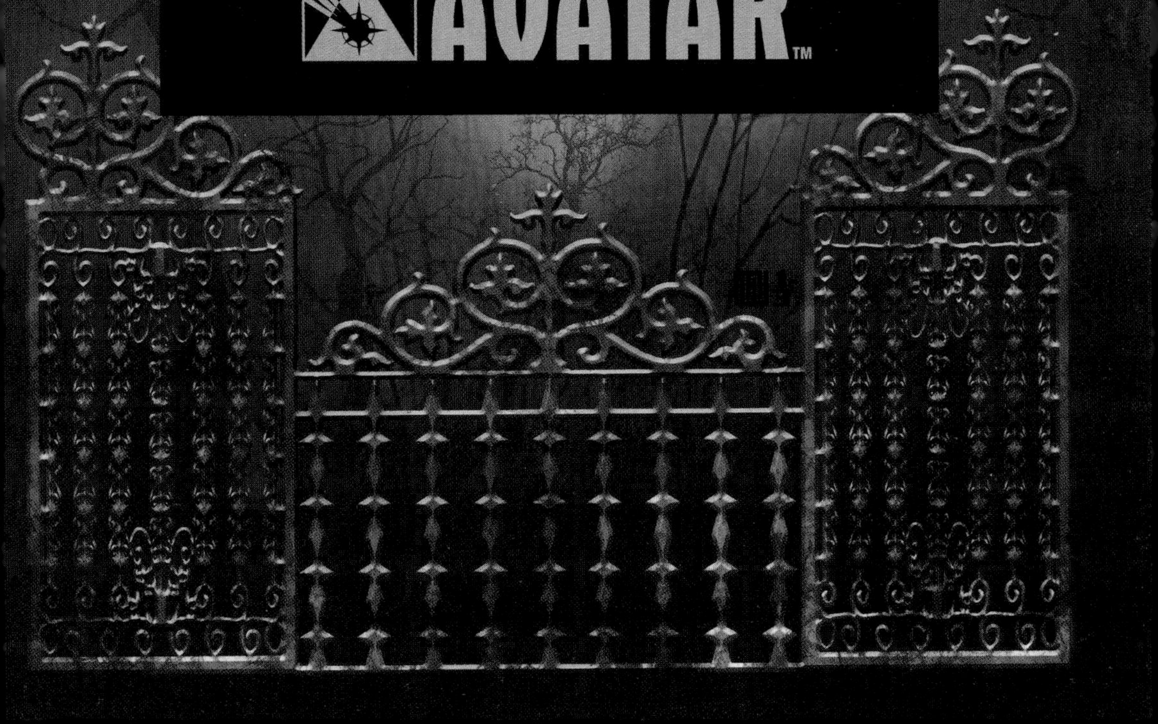

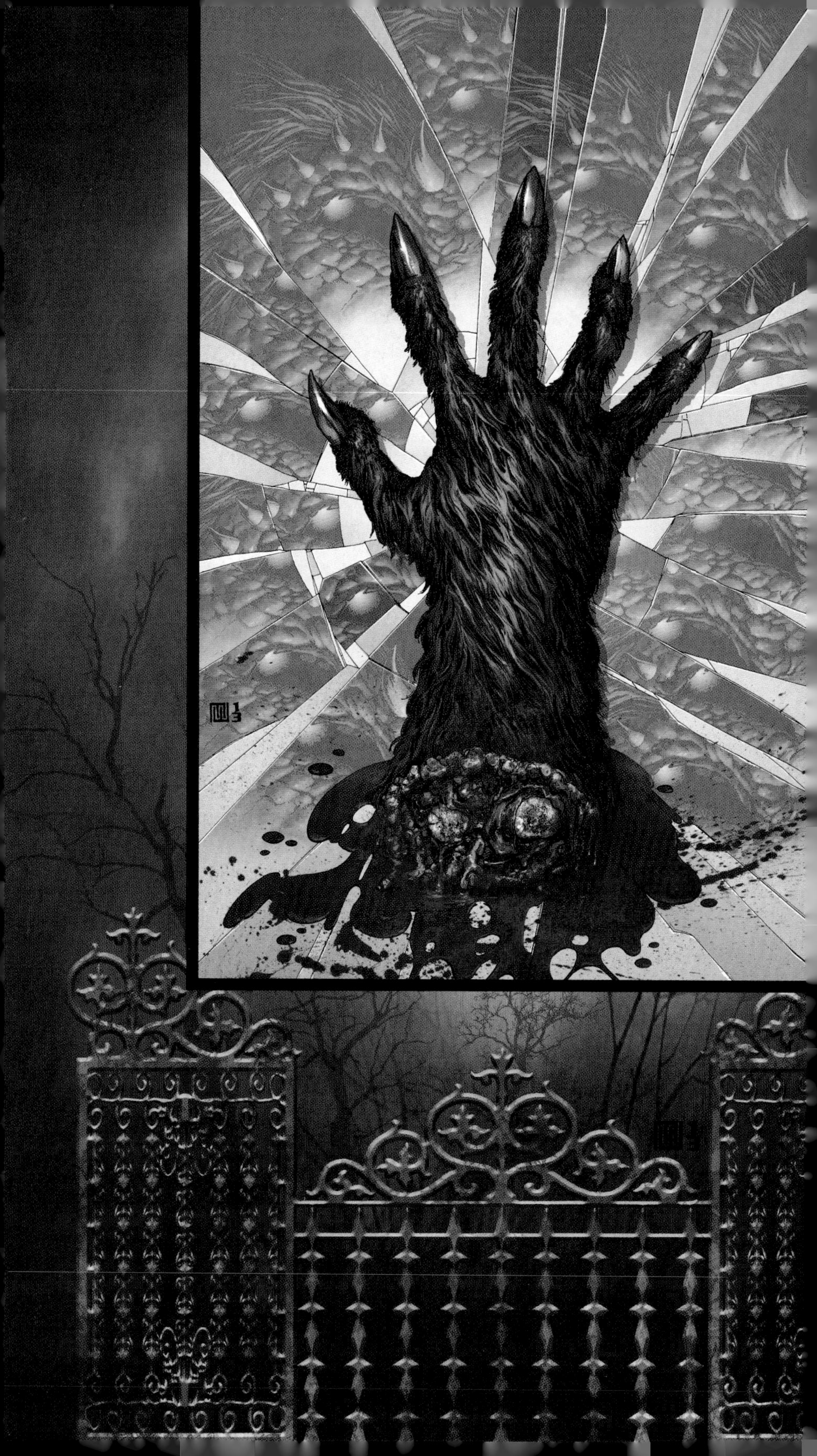

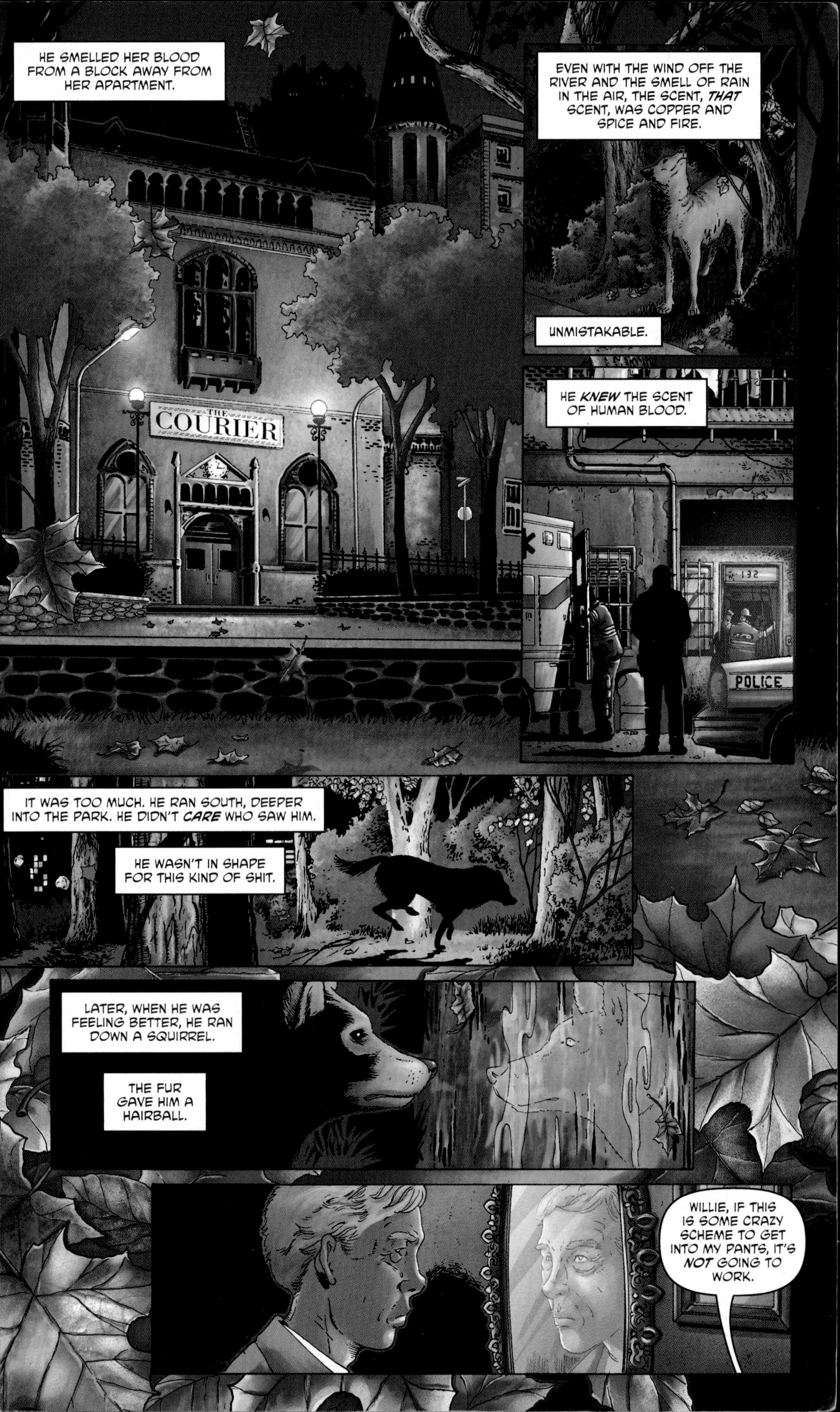
HE SMELLED HER BLOOD FROM A BLOCK AWAY FROM HER APARTMENT.
THE COURIER
EVEN WITH THE WIND OFF THE RIVER AND THE SMELL OF RAIN IN THE AIR, THE SCENT, *THAT* SCENT, WAS COPPER AND SPICE AND FIRE.
UNMISTAKABLE.
HE *KNEW* THE SCENT OF HUMAN BLOOD.
132
POLICE
IT WAS TOO MUCH. HE RAN SOUTH, DEEPER INTO THE PARK. HE DIDN'T *CARE* WHO SAW HIM.
HE WASN'T IN SHAPE FOR THIS KIND OF SHIT.
LATER, WHEN HE WAS FEELING BETTER, HE RAN DOWN A SQUIRREL.
THE FUR GAVE HIM A HAIRBALL.
WILLIE, IF THIS IS SOME CRAZY SCHEME TO GET INTO MY PANTS, IT'S *NOT* GOING TO WORK.

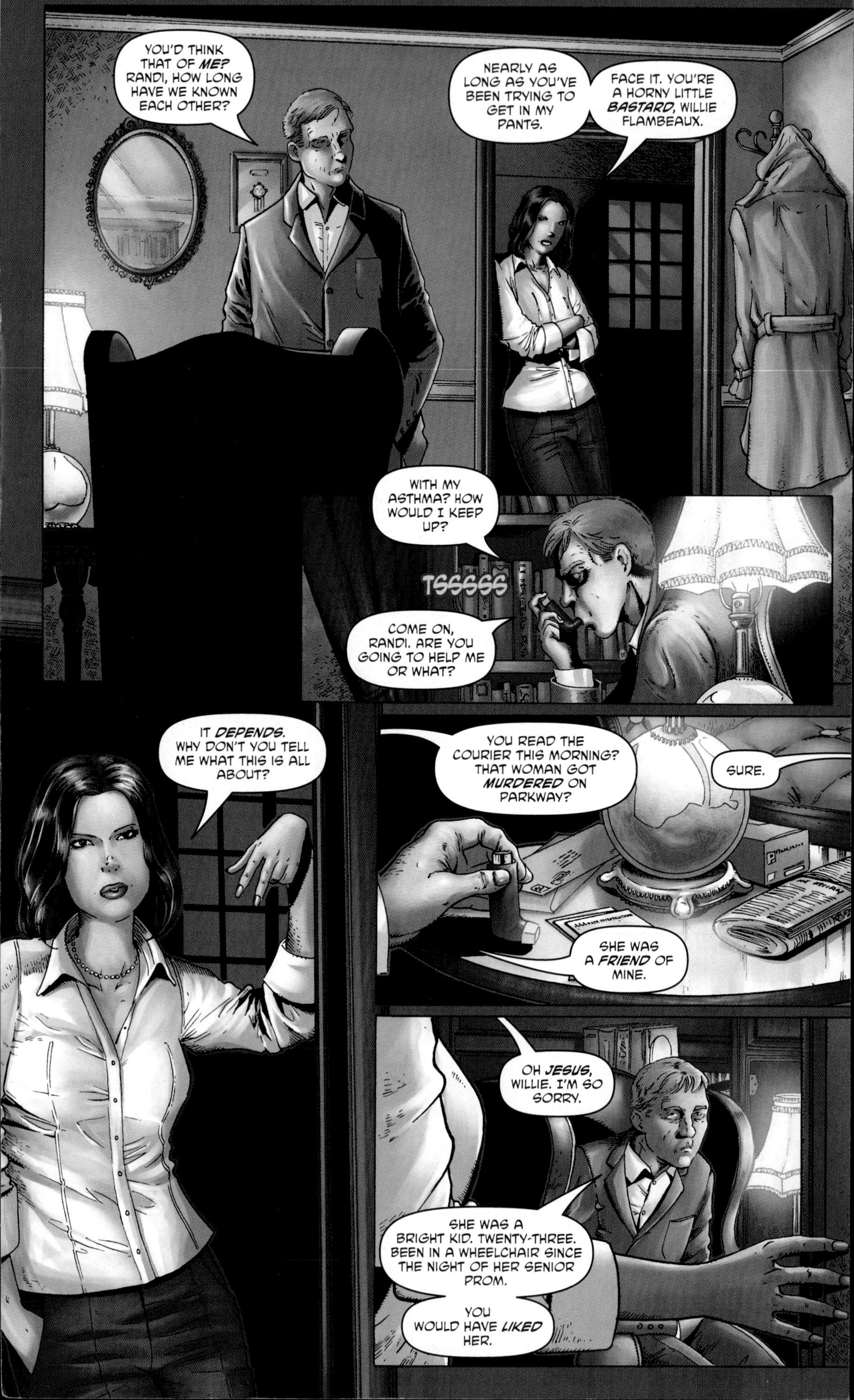
YOU'D THINK THAT OF ME? RANDI, HOW LONG HAVE WE KNOWN EACH OTHER?
NEARLY AS LONG AS YOU'VE BEEN TRYING TO GET IN MY PANTS.
FACE IT. YOU'RE A HORNY LITTLE BASTARD, WILLIE FLAMBEAUX.
WITH MY ASTHMA? HOW WOULD I KEEP UP?
TSSSSS
COME ON, RANDI. ARE YOU GOING TO HELP ME OR WHAT?
IT DEPENDS. WHY DON'T YOU TELL ME WHAT THIS IS ALL ABOUT?
YOU READ THE COURIER THIS MORNING? THAT WOMAN GOT MURDERED ON PARKWAY?
SURE.
SHE WAS A FRIEND OF MINE.
OH JESUS, WILLIE. I'M SO SORRY.
SHE WAS A BRIGHT KID. TWENTY-THREE. BEEN IN A WHEELCHAIR SINCE THE NIGHT OF HER SENIOR PROM.
YOU WOULD HAVE LIKED HER.

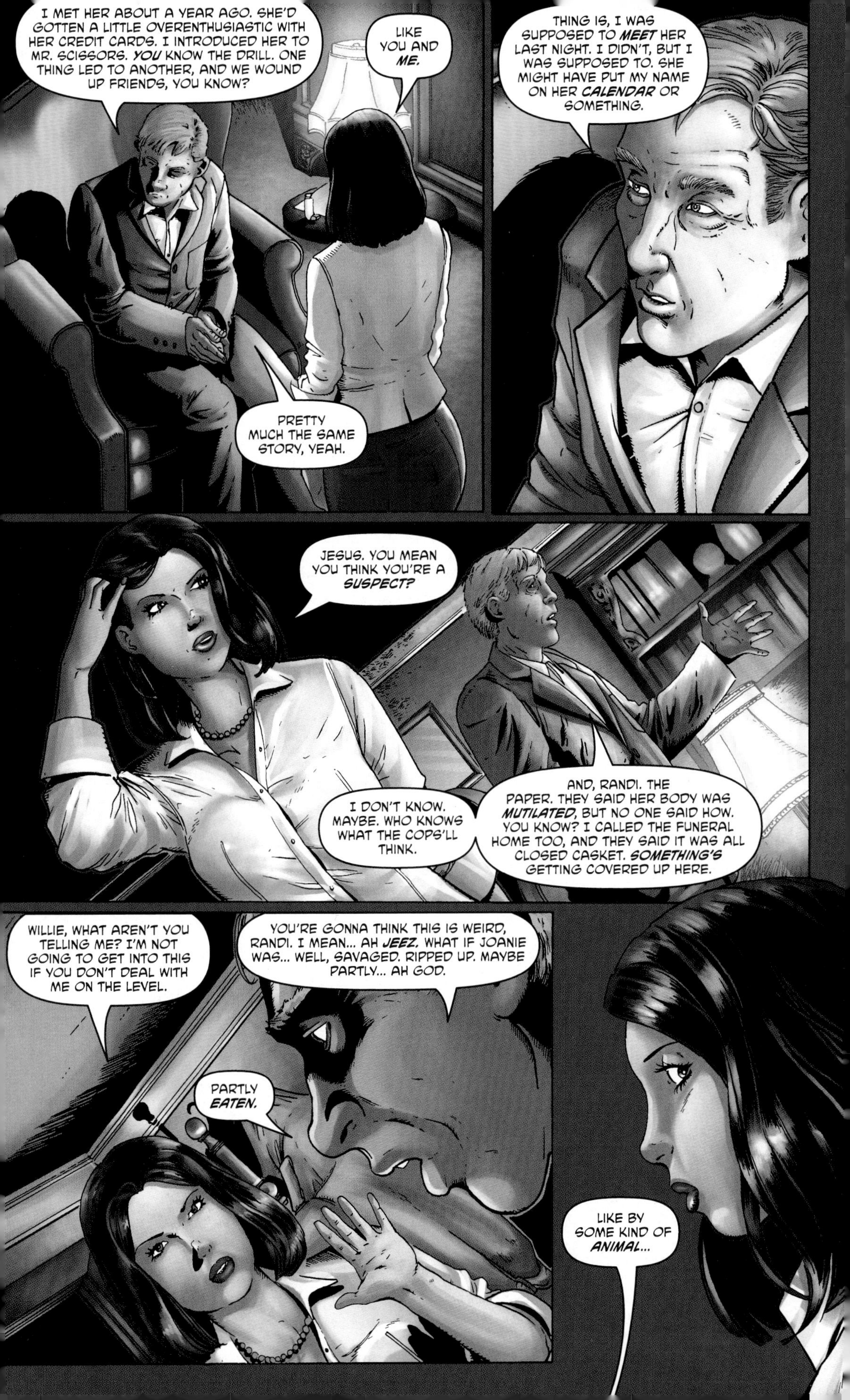
I MET HER ABOUT A YEAR AGO. SHE'D GOTTEN A LITTLE OVERENTHUSIASTIC WITH HER CREDIT CARDS. I INTRODUCED HER TO MR. SCISSORS. *YOU* KNOW THE DRILL. ONE THING LED TO ANOTHER, AND WE WOUND UP FRIENDS, YOU KNOW?
LIKE YOU AND *ME.*
PRETTY MUCH THE SAME STORY, YEAH.
THING IS, I WAS SUPPOSED TO *MEET* HER LAST NIGHT. I DIDN'T, BUT I WAS SUPPOSED TO. SHE MIGHT HAVE PUT MY NAME ON HER *CALENDAR* OR SOMETHING.
JESUS. YOU MEAN YOU THINK YOU'RE A *SUSPECT?*
I DON'T KNOW. MAYBE. WHO KNOWS WHAT THE COPS'LL THINK.
AND, RANDI. THE PAPER. THEY SAID HER BODY WAS *MUTILATED*, BUT NO ONE SAID HOW. YOU KNOW? I CALLED THE FUNERAL HOME TOO, AND THEY SAID IT WAS ALL CLOSED CASKET. *SOMETHING'S* GETTING COVERED UP HERE.
WILLIE, WHAT AREN'T YOU TELLING ME? I'M NOT GOING TO GET INTO THIS IF YOU DON'T DEAL WITH ME ON THE LEVEL.
YOU'RE GONNA THINK THIS IS WEIRD, RANDI. I MEAN... AH *JEEZ.* WHAT IF JOANIE WAS... WELL, SAVAGED. RIPPED UP. MAYBE PARTLY... AH GOD.
PARTLY *EATEN.*
LIKE BY SOME KIND OF *ANIMAL...*

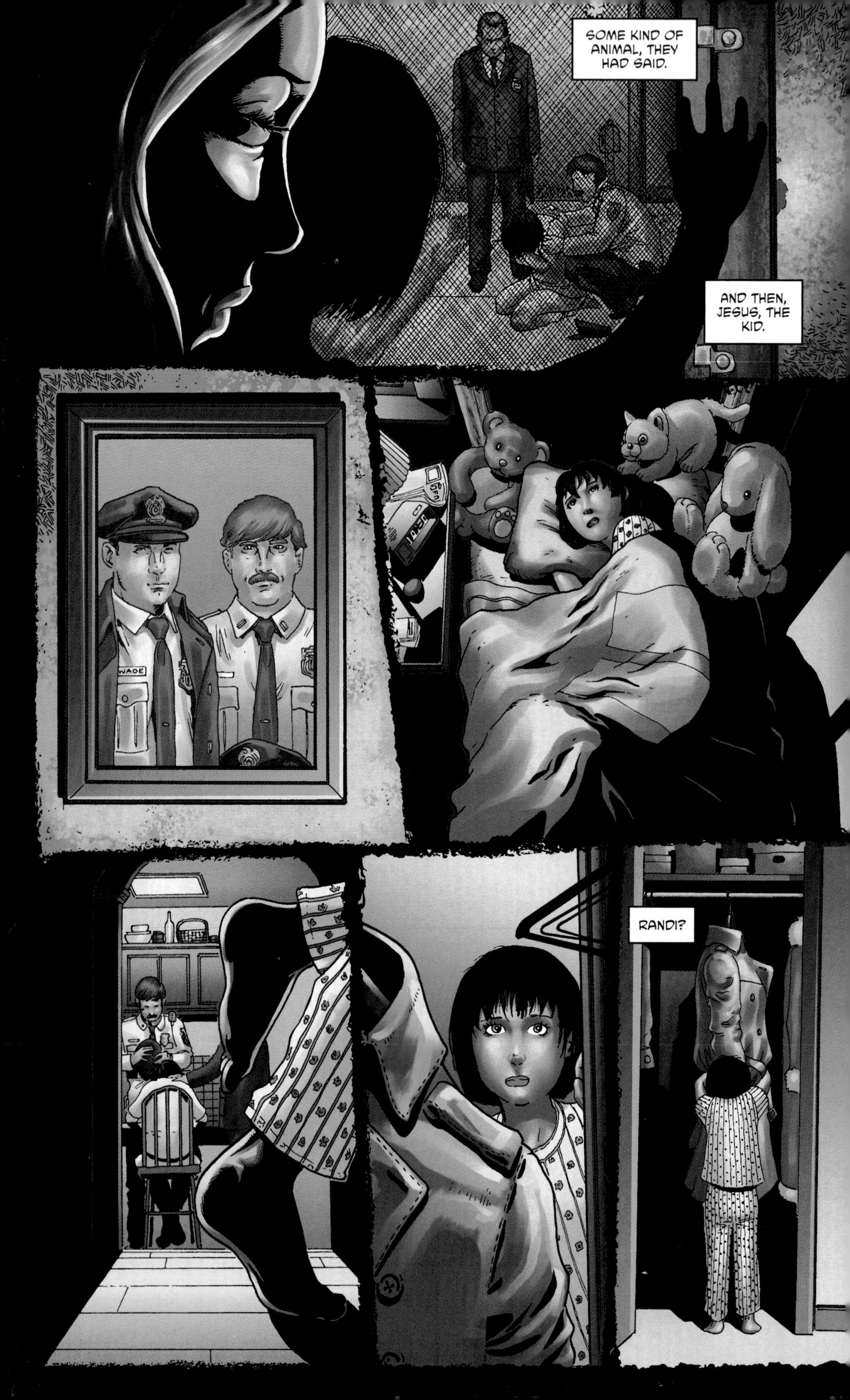
SOME KIND OF ANIMAL, THEY HAD SAID.
AND THEN, JESUS, THE KID.
WADE
RANDI?

HEY. *HEY!* ARE YOU OKAY?

I'M FINE, WILLIE. JUST FINE.

AND I'LL TAKE THE CASE.

RIVER STREET WASN'T EXACTLY A PRESTIGE ADDRESS, BUT HE LIKED IT. HE HAD THE SLAP OF WATER AGAINST THE ROTTING PILINGS, THE FOGHORNS WHEN THE MIST GREW THICK, THE SHOUTS OF PLEASURE-BOATERS ON SUNDAY AFTERNOONS. IT WAS ALL INDUSTRIAL DOWN HERE, SO THERE WEREN'T ANY NEIGHBORS.

HE HAD ELEVEN ROOMS THAT USED TO BE OFFICES. A WOMAN'S ROOM WITH A TAMPAX DISPENSER. A MEN'S ROOM WITH A URINAL. AN ABANDONED BREWERY IF HE EVER DECIDED TO MAKE HIS OWN BEER. SOMEDAY HE'D PUT IN A KITCHEN.

MAYBE HE SHOULD HAVE *TOLD* HER.

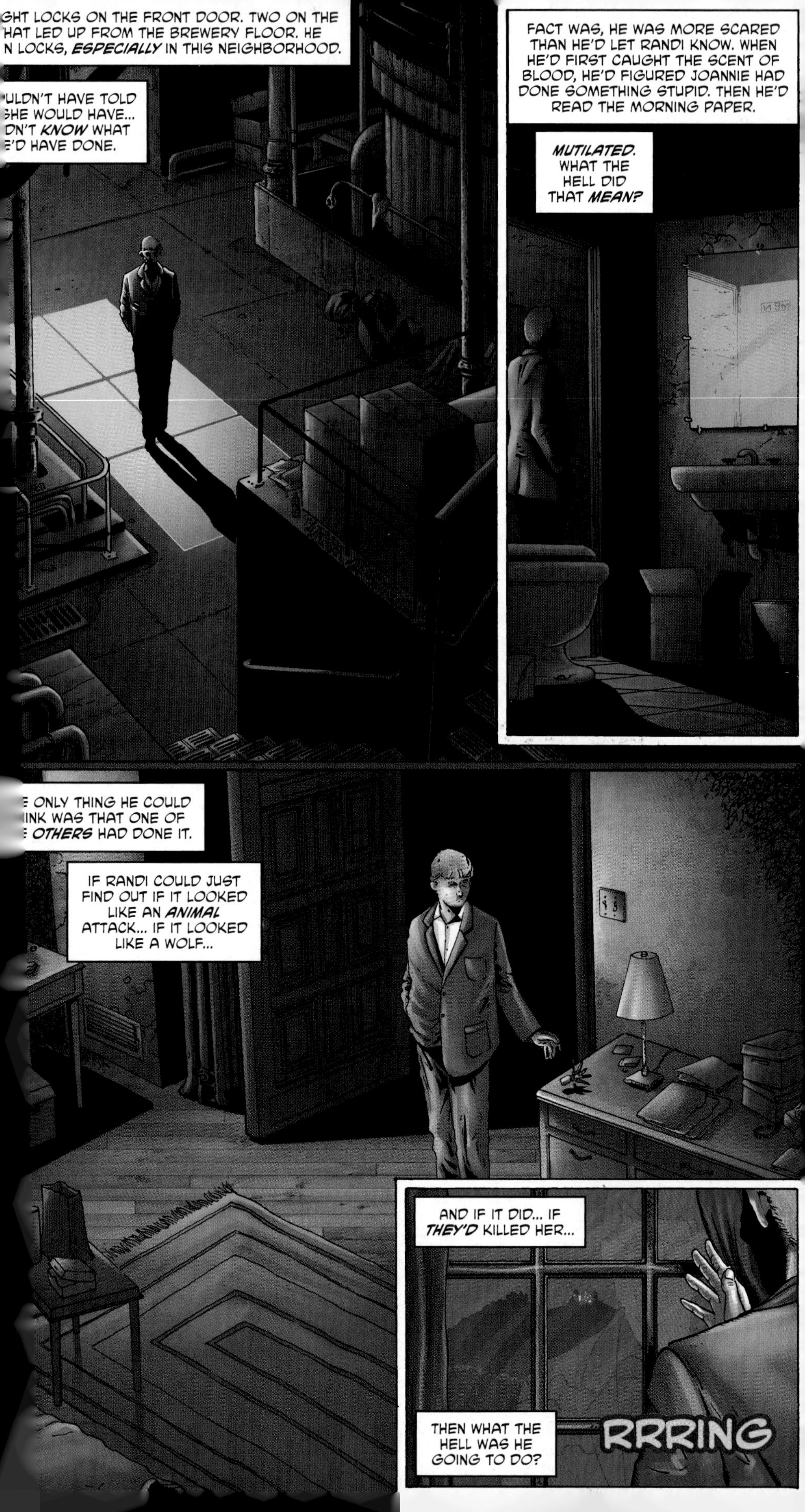

GHT LOCKS ON THE FRONT DOOR. TWO ON THE HAT LED UP FROM THE BREWERY FLOOR. HE N LOCKS, *ESPECIALLY* IN THIS NEIGHBORHOOD.
ULDN'T HAVE TOLD SHE WOULD HAVE... ON'T *KNOW* WHAT E'D HAVE DONE.
FACT WAS, HE WAS MORE SCARED THAN HE'D LET RANDI KNOW. WHEN HE'D FIRST CAUGHT THE SCENT OF BLOOD, HE'D FIGURED JOANNIE HAD DONE SOMETHING STUPID. THEN HE'D READ THE MORNING PAPER.
MUTILATED. WHAT THE HELL DID THAT *MEAN?*
E ONLY THING HE COULD INK WAS THAT ONE OF E *OTHERS* HAD DONE IT.
IF RANDI COULD JUST FIND OUT IF IT LOOKED LIKE AN *ANIMAL* ATTACK... IF IT LOOKED LIKE A WOLF...
AND IF IT DID... IF *THEY'D* KILLED HER...
THEN WHAT THE HELL WAS HE GOING TO DO?
RRRING

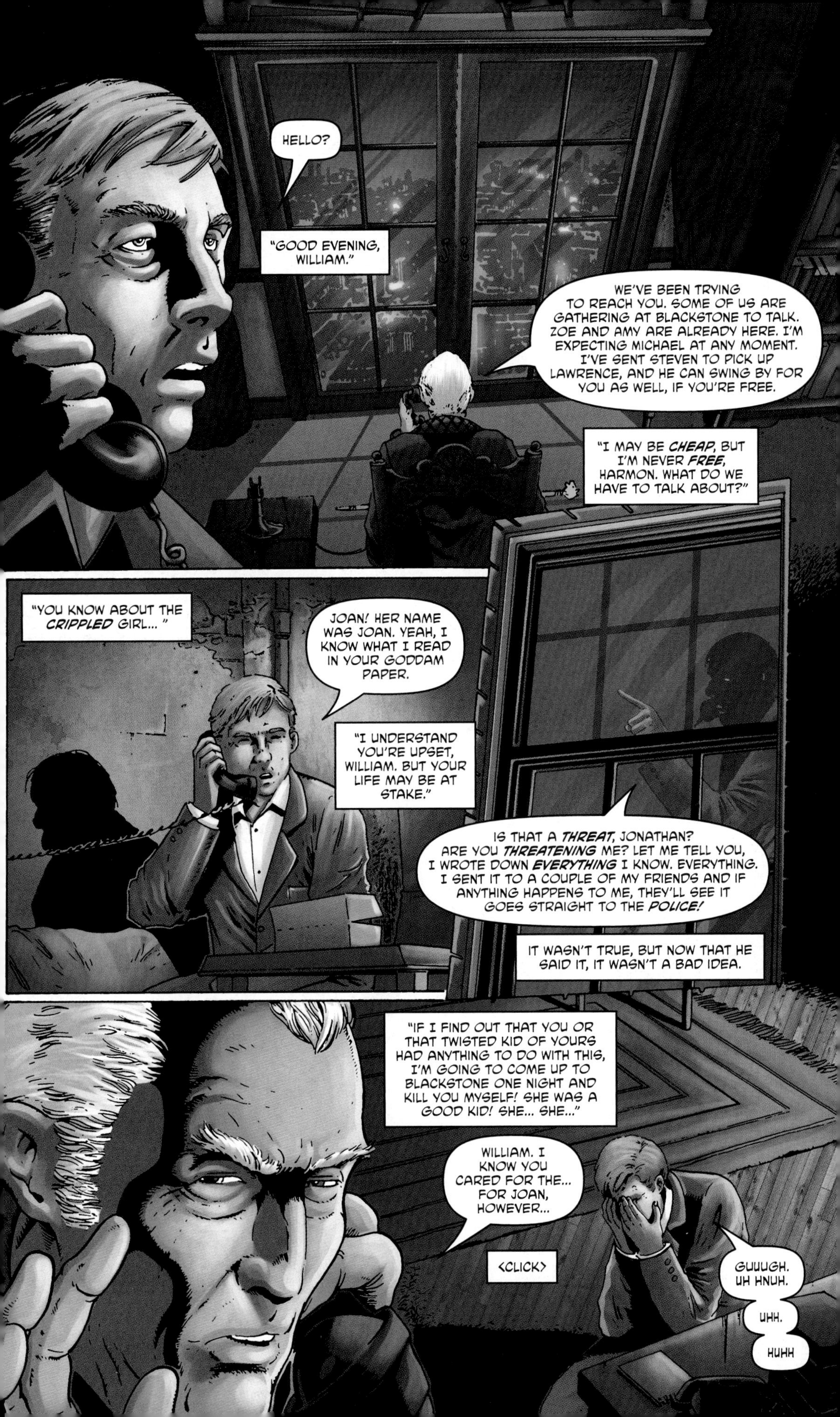
HELLO?
"GOOD EVENING, WILLIAM."
WE'VE BEEN TRYING TO REACH YOU. SOME OF US ARE GATHERING AT BLACKSTONE TO TALK. ZOE AND AMY ARE ALREADY HERE. I'M EXPECTING MICHAEL AT ANY MOMENT. I'VE SENT STEVEN TO PICK UP LAWRENCE, AND HE CAN SWING BY FOR YOU AS WELL, IF YOU'RE FREE.
"I MAY BE *CHEAP*, BUT I'M NEVER *FREE*, HARMON. WHAT DO WE HAVE TO TALK ABOUT?"
"YOU KNOW ABOUT THE *CRIPPLED* GIRL... "
JOAN! HER NAME WAS JOAN. YEAH, I KNOW WHAT I READ IN YOUR GODDAM PAPER.
"I UNDERSTAND YOU'RE UPSET, WILLIAM. BUT YOUR LIFE MAY BE AT STAKE."
IS THAT A *THREAT*, JONATHAN? ARE YOU *THREATENING* ME? LET ME TELL YOU, I WROTE DOWN *EVERYTHING* I KNOW. EVERYTHING. I SENT IT TO A COUPLE OF MY FRIENDS AND IF ANYTHING HAPPENS TO ME, THEY'LL SEE IT GOES STRAIGHT TO THE *POLICE!*
IT WASN'T TRUE, BUT NOW THAT HE SAID IT, IT WASN'T A BAD IDEA.
"IF I FIND OUT THAT YOU OR THAT TWISTED KID OF YOURS HAD ANYTHING TO DO WITH THIS, I'M GOING TO COME UP TO BLACKSTONE ONE NIGHT AND KILL YOU MYSELF! SHE WAS A GOOD KID! SHE... SHE..."
WILLIAM. I KNOW YOU CARED FOR THE... FOR JOAN, HOWEVER...
<CLICK>
GUUUGH. UH HNUH.
UHH.
HUHH

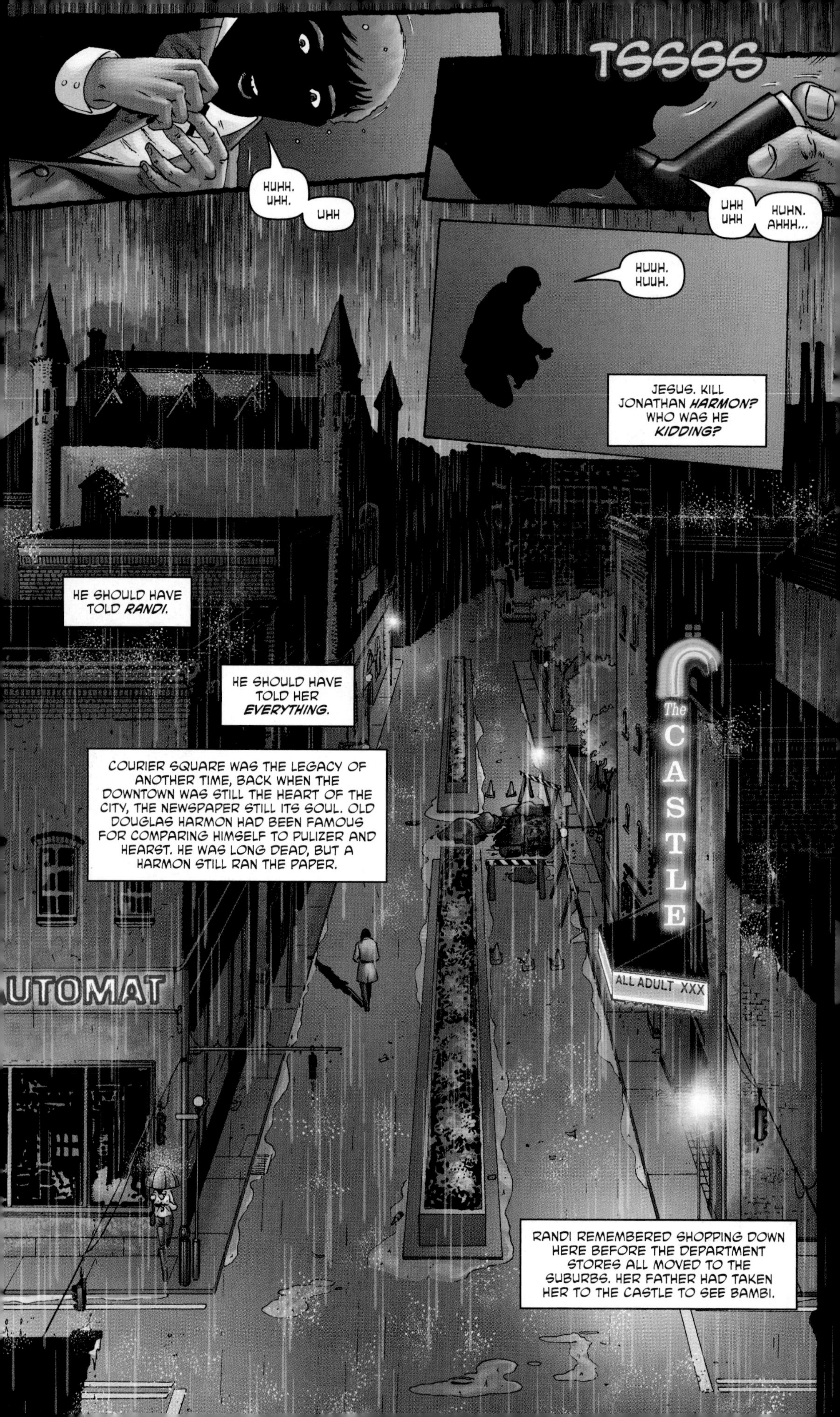
TSSSS
HUHH. UHH.
UHH
UHH UHH
HUHN. AHHH...
HUUH. HUUH.
JESUS. KILL JONATHAN HARMON? WHO WAS HE KIDDING?
HE SHOULD HAVE TOLD RANDI.
HE SHOULD HAVE TOLD HER EVERYTHING.
COURIER SQUARE WAS THE LEGACY OF ANOTHER TIME, BACK WHEN THE DOWNTOWN WAS STILL THE HEART OF THE CITY, THE NEWSPAPER STILL ITS SOUL. OLD DOUGLAS HARMON HAD BEEN FAMOUS FOR COMPARING HIMSELF TO PULIZER AND HEARST. HE WAS LONG DEAD, BUT A HARMON STILL RAN THE PAPER.
The CASTLE
ALL ADULT XXX
UTOMAT
RANDI REMEMBERED SHOPPING DOWN HERE BEFORE THE DEPARTMENT STORES ALL MOVED TO THE SUBURBS. HER FATHER HAD TAKEN HER TO THE CASTLE TO SEE BAMBI.

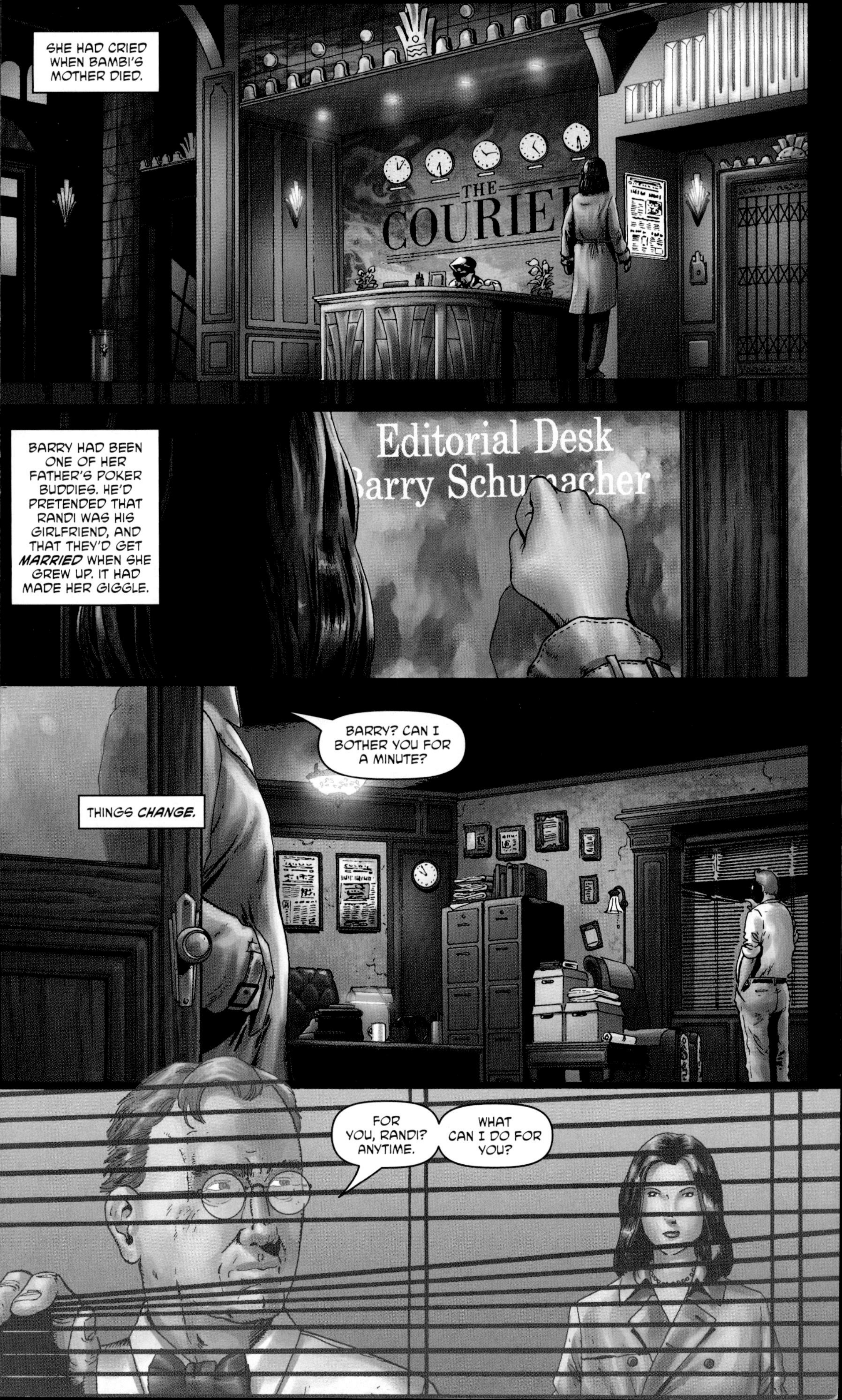
SHE HAD CRIED WHEN BAMBI'S MOTHER DIED.
THE COURIER
BARRY HAD BEEN ONE OF HER FATHER'S POKER BUDDIES. HE'D PRETENDED THAT RANDI WAS HIS GIRLFRIEND, AND THAT THEY'D GET *MARRIED* WHEN SHE GREW UP. IT HAD MADE HER GIGGLE.
Editorial Desk
Barry Schumacher
THINGS *CHANGE.*
BARRY? CAN I BOTHER YOU FOR A MINUTE?
FOR YOU, RANDI? ANYTIME.
WHAT CAN I DO FOR YOU?

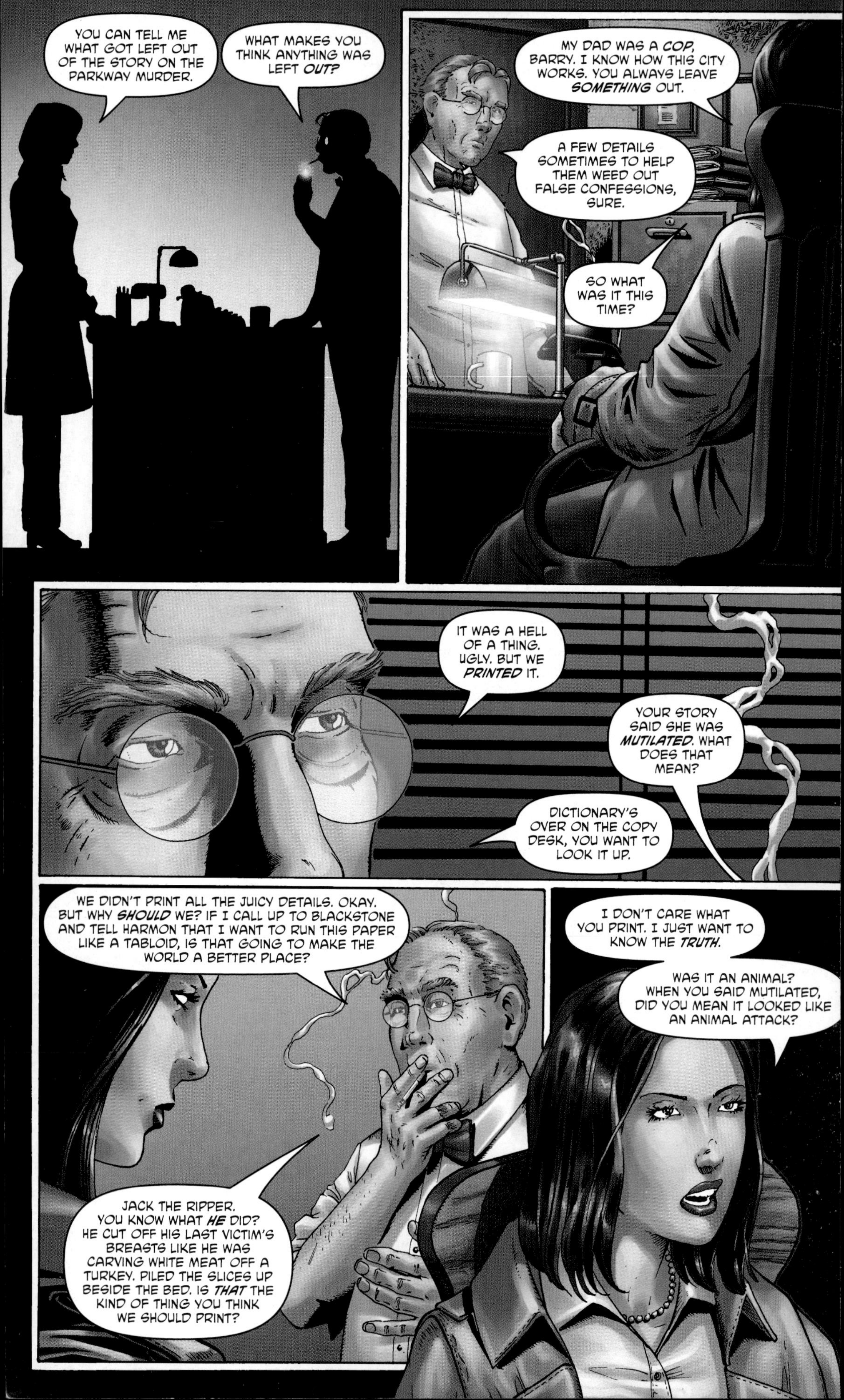

YOU CAN TELL ME WHAT GOT LEFT OUT OF THE STORY ON THE PARKWAY MURDER.
WHAT MAKES YOU THINK ANYTHING WAS LEFT *OUT?*
MY DAD WAS A *COP*, BARRY. I KNOW HOW THIS CITY WORKS. YOU ALWAYS LEAVE *SOMETHING* OUT.
A FEW DETAILS SOMETIMES TO HELP THEM WEED OUT FALSE CONFESSIONS, SURE.
SO WHAT WAS IT THIS TIME?
IT WAS A HELL OF A THING. UGLY. BUT WE *PRINTED* IT.
YOUR STORY SAID SHE WAS *MUTILATED*. WHAT DOES THAT MEAN?
DICTIONARY'S OVER ON THE COPY DESK, YOU WANT TO LOOK IT UP.
WE DIDN'T PRINT ALL THE JUICY DETAILS. OKAY. BUT WHY *SHOULD* WE? IF I CALL UP TO BLACKSTONE AND TELL HARMON THAT I WANT TO RUN THIS PAPER LIKE A TABLOID, IS THAT GOING TO MAKE THE WORLD A BETTER PLACE?
JACK THE RIPPER. YOU KNOW WHAT *HE* DID? HE CUT OFF HIS LAST VICTIM'S BREASTS LIKE HE WAS CARVING WHITE MEAT OFF A TURKEY. PILED THE SLICES UP BESIDE THE BED. IS *THAT* THE KIND OF THING YOU THINK WE SHOULD PRINT?
I DON'T CARE WHAT YOU PRINT. I JUST WANT TO KNOW THE *TRUTH*.
WAS IT AN ANIMAL? WHEN YOU SAID MUTILATED, DID YOU MEAN IT LOOKED LIKE AN ANIMAL ATTACK?

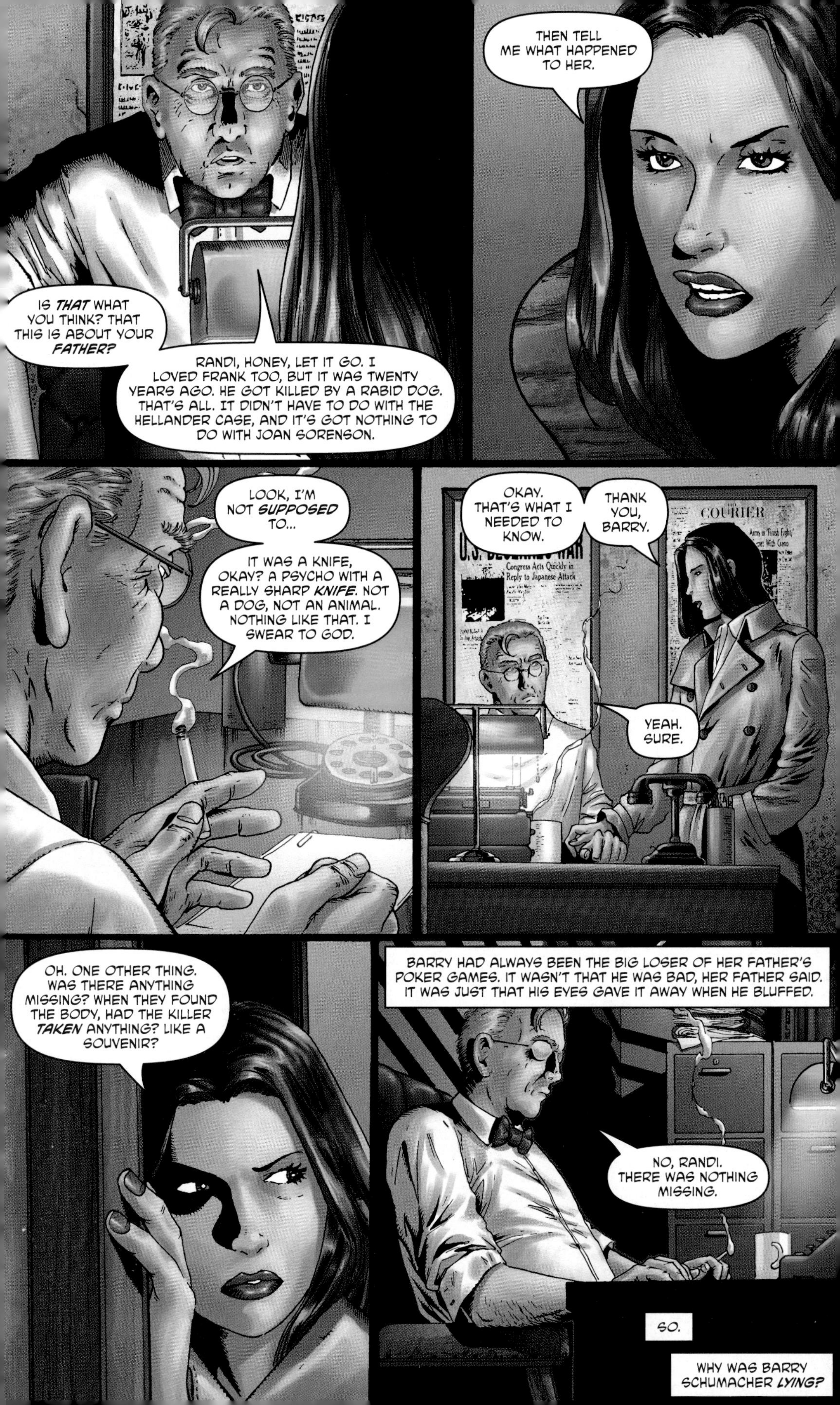
IS THAT WHAT YOU THINK? THAT THIS IS ABOUT YOUR FATHER?
RANDI, HONEY, LET IT GO. I LOVED FRANK TOO, BUT IT WAS TWENTY YEARS AGO. HE GOT KILLED BY A RABID DOG. THAT'S ALL. IT DIDN'T HAVE TO DO WITH THE HELLANDER CASE, AND IT'S GOT NOTHING TO DO WITH JOAN SORENSON.
THEN TELL ME WHAT HAPPENED TO HER.
LOOK, I'M NOT SUPPOSED TO...
IT WAS A KNIFE, OKAY? A PSYCHO WITH A REALLY SHARP KNIFE. NOT A DOG, NOT AN ANIMAL. NOTHING LIKE THAT. I SWEAR TO GOD.
OKAY. THAT'S WHAT I NEEDED TO KNOW.
THANK YOU, BARRY.
COURIER
Congress Acts Quickly in Reply to Japanese Attack
YEAH. SURE.
OH. ONE OTHER THING. WAS THERE ANYTHING MISSING? WHEN THEY FOUND THE BODY, HAD THE KILLER TAKEN ANYTHING? LIKE A SOUVENIR?
BARRY HAD ALWAYS BEEN THE BIG LOSER OF HER FATHER'S POKER GAMES. IT WASN'T THAT HE WAS BAD, HER FATHER SAID. IT WAS JUST THAT HIS EYES GAVE IT AWAY WHEN HE BLUFFED.
NO, RANDI. THERE WAS NOTHING MISSING.
SO.
WHY WAS BARRY SCHUMACHER LYING?

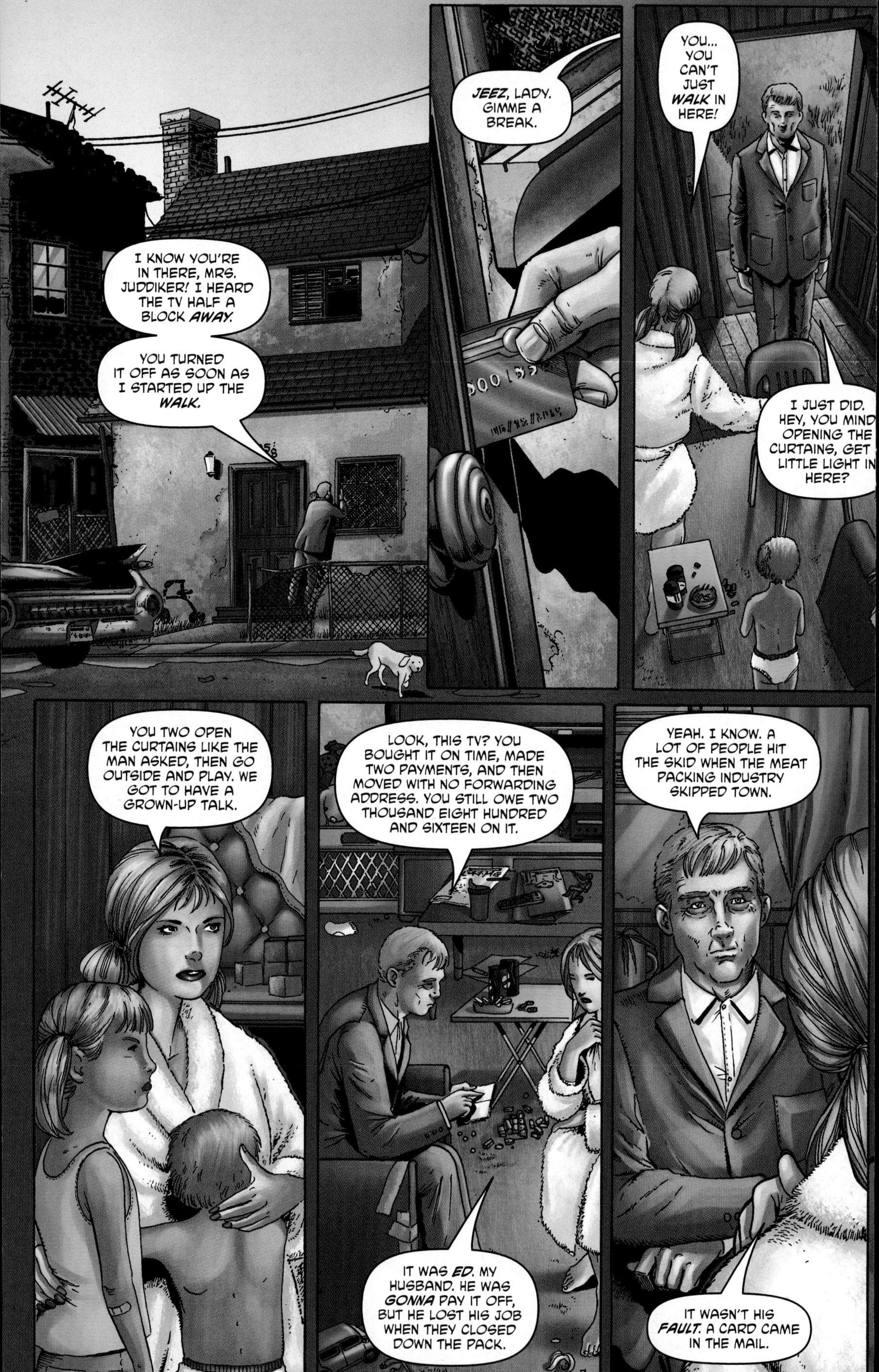
I KNOW YOU'RE IN THERE, MRS. JUDDIKER! I HEARD THE TV HALF A BLOCK *AWAY.*
YOU TURNED IT OFF AS SOON AS I STARTED UP THE *WALK.*
JEEZ, LADY. GIMME A BREAK.
YOU... YOU CAN'T JUST *WALK* IN HERE!
I JUST DID. HEY, YOU MIND OPENING THE CURTAINS, GET LITTLE LIGHT IN HERE?
YOU TWO OPEN THE CURTAINS LIKE THE MAN ASKED, THEN GO OUTSIDE AND PLAY. WE GOT TO HAVE A GROWN-UP TALK.
LOOK, THIS TV? YOU BOUGHT IT ON TIME, MADE TWO PAYMENTS, AND THEN MOVED WITH NO FORWARDING ADDRESS. YOU STILL OWE TWO THOUSAND EIGHT HUNDRED AND SIXTEEN ON IT.
IT WAS *ED*. MY HUSBAND. HE WAS *GONNA* PAY IT OFF, BUT HE LOST HIS JOB WHEN THEY CLOSED DOWN THE PACK.
YEAH. I KNOW. A LOT OF PEOPLE HIT THE SKID WHEN THE MEAT PACKING INDUSTRY SKIPPED TOWN.
IT WASN'T HIS *FAULT.* A CARD CAME IN THE MAIL.

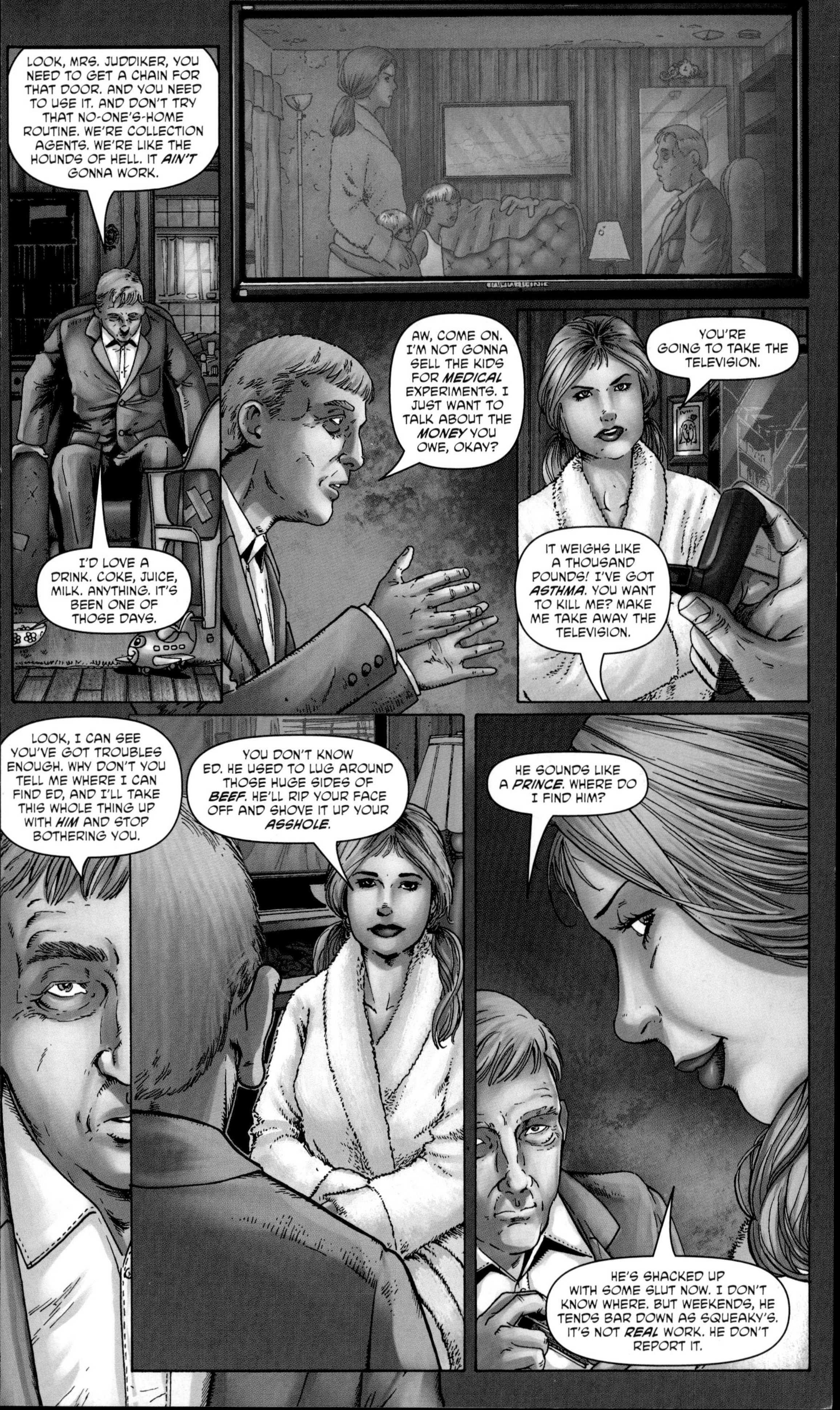
LOOK, MRS. JUDDIKER, YOU NEED TO GET A CHAIN FOR THAT DOOR. AND YOU NEED TO USE IT. AND DON'T TRY THAT NO-ONE'S-HOME ROUTINE. WE'RE COLLECTION AGENTS. WE'RE LIKE THE HOUNDS OF HELL. IT AIN'T GONNA WORK.
I'D LOVE A DRINK. COKE, JUICE, MILK. ANYTHING. IT'S BEEN ONE OF THOSE DAYS.
AW, COME ON. I'M NOT GONNA SELL THE KIDS FOR MEDICAL EXPERIMENTS. I JUST WANT TO TALK ABOUT THE MONEY YOU OWE, OKAY?
YOU'RE GOING TO TAKE THE TELEVISION.
IT WEIGHS LIKE A THOUSAND POUNDS! I'VE GOT ASTHMA. YOU WANT TO KILL ME? MAKE ME TAKE AWAY THE TELEVISION.
LOOK, I CAN SEE YOU'VE GOT TROUBLES ENOUGH. WHY DON'T YOU TELL ME WHERE I CAN FIND ED, AND I'LL TAKE THIS WHOLE THING UP WITH HIM AND STOP BOTHERING YOU.
YOU DON'T KNOW ED. HE USED TO LUG AROUND THOSE HUGE SIDES OF BEEF. HE'LL RIP YOUR FACE OFF AND SHOVE IT UP YOUR ASSHOLE.
HE SOUNDS LIKE A PRINCE. WHERE DO I FIND HIM?
HE'S SHACKED UP WITH SOME SLUT NOW. I DON'T KNOW WHERE. BUT WEEKENDS, HE TENDS BAR DOWN AS SQUEAKY'S. IT'S NOT REAL WORK. HE DON'T REPORT IT.

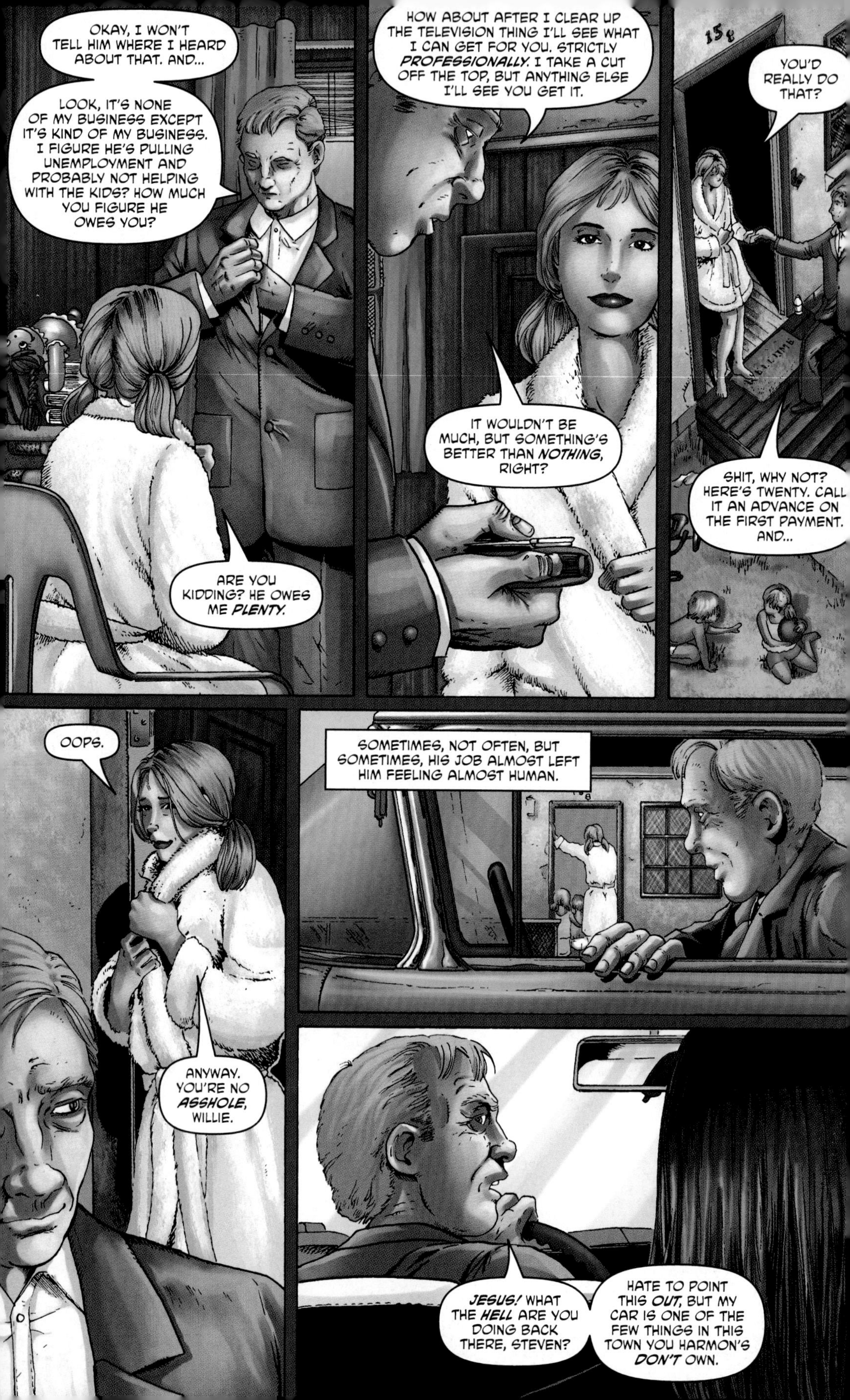
OKAY, I WON'T TELL HIM WHERE I HEARD ABOUT THAT. AND...
LOOK, IT'S NONE OF MY BUSINESS EXCEPT IT'S KIND OF MY BUSINESS. I FIGURE HE'S PULLING UNEMPLOYMENT AND PROBABLY NOT HELPING WITH THE KIDS? HOW MUCH YOU FIGURE HE OWES YOU?
ARE YOU KIDDING? HE OWES ME PLENTY.
HOW ABOUT AFTER I CLEAR UP THE TELEVISION THING I'LL SEE WHAT I CAN GET FOR YOU. STRICTLY PROFESSIONALLY. I TAKE A CUT OFF THE TOP, BUT ANYTHING ELSE I'LL SEE YOU GET IT.
IT WOULDN'T BE MUCH, BUT SOMETHING'S BETTER THAN NOTHING, RIGHT?
YOU'D REALLY DO THAT?
SHIT, WHY NOT? HERE'S TWENTY. CALL IT AN ADVANCE ON THE FIRST PAYMENT. AND...
OOPS.
ANYWAY. YOU'RE NO ASSHOLE, WILLIE.
SOMETIMES, NOT OFTEN, BUT SOMETIMES, HIS JOB ALMOST LEFT HIM FEELING ALMOST HUMAN.
JESUS! WHAT THE HELL ARE YOU DOING BACK THERE, STEVEN?
HATE TO POINT THIS OUT, BUT MY CAR IS ONE OF THE FEW THINGS IN THIS TOWN YOU HARMON'S DON'T OWN.

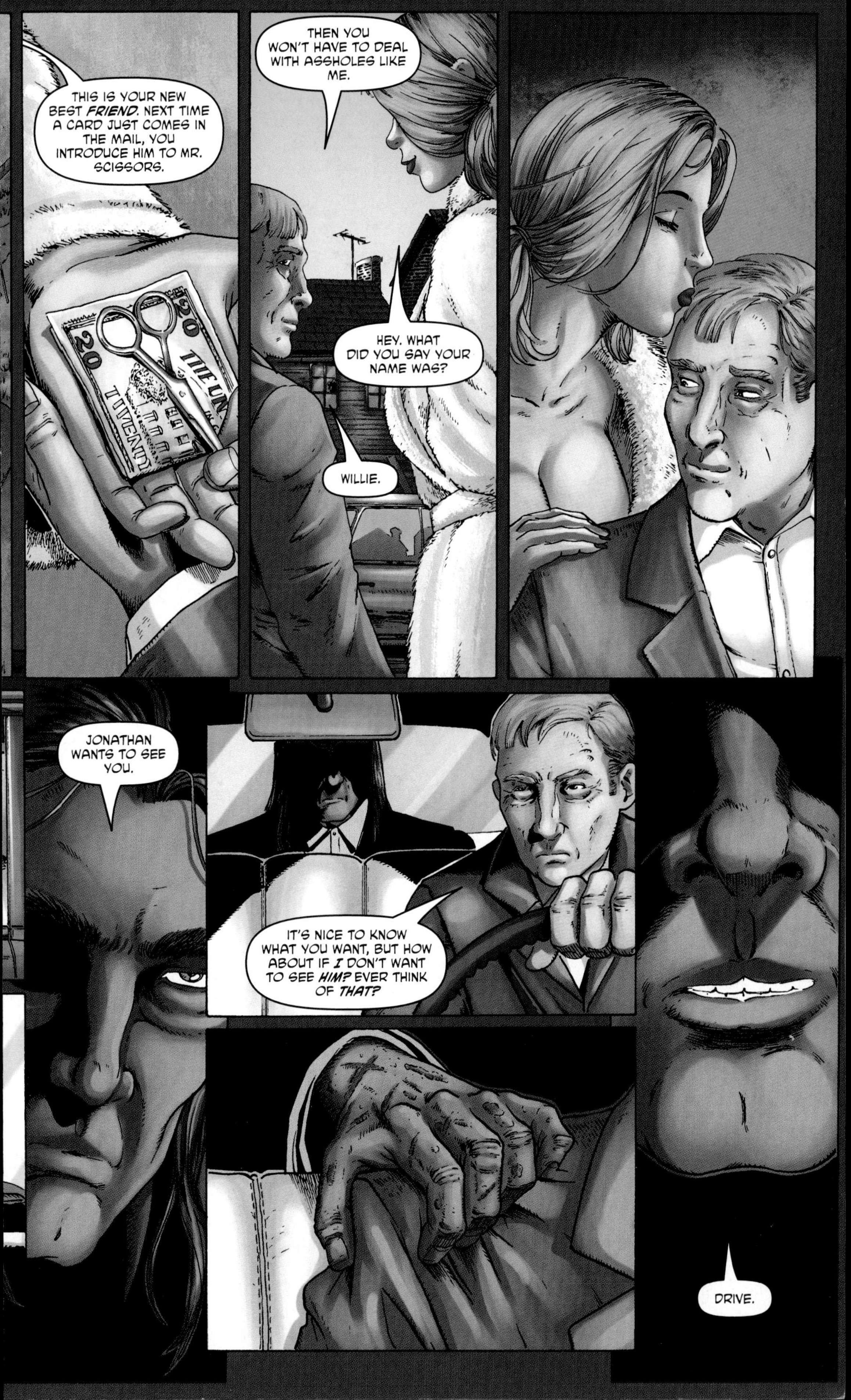
THIS IS YOUR NEW BEST *FRIEND*. NEXT TIME A CARD JUST COMES IN THE MAIL, YOU INTRODUCE HIM TO MR. SCISSORS.
THEN YOU WON'T HAVE TO DEAL WITH ASSHOLES LIKE ME.
HEY. WHAT DID YOU SAY YOUR NAME WAS?
WILLIE.
JONATHAN WANTS TO SEE YOU.
IT'S NICE TO KNOW WHAT YOU WANT, BUT HOW ABOUT IF *I* DON'T WANT TO SEE *HIM?* EVER THINK OF *THAT?*
DRIVE.

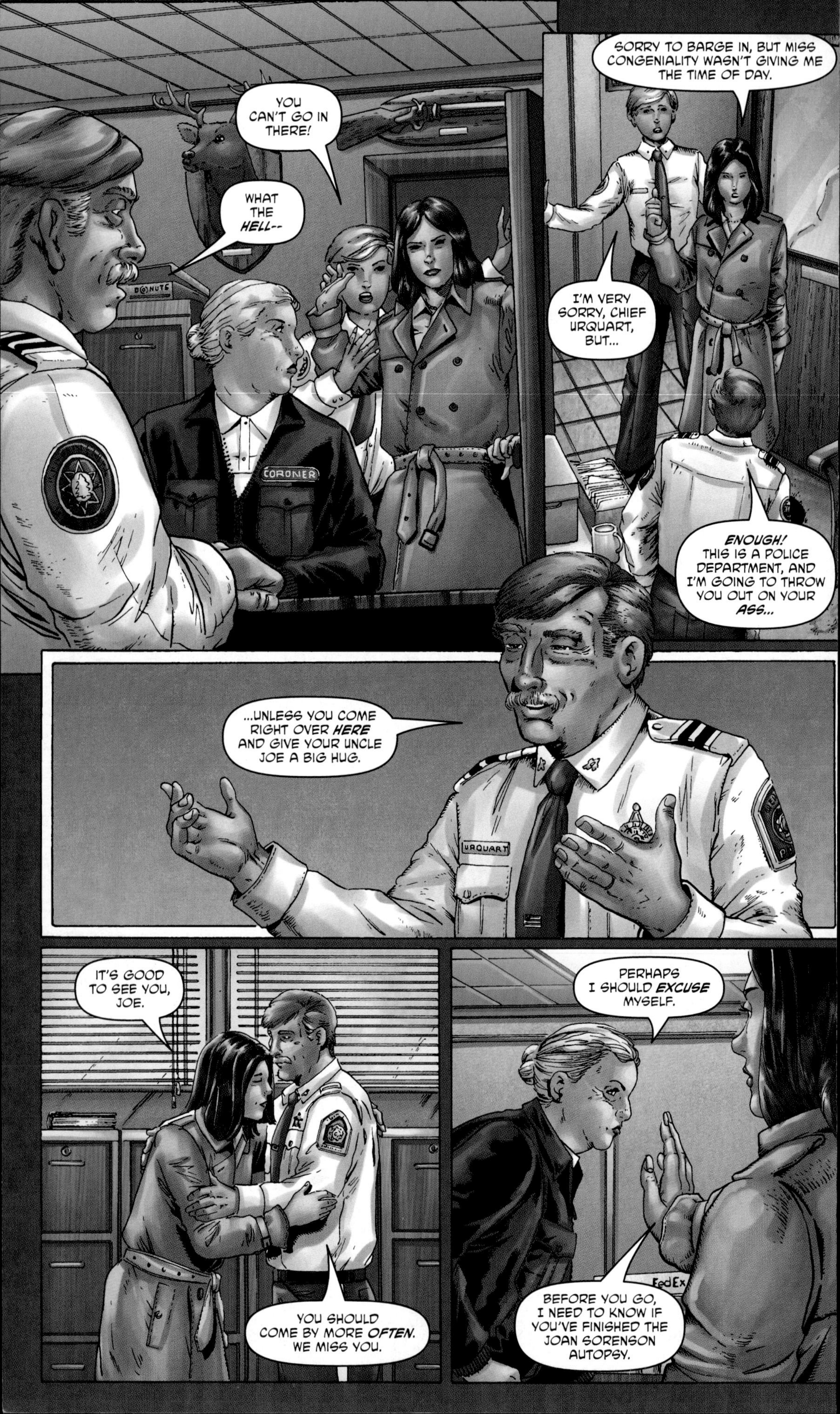
YOU CAN'T GO IN THERE!
WHAT THE HELL--
SORRY TO BARGE IN, BUT MISS CONGENIALITY WASN'T GIVING ME THE TIME OF DAY.
I'M VERY SORRY, CHIEF URQUART, BUT...
ENOUGH! THIS IS A POLICE DEPARTMENT, AND I'M GOING TO THROW YOU OUT ON YOUR ASS...
CORONER
...UNLESS YOU COME RIGHT OVER HERE AND GIVE YOUR UNCLE JOE A BIG HUG.
URQUART
IT'S GOOD TO SEE YOU, JOE.
YOU SHOULD COME BY MORE OFTEN. WE MISS YOU.
PERHAPS I SHOULD EXCUSE MYSELF.
BEFORE YOU GO, I NEED TO KNOW IF YOU'VE FINISHED THE JOAN SORENSON AUTOPSY.
FedEx

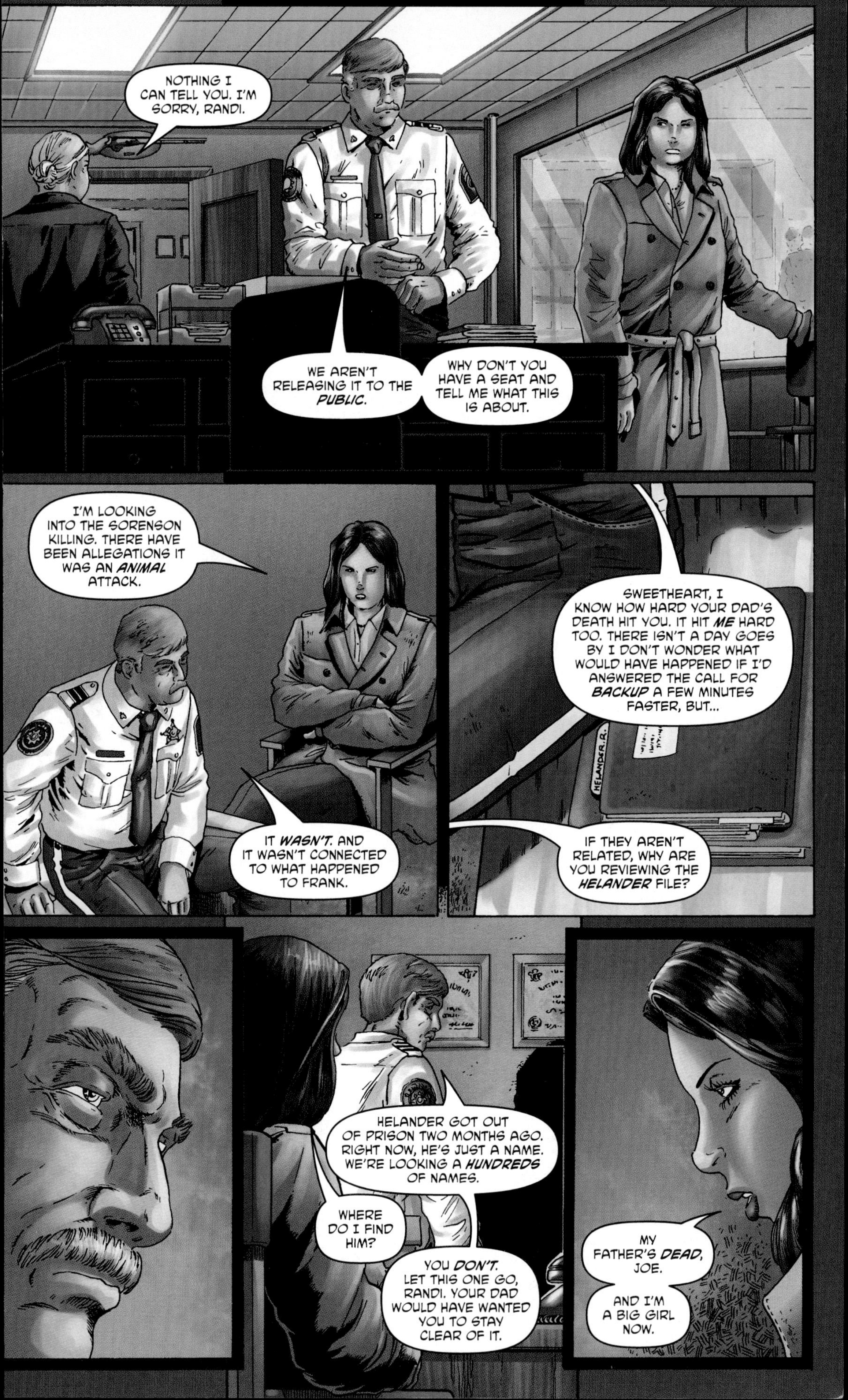
NOTHING I CAN TELL YOU. I'M SORRY, RANDI.
WE AREN'T RELEASING IT TO THE *PUBLIC*.
WHY DON'T YOU HAVE A SEAT AND TELL ME WHAT THIS IS ABOUT.
I'M LOOKING INTO THE SORENSON KILLING. THERE HAVE BEEN ALLEGATIONS IT WAS AN *ANIMAL* ATTACK.
IT *WASN'T.* AND IT WASN'T CONNECTED TO WHAT HAPPENED TO FRANK.
SWEETHEART, I KNOW HOW HARD YOUR DAD'S DEATH HIT YOU. IT HIT *ME* HARD TOO. THERE ISN'T A DAY GOES BY I DON'T WONDER WHAT WOULD HAVE HAPPENED IF I'D ANSWERED THE CALL FOR *BACKUP* A FEW MINUTES FASTER, BUT...
HELANDER, R.
IF THEY AREN'T RELATED, WHY ARE YOU REVIEWING THE *HELANDER* FILE?
HELANDER GOT OUT OF PRISON TWO MONTHS AGO. RIGHT NOW, HE'S JUST A NAME. WE'RE LOOKING A *HUNDREDS* OF NAMES.
WHERE DO I FIND HIM?
YOU *DON'T.* LET THIS ONE GO, RANDI. YOUR DAD WOULD HAVE WANTED YOU TO STAY CLEAR OF IT.
MY FATHER'S *DEAD*, JOE.
AND I'M A BIG GIRL NOW.

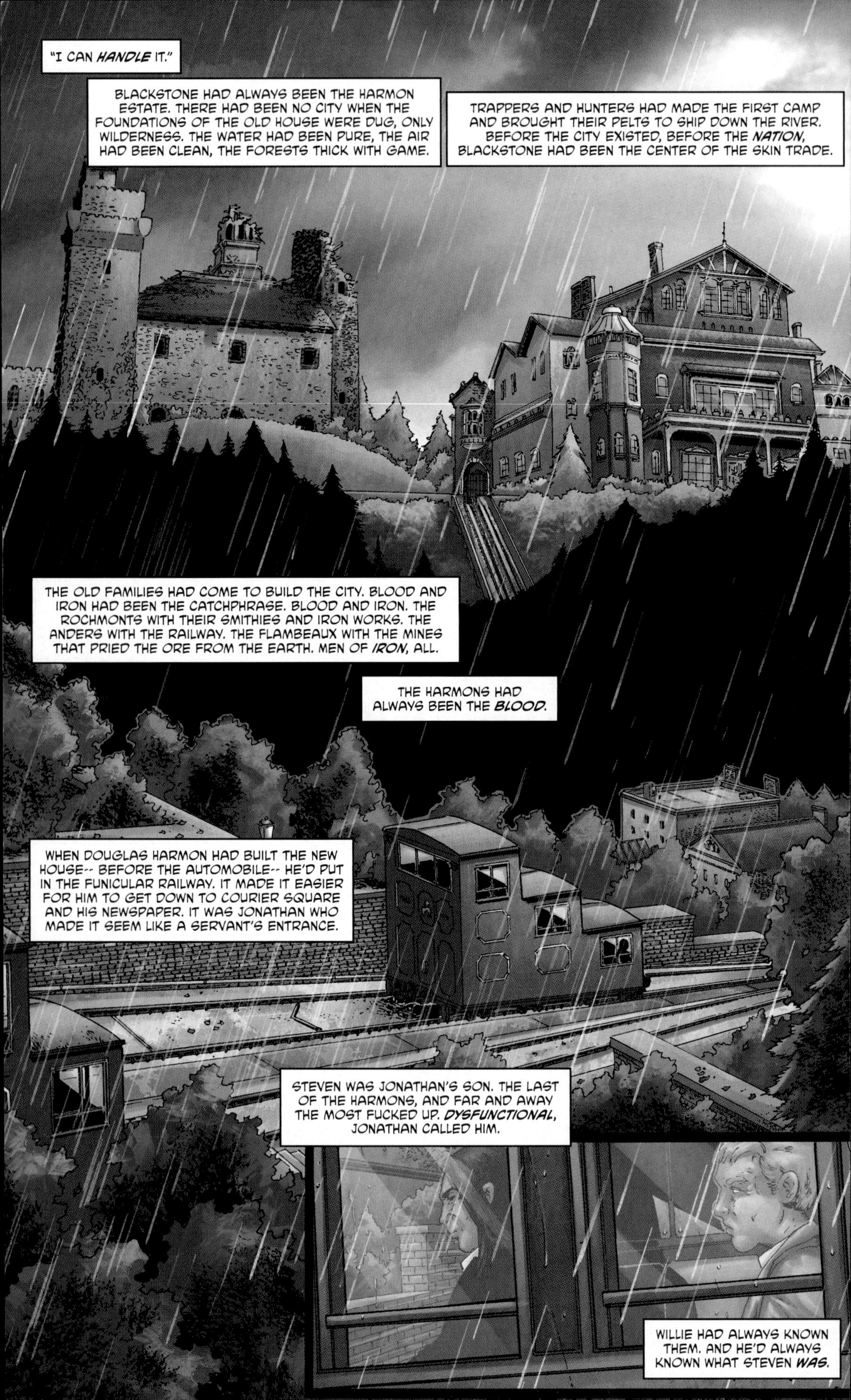
"I CAN HANDLE IT."
BLACKSTONE HAD ALWAYS BEEN THE HARMON ESTATE. THERE HAD BEEN NO CITY WHEN THE FOUNDATIONS OF THE OLD HOUSE WERE DUG, ONLY WILDERNESS. THE WATER HAD BEEN PURE, THE AIR HAD BEEN CLEAN, THE FORESTS THICK WITH GAME.
TRAPPERS AND HUNTERS HAD MADE THE FIRST CAMP AND BROUGHT THEIR PELTS TO SHIP DOWN THE RIVER. BEFORE THE CITY EXISTED, BEFORE THE NATION, BLACKSTONE HAD BEEN THE CENTER OF THE SKIN TRADE.
THE OLD FAMILIES HAD COME TO BUILD THE CITY. BLOOD AND IRON HAD BEEN THE CATCHPHRASE. BLOOD AND IRON. THE ROCHMONTS WITH THEIR SMITHIES AND IRON WORKS. THE ANDERS WITH THE RAILWAY. THE FLAMBEAUX WITH THE MINES THAT PRIED THE ORE FROM THE EARTH. MEN OF IRON, ALL.
THE HARMONS HAD ALWAYS BEEN THE BLOOD.
WHEN DOUGLAS HARMON HAD BUILT THE NEW HOUSE-- BEFORE THE AUTOMOBILE-- HE'D PUT IN THE FUNICULAR RAILWAY. IT MADE IT EASIER FOR HIM TO GET DOWN TO COURIER SQUARE AND HIS NEWSPAPER. IT WAS JONATHAN WHO MADE IT SEEM LIKE A SERVANT'S ENTRANCE.
STEVEN WAS JONATHAN'S SON. THE LAST OF THE HARMONS, AND FAR AND AWAY THE MOST FUCKED UP. DYSFUNCTIONAL, JONATHAN CALLED HIM.
WILLIE HAD ALWAYS KNOWN THEM. AND HE'D ALWAYS KNOWN WHAT STEVEN WAS.

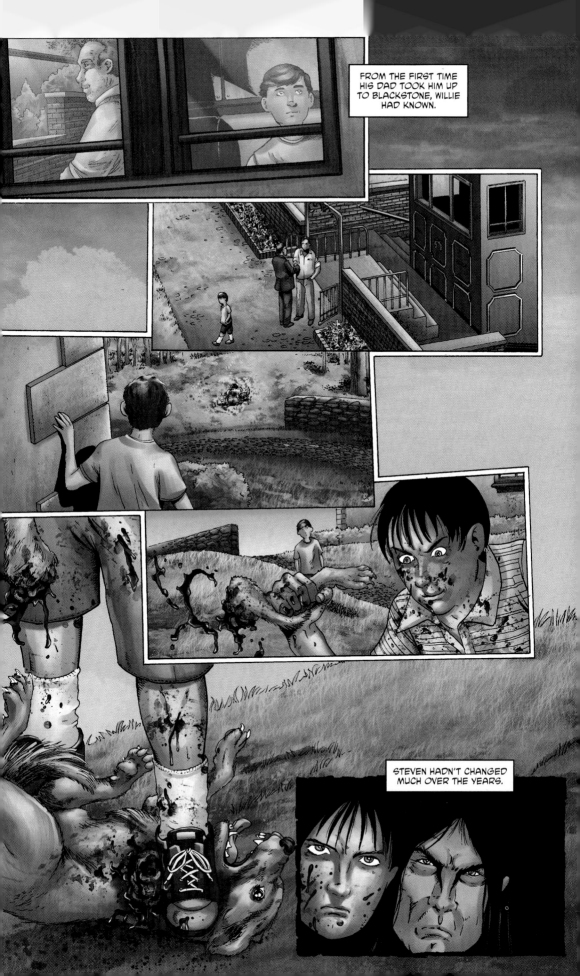

FROM THE FIRST TIME HIS DAD TOOK HIM UP TO BLACKSTONE, WILLIE HAD KNOWN.

STEVEN HADN'T CHANGED MUCH OVER THE YEARS.

SO MAYBE *HE'D* DONE IT. COULD STEVEN HAVE BEEN THE ONE THAT KILLED JOANIE?

AND IF HE DID, WHAT THE FUCK DID OLD JONATHAN WANT? TO TALK?

IT *MUST* BE. IF HE'D WANTED WILLIE DEAD, IT WOULD ALREADY HAVE HAPPENED.

HELLO, WILLIAM. I'M GLAD YOU COULD JOIN US.

YEAH, WELL, I WAS IN THE *NEIGHBORHOOD*, THOUGHT I'D STOP BY. BUT I THINK I GOT SOME WINDOWS OPEN BACK AT THE BREWERY, SO I'D BETTER BE MOVING ON.

I THINK NOT, STEVEN! GET OUR GUEST SOMETHING WARMING TO DRINK. REMY MARTIN.

FORGIVE ME FOR NOT MEETING YOU OUTSIDE. THE *DAMP* AGGRAVATES MY WAR WOUNDS.

BUT PERHAPS *YOU* SHOULD BE APOLOGIZING TO ME.

YOU ALL BUT ACCUSED ME OF COMPLICITY IN THE CRIPPLED GIRL'S DEATH, WILLIAM. *WHY* WOULD YOU DO THAT?

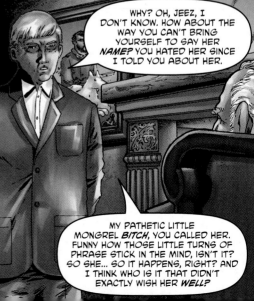

WHY? OH, JEEZ, I DON'T KNOW. HOW ABOUT THE WAY YOU CAN'T BRING YOURSELF TO SAY HER *NAME?* YOU HATED HER SINCE I TOLD YOU ABOUT HER.

MY PATHETIC LITTLE MONGREL *BITCH*, YOU CALLED HER. FUNNY HOW THOSE LITTLE TURNS OF PHRASE STICK IN THE MIND, ISN'T IT? SO SHE... SO IT HAPPENS, RIGHT? AND I THINK WHO IS IT THAT DIDN'T EXACTLY WISH HER *WELL?*

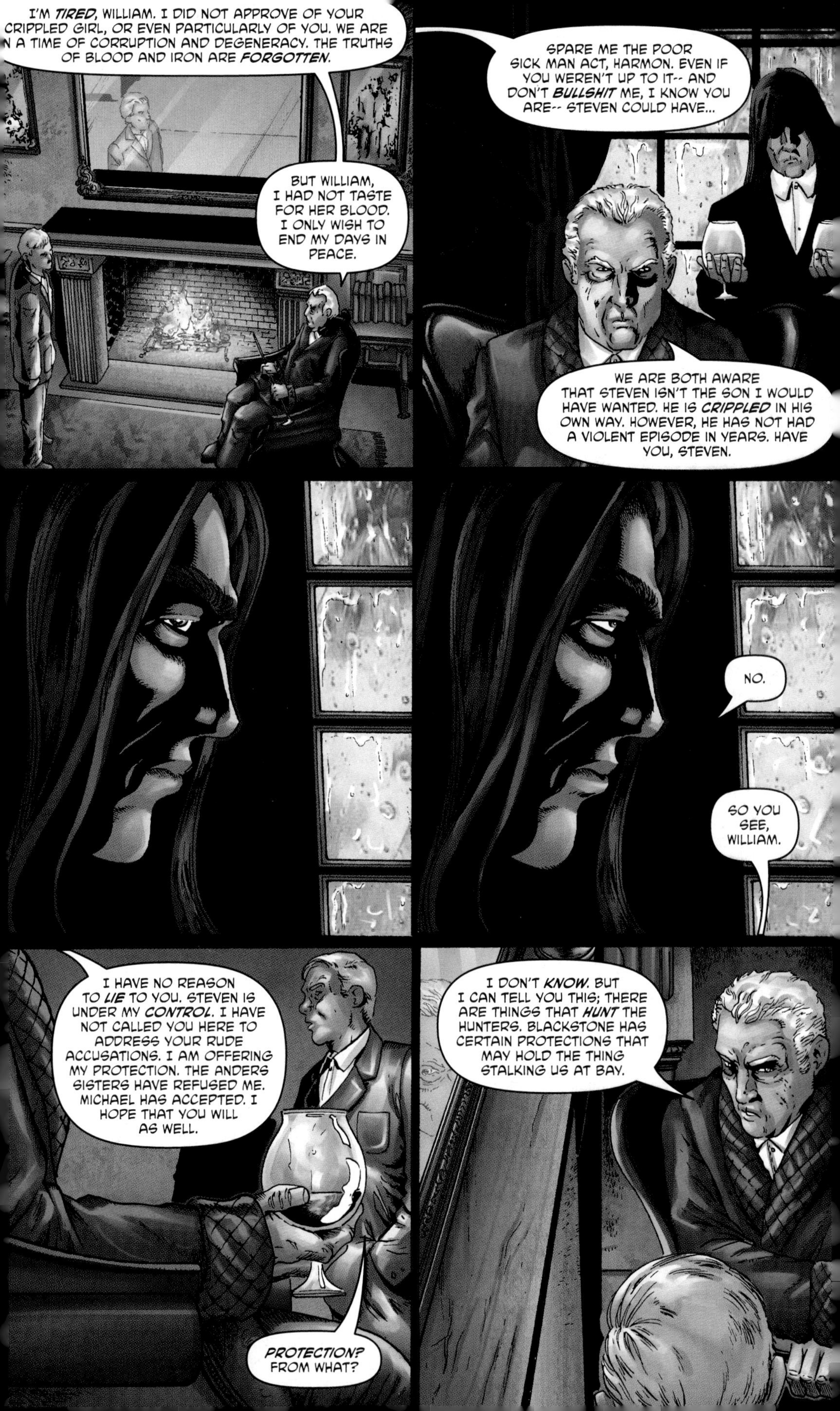
I'M *TIRED*, WILLIAM. I DID NOT APPROVE OF YOUR CRIPPLED GIRL, OR EVEN PARTICULARLY OF YOU. WE ARE IN A TIME OF CORRUPTION AND DEGENERACY. THE TRUTHS OF BLOOD AND IRON ARE *FORGOTTEN*.
BUT WILLIAM, I HAD NOT TASTE FOR HER BLOOD. I ONLY WISH TO END MY DAYS IN PEACE.
SPARE ME THE POOR SICK MAN ACT, HARMON. EVEN IF YOU WEREN'T UP TO IT-- AND DON'T *BULLSHIT* ME, I KNOW YOU ARE-- STEVEN COULD HAVE...
WE ARE BOTH AWARE THAT STEVEN ISN'T THE SON I WOULD HAVE WANTED. HE IS *CRIPPLED* IN HIS OWN WAY. HOWEVER, HE HAS NOT HAD A VIOLENT EPISODE IN YEARS. HAVE YOU, STEVEN.
NO.
SO YOU SEE, WILLIAM.
I HAVE NO REASON TO *LIE* TO YOU. STEVEN IS UNDER MY *CONTROL*. I HAVE NOT CALLED YOU HERE TO ADDRESS YOUR RUDE ACCUSATIONS. I AM OFFERING MY PROTECTION. THE ANDERS SISTERS HAVE REFUSED ME. MICHAEL HAS ACCEPTED. I HOPE THAT YOU WILL AS WELL.
PROTECTION? FROM WHAT?
I DON'T *KNOW*. BUT I CAN TELL YOU THIS; THERE ARE THINGS THAT *HUNT* THE HUNTERS. BLACKSTONE HAS CERTAIN PROTECTIONS THAT MAY HOLD THE THING STALKING US AT BAY.

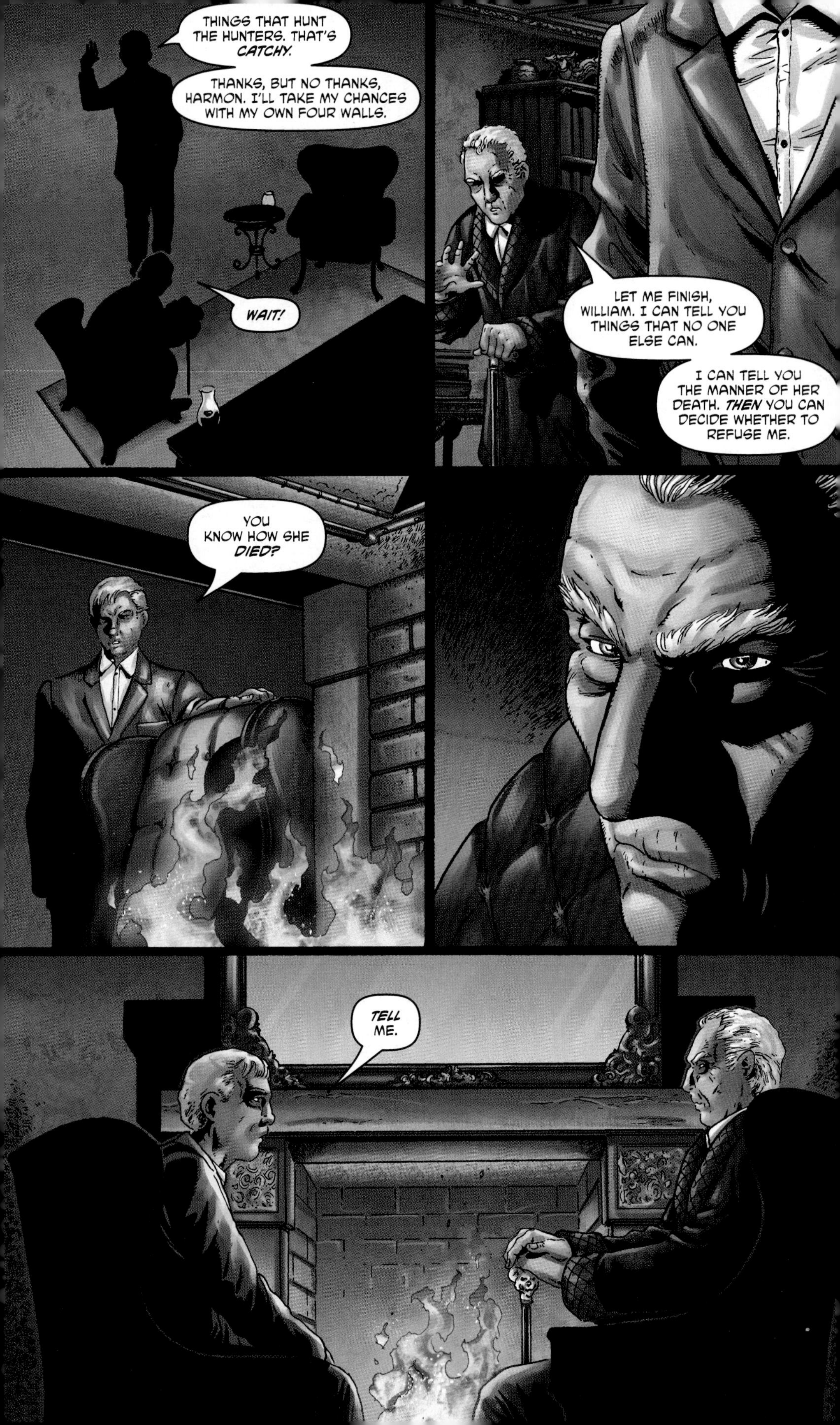
THINGS THAT HUNT THE HUNTERS. THAT'S *CATCHY.*
THANKS, BUT NO THANKS, HARMON. I'LL TAKE MY CHANCES WITH MY OWN FOUR WALLS.
WAIT!
LET ME FINISH, WILLIAM. I CAN TELL YOU THINGS THAT NO ONE ELSE CAN.
I CAN TELL YOU THE MANNER OF HER DEATH. *THEN* YOU CAN DECIDE WHETHER TO REFUSE ME.
YOU KNOW HOW SHE *DIED?*
TELL ME.

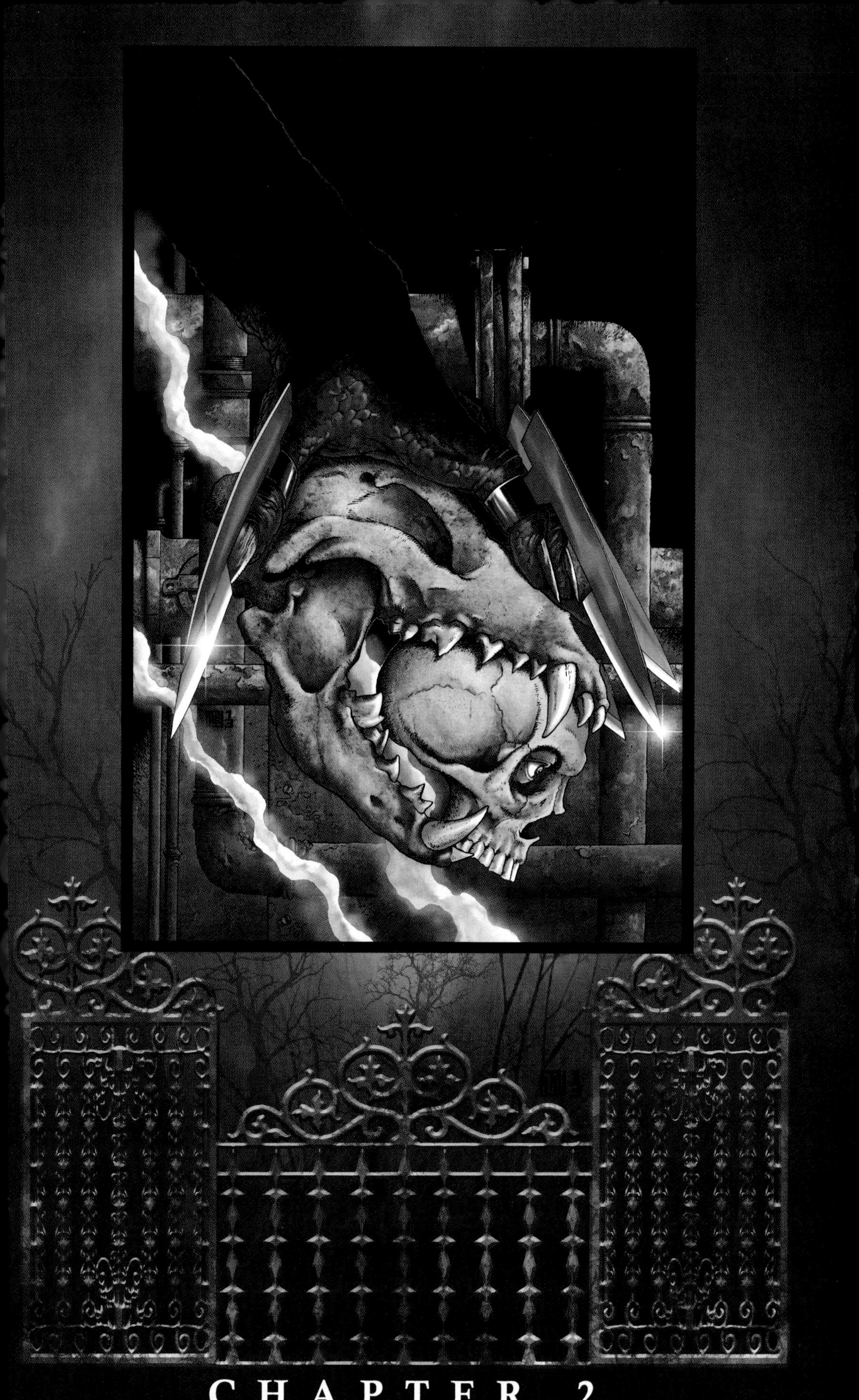

CHAPTER 2

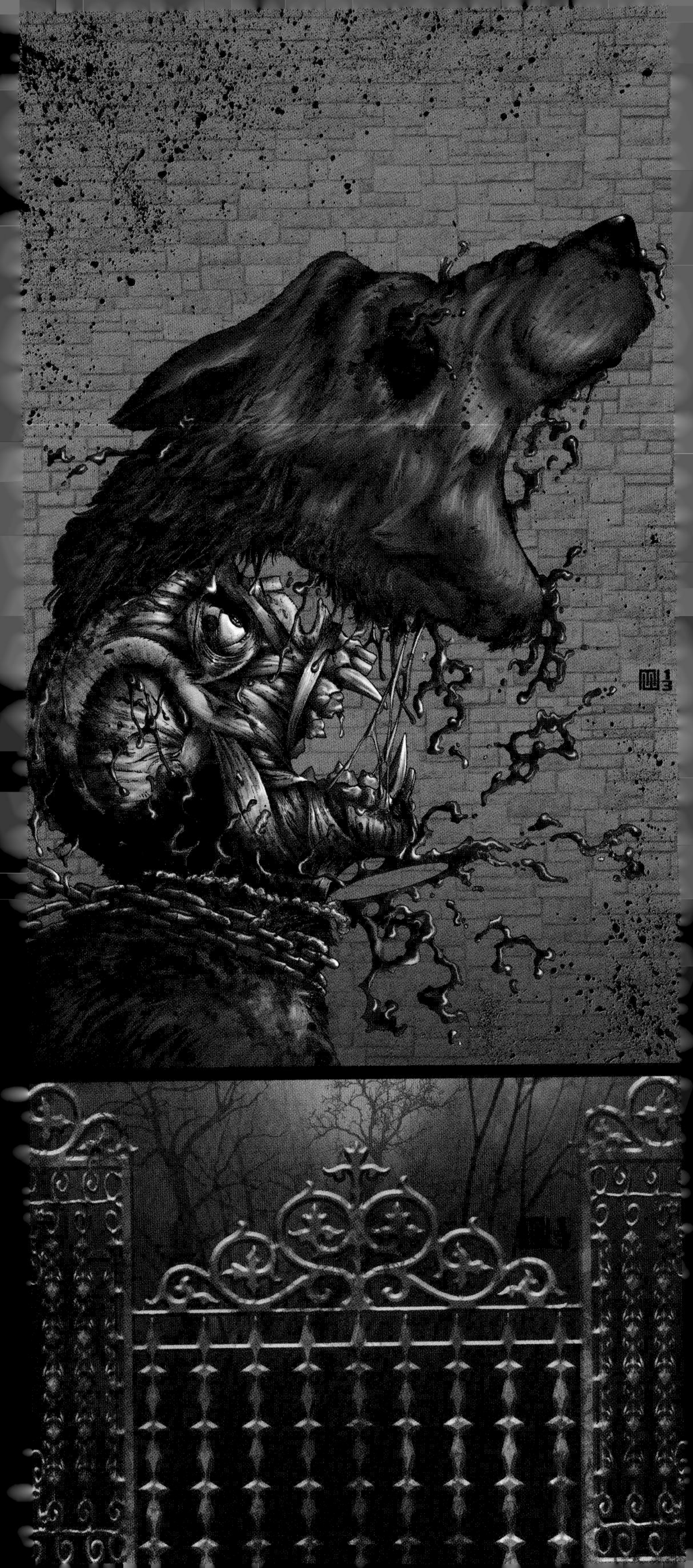

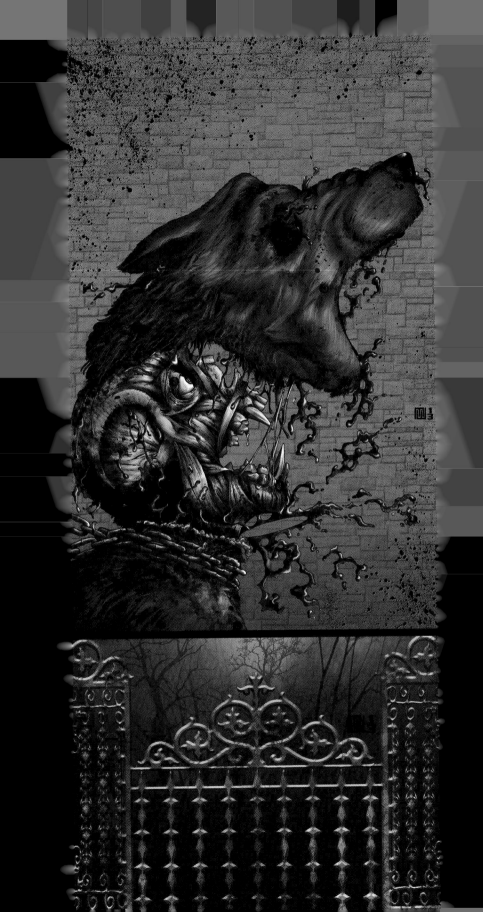

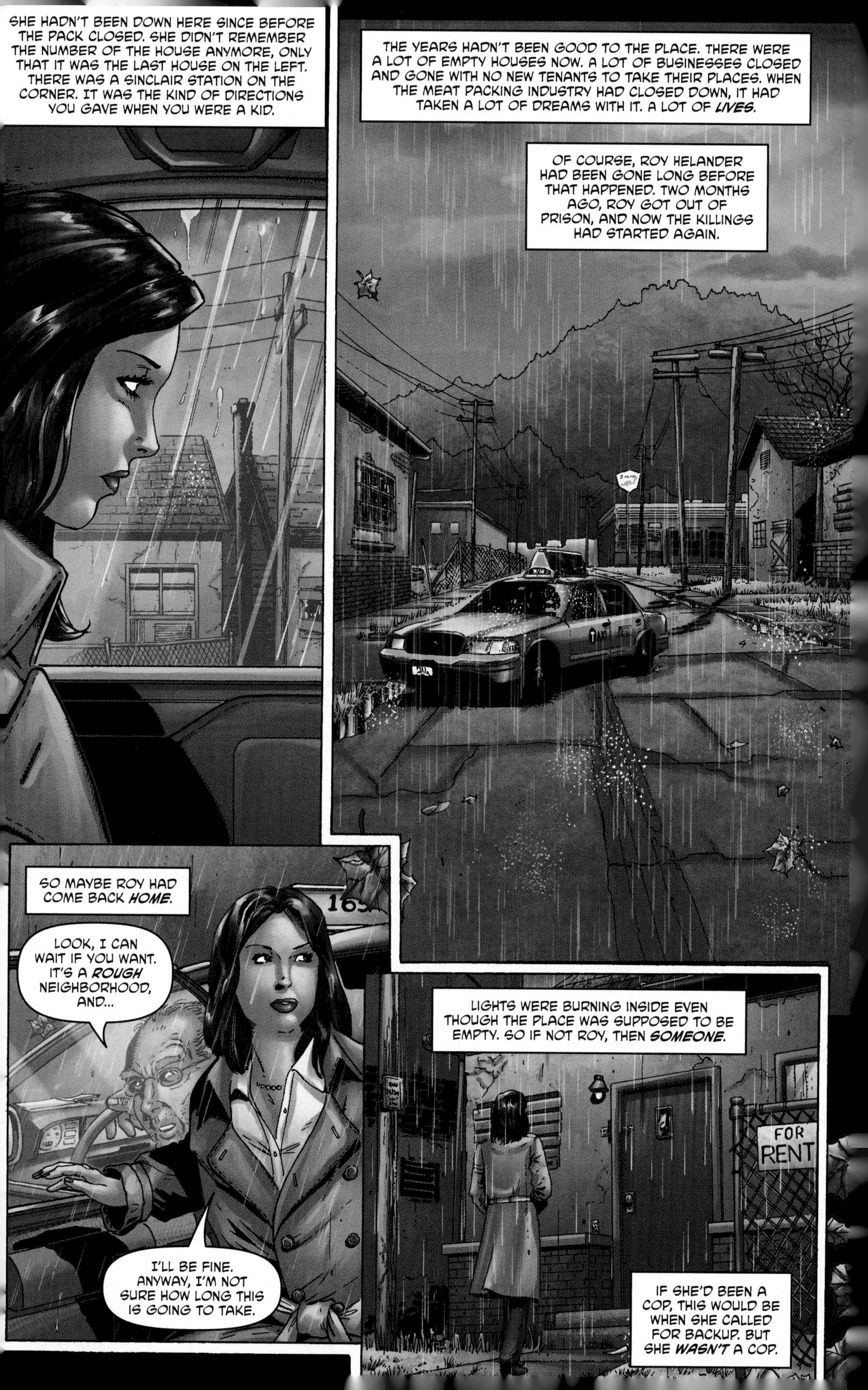

SHE HADN'T BEEN DOWN HERE SINCE BEFORE THE PACK CLOSED. SHE DIDN'T REMEMBER THE NUMBER OF THE HOUSE ANYMORE, ONLY THAT IT WAS THE LAST HOUSE ON THE LEFT. THERE WAS A SINCLAIR STATION ON THE CORNER. IT WAS THE KIND OF DIRECTIONS YOU GAVE WHEN YOU WERE A KID.
THE YEARS HADN'T BEEN GOOD TO THE PLACE. THERE WERE A LOT OF EMPTY HOUSES NOW. A LOT OF BUSINESSES CLOSED AND GONE WITH NO NEW TENANTS TO TAKE THEIR PLACES. WHEN THE MEAT PACKING INDUSTRY HAD CLOSED DOWN, IT HAD TAKEN A LOT OF DREAMS WITH IT. A LOT OF *LIVES*.
OF COURSE, ROY HELANDER HAD BEEN GONE LONG BEFORE THAT HAPPENED. TWO MONTHS AGO, ROY GOT OUT OF PRISON, AND NOW THE KILLINGS HAD STARTED AGAIN.
TAXI
SO MAYBE ROY HAD COME BACK *HOME*.
LOOK, I CAN WAIT IF YOU WANT. IT'S A *ROUGH* NEIGHBORHOOD, AND...
I'LL BE FINE. ANYWAY, I'M NOT SURE HOW LONG THIS IS GOING TO TAKE.
LIGHTS WERE BURNING INSIDE EVEN THOUGH THE PLACE WAS SUPPOSED TO BE EMPTY. SO IF NOT ROY, THEN *SOMEONE*.
FOR RENT
IF SHE'D BEEN A COP, THIS WOULD BE WHEN SHE CALLED FOR BACKUP. BUT SHE *WASN'T* A COP.

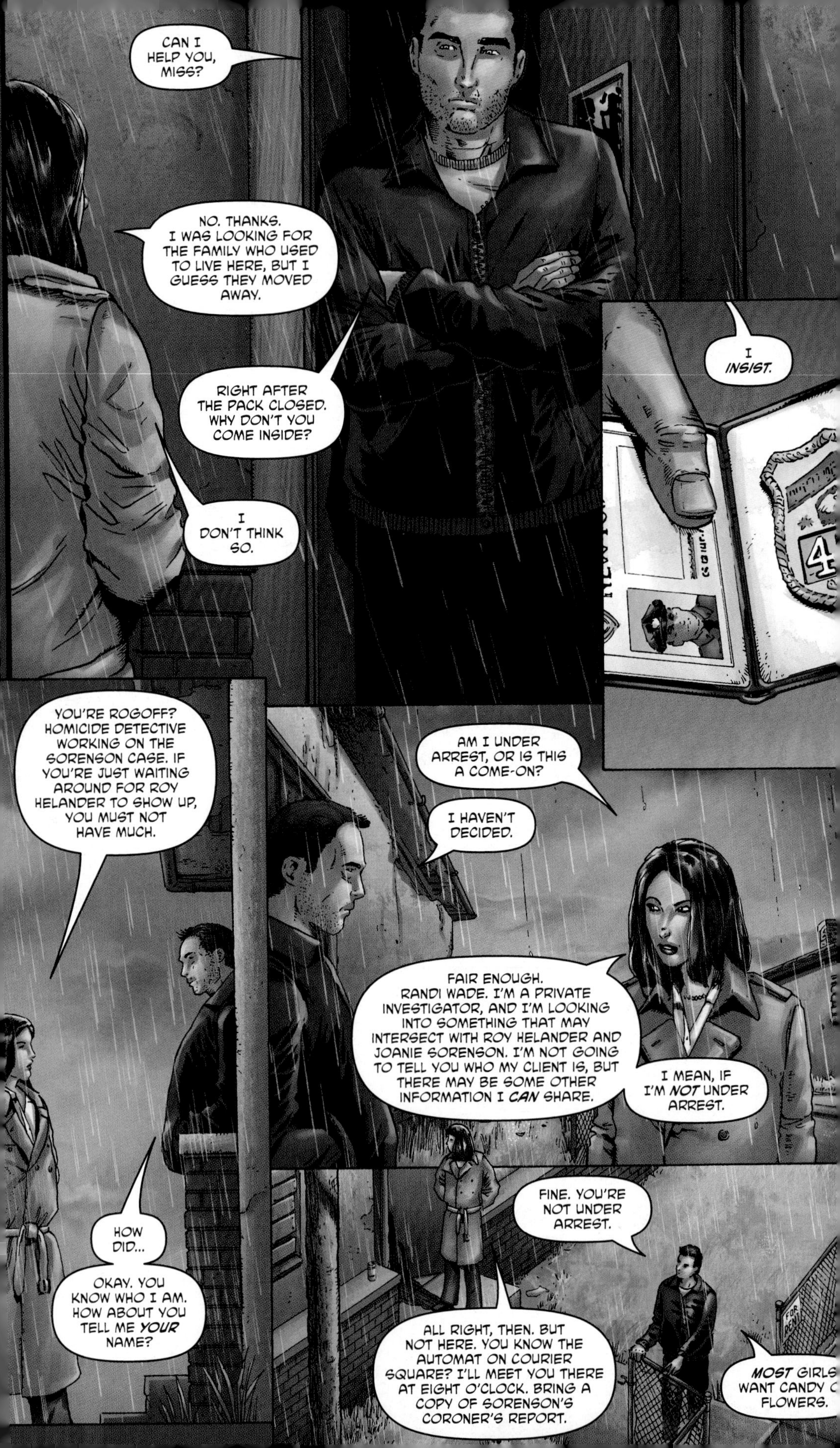

CAN I HELP YOU, MISS?
NO. THANKS. I WAS LOOKING FOR THE FAMILY WHO USED TO LIVE HERE, BUT I GUESS THEY MOVED AWAY.
RIGHT AFTER THE PACK CLOSED. WHY DON'T YOU COME INSIDE?
I DON'T THINK SO.
I INSIST.
YOU'RE ROGOFF? HOMICIDE DETECTIVE WORKING ON THE SORENSON CASE. IF YOU'RE JUST WAITING AROUND FOR ROY HELANDER TO SHOW UP, YOU MUST NOT HAVE MUCH.
AM I UNDER ARREST, OR IS THIS A COME-ON?
I HAVEN'T DECIDED.
FAIR ENOUGH. RANDI WADE. I'M A PRIVATE INVESTIGATOR, AND I'M LOOKING INTO SOMETHING THAT MAY INTERSECT WITH ROY HELANDER AND JOANIE SORENSON. I'M NOT GOING TO TELL YOU WHO MY CLIENT IS, BUT THERE MAY BE SOME OTHER INFORMATION I CAN SHARE.
I MEAN, IF I'M NOT UNDER ARREST.
HOW DID...
OKAY. YOU KNOW WHO I AM. HOW ABOUT YOU TELL ME YOUR NAME?
FINE. YOU'RE NOT UNDER ARREST.
ALL RIGHT, THEN. BUT NOT HERE. YOU KNOW THE AUTOMAT ON COURIER SQUARE? I'LL MEET YOU THERE AT EIGHT O'CLOCK. BRING A COPY OF SORENSON'S CORONER'S REPORT.
MOST GIRLS WANT CANDY O
FLOWERS.

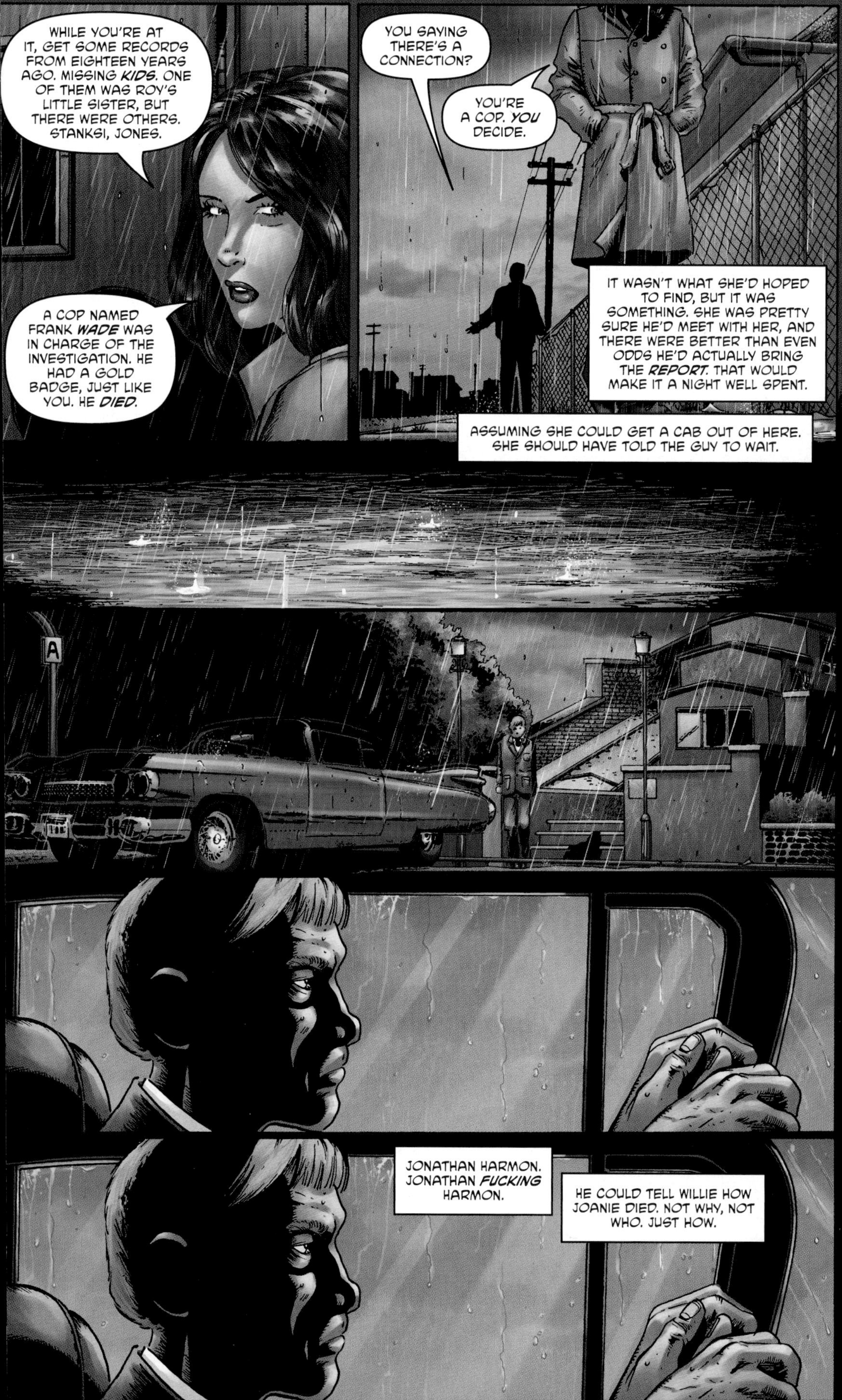
WHILE YOU'RE AT IT, GET SOME RECORDS FROM EIGHTEEN YEARS AGO. MISSING KIDS. ONE OF THEM WAS ROY'S LITTLE SISTER, BUT THERE WERE OTHERS. STANKSI, JONES.
A COP NAMED FRANK WADE WAS IN CHARGE OF THE INVESTIGATION. HE HAD A GOLD BADGE, JUST LIKE YOU. HE DIED.
YOU SAYING THERE'S A CONNECTION?
YOU'RE A COP. YOU DECIDE.
IT WASN'T WHAT SHE'D HOPED TO FIND, BUT IT WAS SOMETHING. SHE WAS PRETTY SURE HE'D MEET WITH HER, AND THERE WERE BETTER THAN EVEN ODDS HE'D ACTUALLY BRING THE REPORT. THAT WOULD MAKE IT A NIGHT WELL SPENT.
ASSUMING SHE COULD GET A CAB OUT OF HERE. SHE SHOULD HAVE TOLD THE GUY TO WAIT.
A
JONATHAN HARMON. JONATHAN FUCKING HARMON.
HE COULD TELL WILLIE HOW JOANIE DIED. NOT WHY, NOT WHO. JUST HOW.

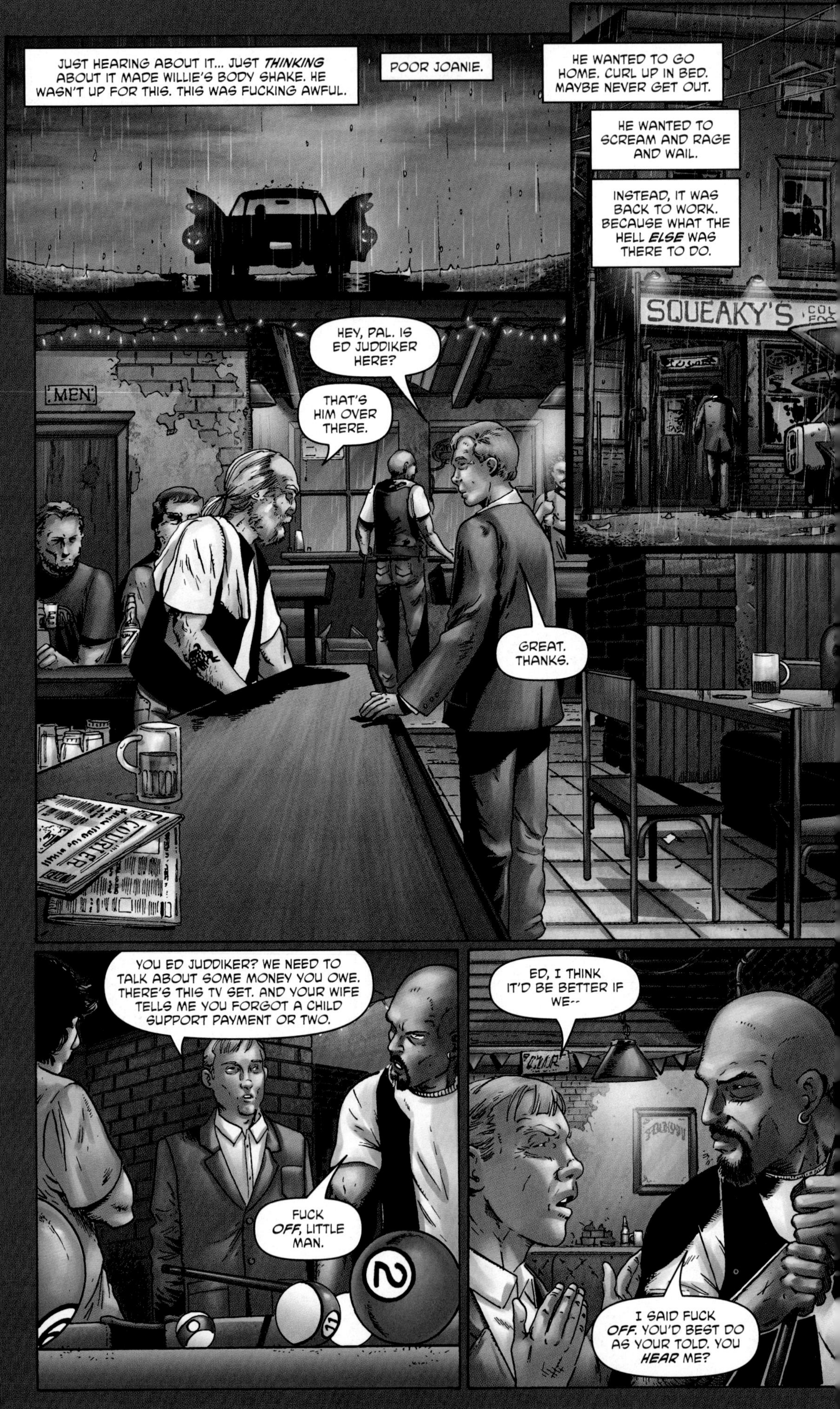

JUST HEARING ABOUT IT... JUST THINKING ABOUT IT MADE WILLIE'S BODY SHAKE. HE WASN'T UP FOR THIS. THIS WAS FUCKING AWFUL.
POOR JOANIE.
HE WANTED TO GO HOME. CURL UP IN BED. MAYBE NEVER GET OUT.
HE WANTED TO SCREAM AND RAGE AND WAIL.
INSTEAD, IT WAS BACK TO WORK. BECAUSE WHAT THE HELL ELSE WAS THERE TO DO.
SQUEAKY'S
MEN
HEY, PAL. IS ED JUDDIKER HERE?
THAT'S HIM OVER THERE.
GREAT. THANKS.
COURIER
YOU ED JUDDIKER? WE NEED TO TALK ABOUT SOME MONEY YOU OWE. THERE'S THIS TV SET. AND YOUR WIFE TELLS ME YOU FORGOT A CHILD SUPPORT PAYMENT OR TWO.
FUCK OFF, LITTLE MAN.
ED, I THINK IT'D BE BETTER IF WE--
I SAID FUCK OFF. YOU'D BEST DO AS YOUR TOLD. YOU HEAR ME?

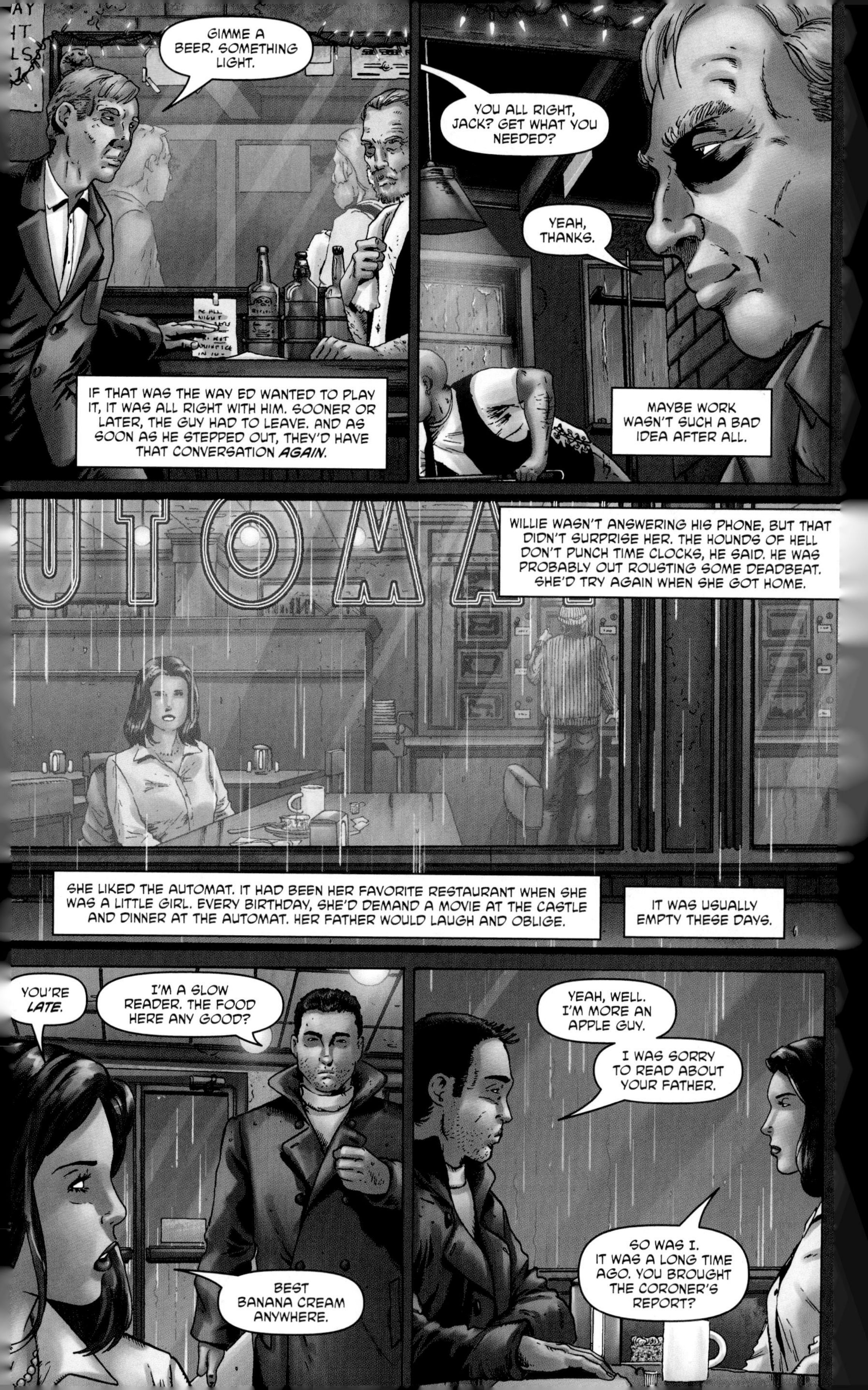
GIMME A BEER. SOMETHING LIGHT.
IF THAT WAS THE WAY ED WANTED TO PLAY IT, IT WAS ALL RIGHT WITH HIM. SOONER OR LATER, THE GUY HAD TO LEAVE. AND AS SOON AS HE STEPPED OUT, THEY'D HAVE THAT CONVERSATION *AGAIN*.
YOU ALL RIGHT, JACK? GET WHAT YOU NEEDED?
YEAH, THANKS.
MAYBE WORK WASN'T SUCH A BAD IDEA AFTER ALL.
WILLIE WASN'T ANSWERING HIS PHONE, BUT THAT DIDN'T SURPRISE HER. THE HOUNDS OF HELL DON'T PUNCH TIME CLOCKS, HE SAID. HE WAS PROBABLY OUT ROUSTING SOME DEADBEAT. SHE'D TRY AGAIN WHEN SHE GOT HOME.
SHE LIKED THE AUTOMAT. IT HAD BEEN HER FAVORITE RESTAURANT WHEN SHE WAS A LITTLE GIRL. EVERY BIRTHDAY, SHE'D DEMAND A MOVIE AT THE CASTLE AND DINNER AT THE AUTOMAT. HER FATHER WOULD LAUGH AND OBLIGE.
IT WAS USUALLY EMPTY THESE DAYS.
YOU'RE *LATE*.
I'M A SLOW READER. THE FOOD HERE ANY GOOD?
BEST BANANA CREAM ANYWHERE.
YEAH, WELL. I'M MORE AN APPLE GUY.
I WAS SORRY TO READ ABOUT YOUR FATHER.
SO WAS I. IT WAS A LONG TIME AGO. YOU BROUGHT THE CORONER'S REPORT?

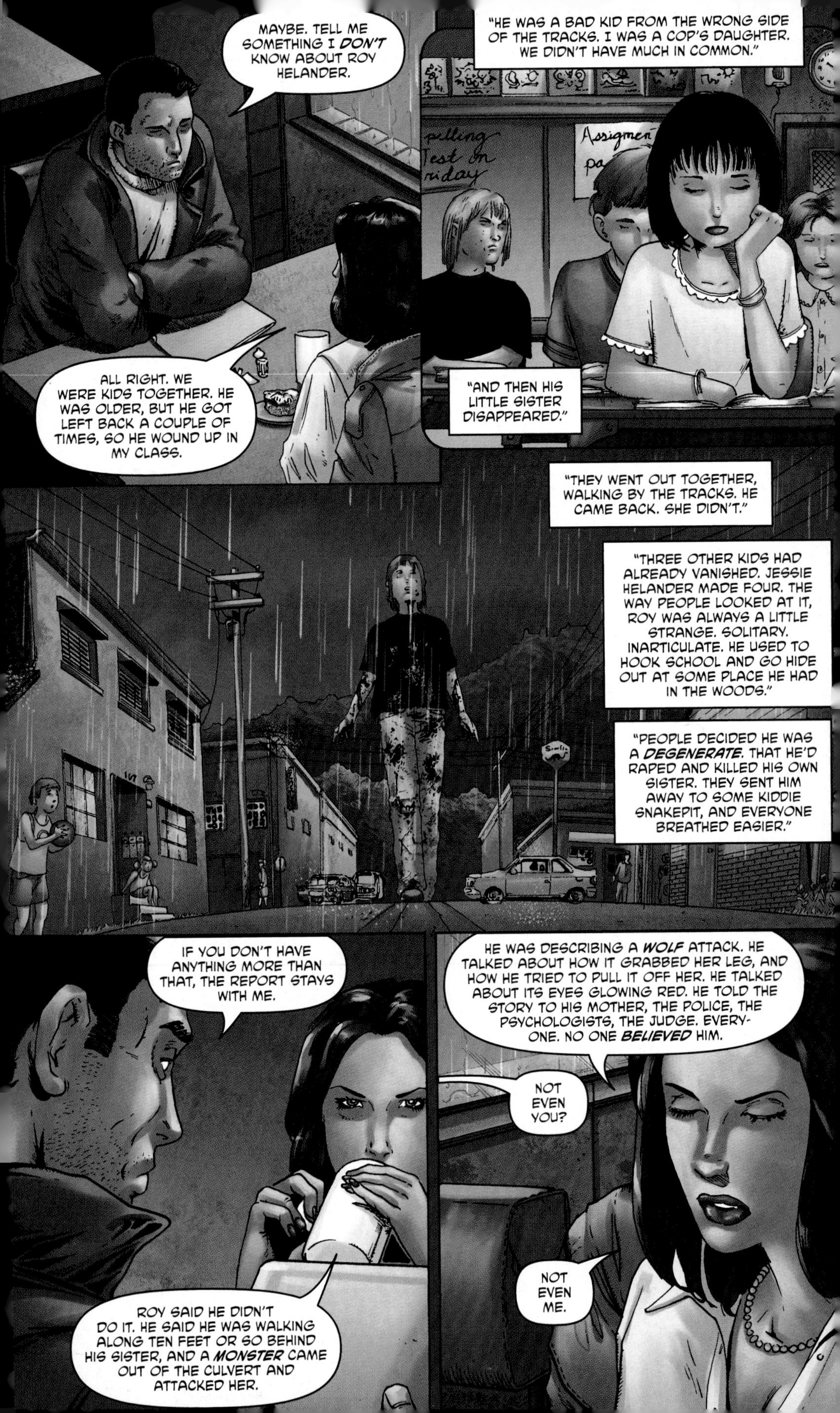
MAYBE. TELL ME SOMETHING I DON'T KNOW ABOUT ROY HELANDER.
ALL RIGHT. WE WERE KIDS TOGETHER. HE WAS OLDER, BUT HE GOT LEFT BACK A COUPLE OF TIMES, SO HE WOUND UP IN MY CLASS.
"HE WAS A BAD KID FROM THE WRONG SIDE OF THE TRACKS. I WAS A COP'S DAUGHTER. WE DIDN'T HAVE MUCH IN COMMON."
"AND THEN HIS LITTLE SISTER DISAPPEARED."
"THEY WENT OUT TOGETHER, WALKING BY THE TRACKS. HE CAME BACK. SHE DIDN'T."
"THREE OTHER KIDS HAD ALREADY VANISHED. JESSIE HELANDER MADE FOUR. THE WAY PEOPLE LOOKED AT IT, ROY WAS ALWAYS A LITTLE STRANGE. SOLITARY. INARTICULATE. HE USED TO HOOK SCHOOL AND GO HIDE OUT AT SOME PLACE HE HAD IN THE WOODS."
"PEOPLE DECIDED HE WAS A DEGENERATE. THAT HE'D RAPED AND KILLED HIS OWN SISTER. THEY SENT HIM AWAY TO SOME KIDDIE SNAKEPIT, AND EVERYONE BREATHED EASIER."
IF YOU DON'T HAVE ANYTHING MORE THAN THAT, THE REPORT STAYS WITH ME.
ROY SAID HE DIDN'T DO IT. HE SAID HE WAS WALKING ALONG TEN FEET OR SO BEHIND HIS SISTER, AND A MONSTER CAME OUT OF THE CULVERT AND ATTACKED HER.
HE WAS DESCRIBING A WOLF ATTACK. HE TALKED ABOUT HOW IT GRABBED HER LEG, AND HOW HE TRIED TO PULL IT OFF HER. HE TALKED ABOUT ITS EYES GLOWING RED. HE TOLD THE STORY TO HIS MOTHER, THE POLICE, THE PSYCHOLOGISTS, THE JUDGE. EVERY-ONE. NO ONE BELIEVED HIM.
NOT EVEN YOU?
NOT EVEN ME.

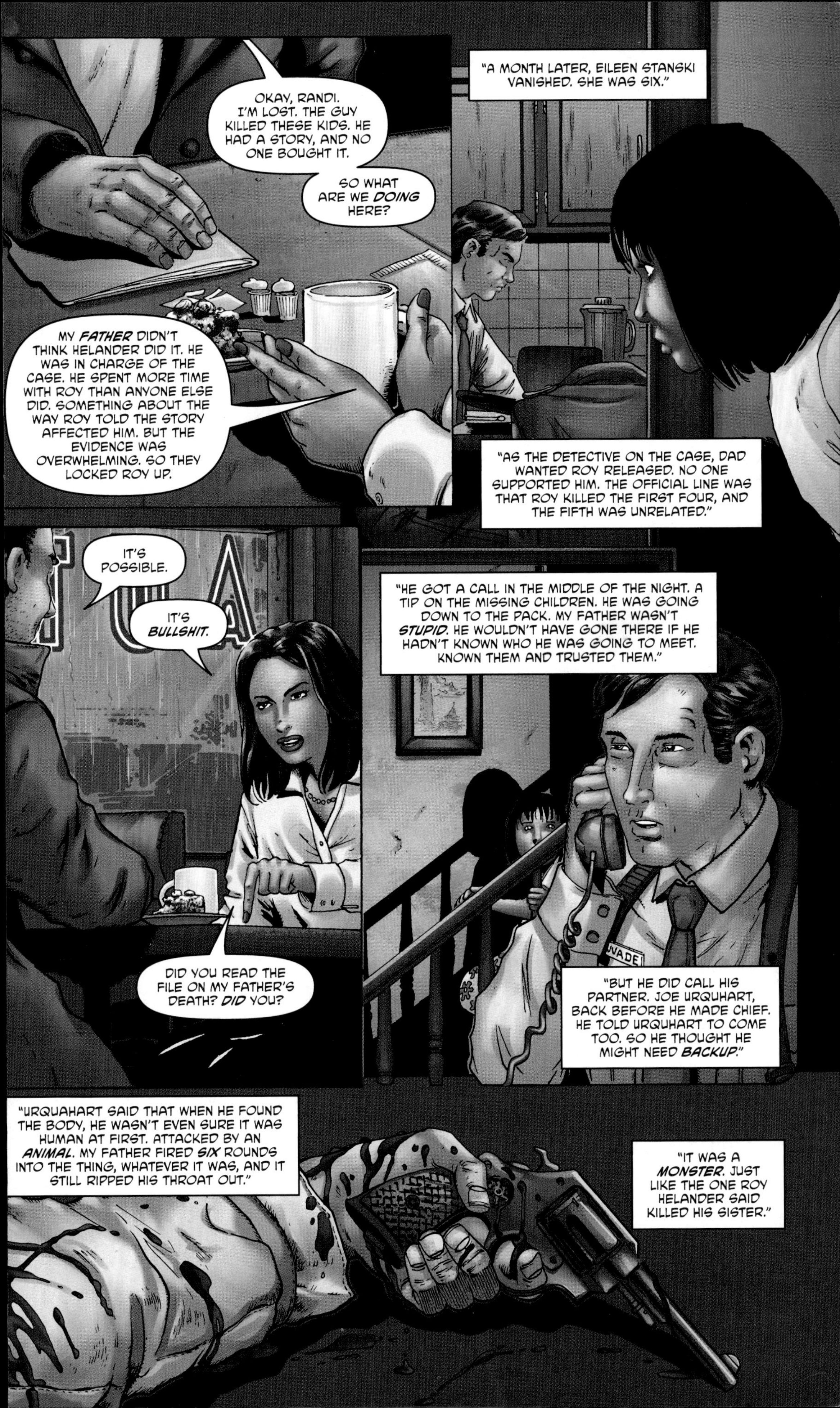

OKAY, RANDI. I'M LOST. THE GUY KILLED THESE KIDS. HE HAD A STORY, AND NO ONE BOUGHT IT.
SO WHAT ARE WE *DOING* HERE?
MY *FATHER* DIDN'T THINK HELANDER DID IT. HE WAS IN CHARGE OF THE CASE. HE SPENT MORE TIME WITH ROY THAN ANYONE ELSE DID. SOMETHING ABOUT THE WAY ROY TOLD THE STORY AFFECTED HIM. BUT THE EVIDENCE WAS OVERWHELMING. SO THEY LOCKED ROY UP.
"A MONTH LATER, EILEEN STANSKI VANISHED. SHE WAS SIX."
"AS THE DETECTIVE ON THE CASE, DAD WANTED ROY RELEASED. NO ONE SUPPORTED HIM. THE OFFICIAL LINE WAS THAT ROY KILLED THE FIRST FOUR, AND THE FIFTH WAS UNRELATED."
IT'S POSSIBLE.
IT'S *BULLSHIT*.
DID YOU READ THE FILE ON MY FATHER'S DEATH? *DID* YOU?
"HE GOT A CALL IN THE MIDDLE OF THE NIGHT. A TIP ON THE MISSING CHILDREN. HE WAS GOING DOWN TO THE PACK. MY FATHER WASN'T *STUPID*. HE WOULDN'T HAVE GONE THERE IF HE HADN'T KNOWN WHO HE WAS GOING TO MEET. KNOWN THEM AND TRUSTED THEM."
WADE
"BUT HE DID CALL HIS PARTNER. JOE URQUHART, BACK BEFORE HE MADE CHIEF. HE TOLD URQUHART TO COME TOO. SO HE THOUGHT HE MIGHT NEED *BACKUP*."
"URQUAHART SAID THAT WHEN HE FOUND THE BODY, HE WASN'T EVEN SURE IT WAS HUMAN AT FIRST. ATTACKED BY AN *ANIMAL*. MY FATHER FIRED *SIX* ROUNDS INTO THE THING, WHATEVER IT WAS, AND IT STILL RIPPED HIS THROAT OUT."
"IT WAS A *MONSTER*. JUST LIKE THE ONE ROY HELANDER SAID KILLED HIS SISTER."

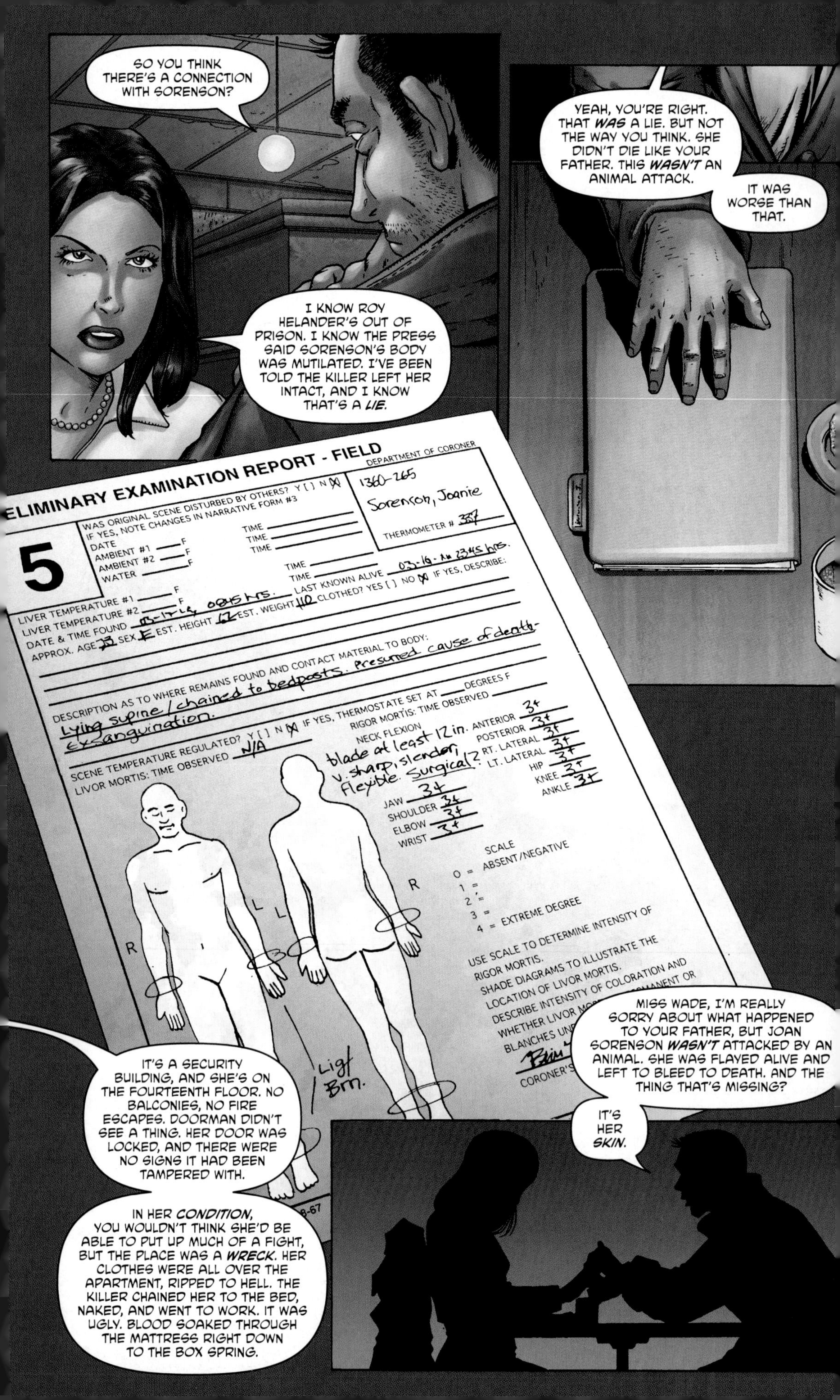
SO YOU THINK THERE'S A CONNECTION WITH SORENSON?
I KNOW ROY HELANDER'S OUT OF PRISON. I KNOW THE PRESS SAID SORENSON'S BODY WAS MUTILATED. I'VE BEEN TOLD THE KILLER LEFT HER INTACT, AND I KNOW THAT'S A *LIE*.
YEAH, YOU'RE RIGHT. THAT *WAS* A LIE. BUT NOT THE WAY YOU THINK. SHE DIDN'T DIE LIKE YOUR FATHER. THIS *WASN'T* AN ANIMAL ATTACK.
IT WAS WORSE THAN THAT.
ELIMINARY EXAMINATION REPORT - FIELD
DEPARTMENT OF CORONER
1360-265
Sorenson, Joanie
5
WAS ORIGINAL SCENE DISTURBED BY OTHERS? Y [ ] N [X]
IF YES, NOTE CHANGES IN NARRATIVE FORM #3
THERMOMETER # 337
LAST KNOWN ALIVE 03-16 2345 hrs.
CLOTHED? YES [ ] NO [X] IF YES, DESCRIBE:
DESCRIPTION AS TO WHERE REMAINS FOUND AND CONTACT MATERIAL TO BODY:
Lying supine / chained to bedposts. Presumed cause of death - exsanguination.
SCENE TEMPERATURE REGULATED? Y [ ] N [X] IF YES, THERMOSTAT SET AT ___ DEGREES F
LIVOR MORTIS: TIME OBSERVED N/A
RIGOR MORTIS: TIME OBSERVED
blade at least 12 in. v. sharp, slender, flexible. Surgical?
SCALE
0 = ABSENT/NEGATIVE
4 = EXTREME DEGREE
USE SCALE TO DETERMINE INTENSITY OF RIGOR MORTIS.
SHADE DIAGRAMS TO ILLUSTRATE THE LOCATION OF LIVOR MORTIS.
Lig / Brn.
IT'S A SECURITY BUILDING, AND SHE'S ON THE FOURTEENTH FLOOR. NO BALCONIES, NO FIRE ESCAPES. DOORMAN DIDN'T SEE A THING. HER DOOR WAS LOCKED, AND THERE WERE NO SIGNS IT HAD BEEN TAMPERED WITH.
IN HER *CONDITION*, YOU WOULDN'T THINK SHE'D BE ABLE TO PUT UP MUCH OF A FIGHT, BUT THE PLACE WAS A *WRECK*. HER CLOTHES WERE ALL OVER THE APARTMENT, RIPPED TO HELL. THE KILLER CHAINED HER TO THE BED, NAKED, AND WENT TO WORK. IT WAS UGLY. BLOOD SOAKED THROUGH THE MATTRESS RIGHT DOWN TO THE BOX SPRING.
MISS WADE, I'M REALLY SORRY ABOUT WHAT HAPPENED TO YOUR FATHER, BUT JOAN SORENSON *WASN'T* ATTACKED BY AN ANIMAL. SHE WAS FLAYED ALIVE AND LEFT TO BLEED TO DEATH. AND THE THING THAT'S MISSING?
IT'S HER *SKIN*.

ED
JUDDIKER.

GOOD
OLD *ED*.

HE ONLY HAD SEVENTY-NINE
BUCKS ON HIM, BUT IT WAS A
START. HE FIGURED HE GIVE
HALF TO BETSY AND PUT THE
REST TOWARD ED'S ACCOUNT.

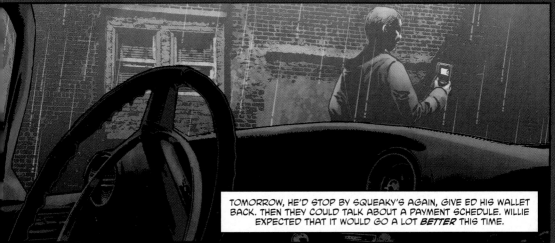

TOMORROW, HE'D STOP BY SQUEAKY'S AGAIN, GIVE ED HIS WALLET
BACK. THEN THEY COULD TALK ABOUT A PAYMENT SCHEDULE. WILLIE
EXPECTED THAT IT WOULD GO A LOT *BETTER* THIS TIME.

HE NEEDED TO STOP
CARRYING SO MANY
THINGS. HIS INHALER,
SIX GIVE-AWAY
CREDIT CARD
SCISSORS, HIS PILL
BOX, A COUPLE
HANDKERCHIEFS. HE
COULD *NEVER* GET
HIS KEYS OUT THE
FIRST TIME. HE
ALWAYS WOUND UP
STANDING IN THE
RAIN IN FRONT OF A
LOCKED DOOR...

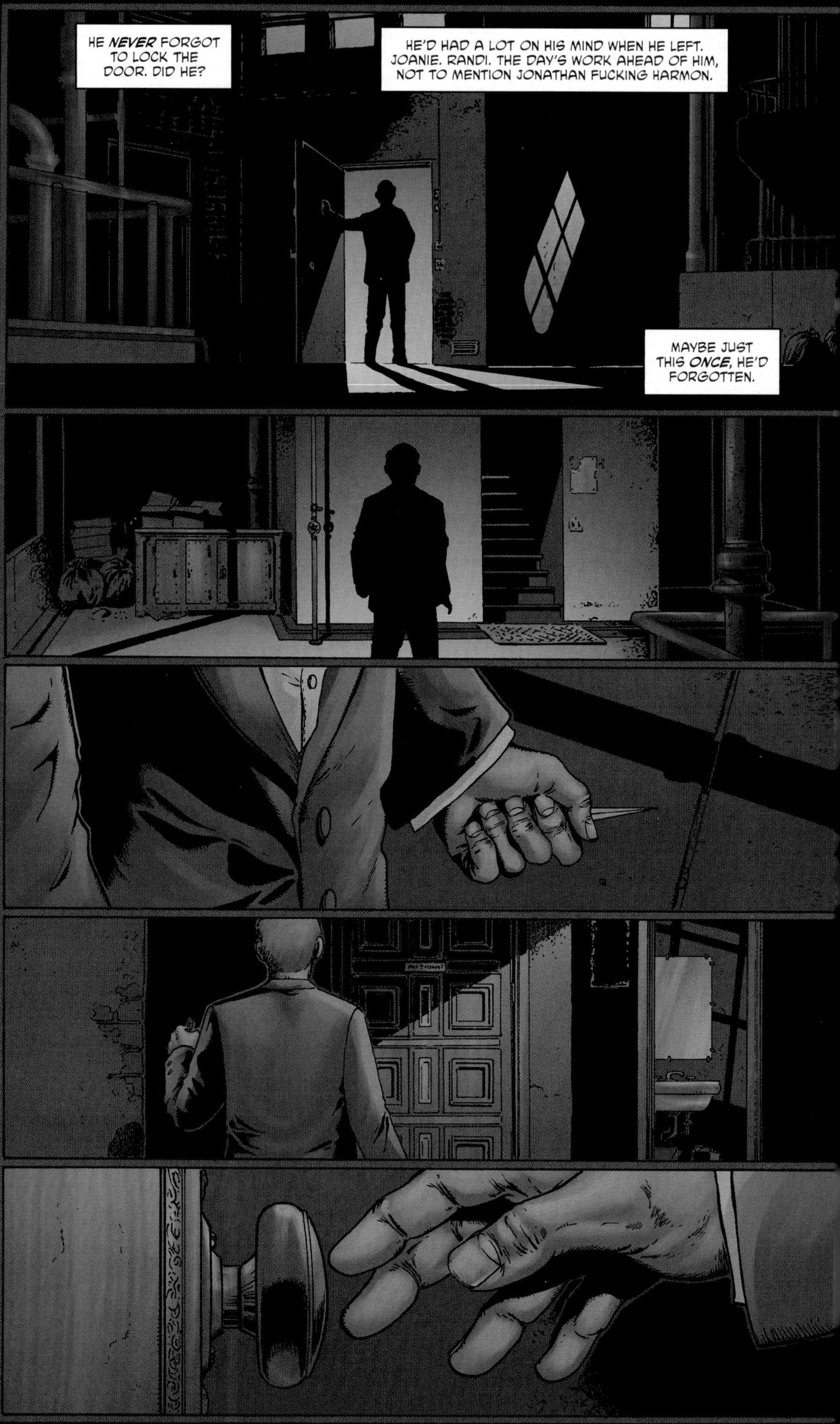

HE *NEVER* FORGOT TO LOCK THE DOOR. DID HE?
HE'D HAD A LOT ON HIS MIND WHEN HE LEFT. JOANIE. RANDI. THE DAY'S WORK AHEAD OF HIM, NOT TO MENTION JONATHAN FUCKING HARMON.
MAYBE JUST THIS *ONCE*, HE'D FORGOTTEN.

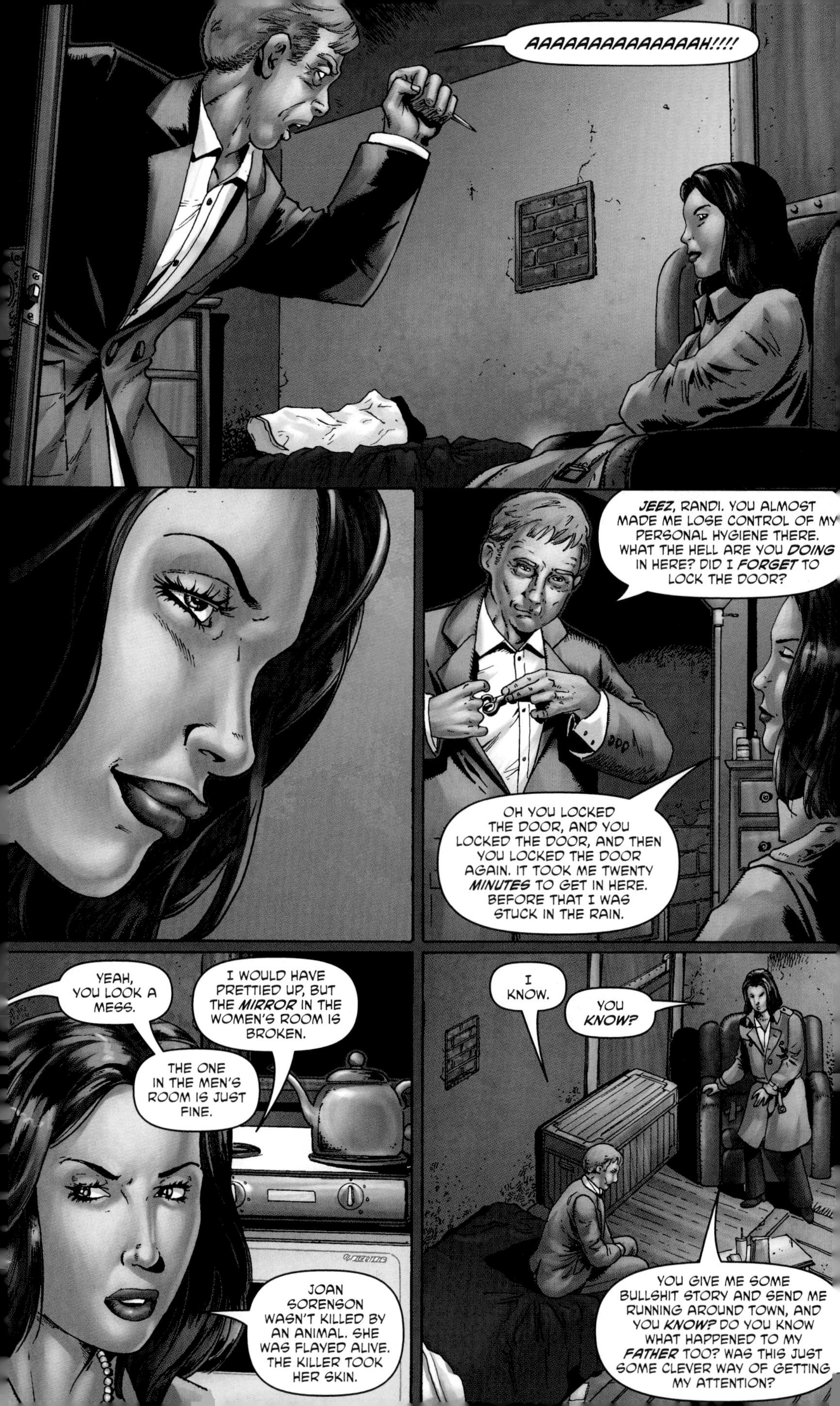
AAAAAAAAAAAAAAAH!!!!
JEEZ, RANDI. YOU ALMOST MADE ME LOSE CONTROL OF MY PERSONAL HYGIENE THERE. WHAT THE HELL ARE YOU DOING IN HERE? DID I FORGET TO LOCK THE DOOR?
OH YOU LOCKED THE DOOR, AND YOU LOCKED THE DOOR, AND THEN YOU LOCKED THE DOOR AGAIN. IT TOOK ME TWENTY MINUTES TO GET IN HERE. BEFORE THAT I WAS STUCK IN THE RAIN.
YEAH, YOU LOOK A MESS.
I WOULD HAVE PRETTIED UP, BUT THE MIRROR IN THE WOMEN'S ROOM IS BROKEN.
THE ONE IN THE MEN'S ROOM IS JUST FINE.
JOAN SORENSON WASN'T KILLED BY AN ANIMAL. SHE WAS FLAYED ALIVE. THE KILLER TOOK HER SKIN.
I KNOW.
YOU KNOW?
YOU GIVE ME SOME BULLSHIT STORY AND SEND ME RUNNING AROUND TOWN, AND YOU KNOW? DO YOU KNOW WHAT HAPPENED TO MY FATHER TOO? WAS THIS JUST SOME CLEVER WAY OF GETTING MY ATTENTION?

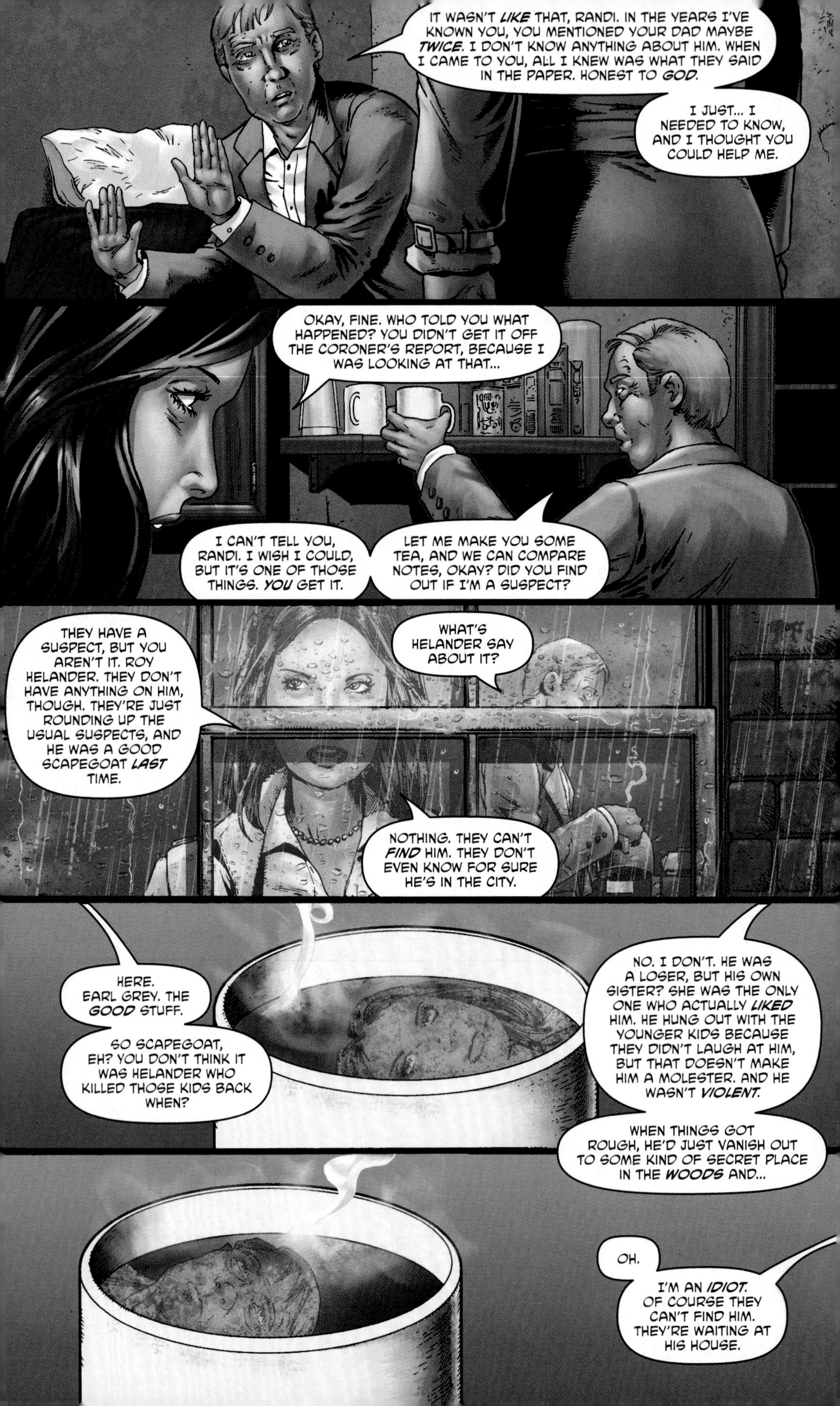
IT WASN'T *LIKE* THAT, RANDI. IN THE YEARS I'VE KNOWN YOU, YOU MENTIONED YOUR DAD MAYBE *TWICE*. I DON'T KNOW ANYTHING ABOUT HIM. WHEN I CAME TO YOU, ALL I KNEW WAS WHAT THEY SAID IN THE PAPER. HONEST TO *GOD*.
I JUST... I NEEDED TO KNOW, AND I THOUGHT YOU COULD HELP ME.
OKAY, FINE. WHO TOLD YOU WHAT HAPPENED? YOU DIDN'T GET IT OFF THE CORONER'S REPORT, BECAUSE I WAS LOOKING AT THAT...
I CAN'T TELL YOU, RANDI. I WISH I COULD, BUT IT'S ONE OF THOSE THINGS. *YOU* GET IT.
LET ME MAKE YOU SOME TEA, AND WE CAN COMPARE NOTES, OKAY? DID YOU FIND OUT IF I'M A SUSPECT?
THEY HAVE A SUSPECT, BUT YOU AREN'T IT. ROY HELANDER. THEY DON'T HAVE ANYTHING ON HIM, THOUGH. THEY'RE JUST ROUNDING UP THE USUAL SUSPECTS, AND HE WAS A GOOD SCAPEGOAT *LAST* TIME.
WHAT'S HELANDER SAY ABOUT IT?
NOTHING. THEY CAN'T *FIND* HIM. THEY DON'T EVEN KNOW FOR SURE HE'S IN THE CITY.
HERE. EARL GREY. THE *GOOD* STUFF.
SO SCAPEGOAT, EH? YOU DON'T THINK IT WAS HELANDER WHO KILLED THOSE KIDS BACK WHEN?
NO. I DON'T. HE WAS A LOSER, BUT HIS OWN SISTER? SHE WAS THE ONLY ONE WHO ACTUALLY *LIKED* HIM. HE HUNG OUT WITH THE YOUNGER KIDS BECAUSE THEY DIDN'T LAUGH AT HIM, BUT THAT DOESN'T MAKE HIM A MOLESTER. AND HE WASN'T *VIOLENT*.
WHEN THINGS GOT ROUGH, HE'D JUST VANISH OUT TO SOME KIND OF SECRET PLACE IN THE *WOODS* AND...
OH.
I'M AN *IDIOT*. OF COURSE THEY CAN'T FIND HIM. THEY'RE WAITING AT HIS HOUSE.

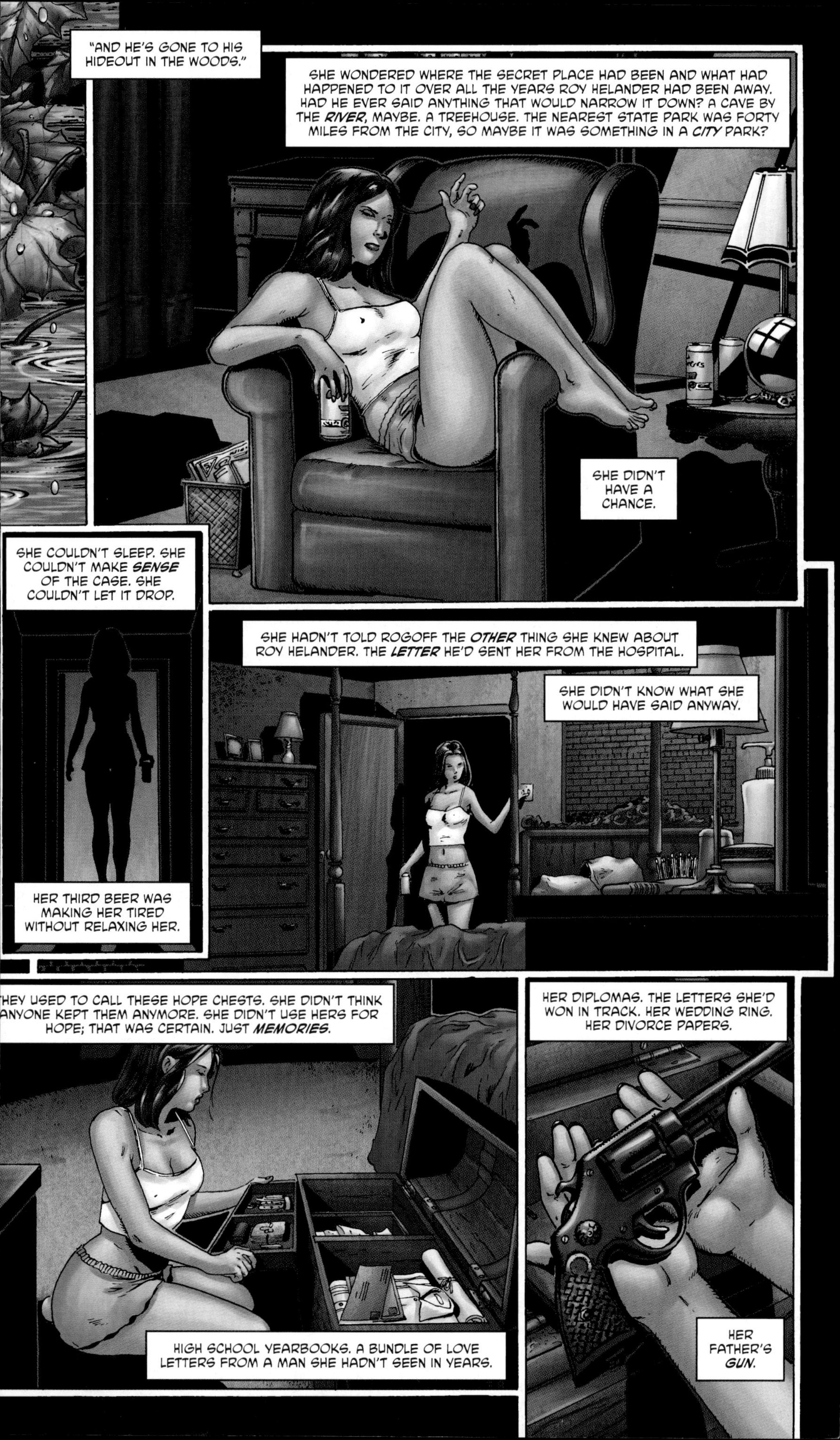
"AND HE'S GONE TO HIS HIDEOUT IN THE WOODS."
SHE WONDERED WHERE THE SECRET PLACE HAD BEEN AND WHAT HAD HAPPENED TO IT OVER ALL THE YEARS ROY HELANDER HAD BEEN AWAY. HAD HE EVER SAID ANYTHING THAT WOULD NARROW IT DOWN? A CAVE BY THE *RIVER*, MAYBE. A TREEHOUSE. THE NEAREST STATE PARK WAS FORTY MILES FROM THE CITY, SO MAYBE IT WAS SOMETHING IN A *CITY* PARK?
SHE DIDN'T HAVE A CHANCE.
SHE COULDN'T SLEEP. SHE COULDN'T MAKE *SENSE* OF THE CASE. SHE COULDN'T LET IT DROP.
HER THIRD BEER WAS MAKING HER TIRED WITHOUT RELAXING HER.
SHE HADN'T TOLD ROGOFF THE *OTHER* THING SHE KNEW ABOUT ROY HELANDER. THE *LETTER* HE'D SENT HER FROM THE HOSPITAL.
SHE DIDN'T KNOW WHAT SHE WOULD HAVE SAID ANYWAY.
HEY USED TO CALL THESE HOPE CHESTS. SHE DIDN'T THINK ANYONE KEPT THEM ANYMORE. SHE DIDN'T USE HERS FOR HOPE; THAT WAS CERTAIN. JUST *MEMORIES*.
HIGH SCHOOL YEARBOOKS. A BUNDLE OF LOVE LETTERS FROM A MAN SHE HADN'T SEEN IN YEARS.
HER DIPLOMAS. THE LETTERS SHE'D WON IN TRACK. HER WEDDING RING. HER DIVORCE PAPERS.
HER FATHER'S *GUN*.

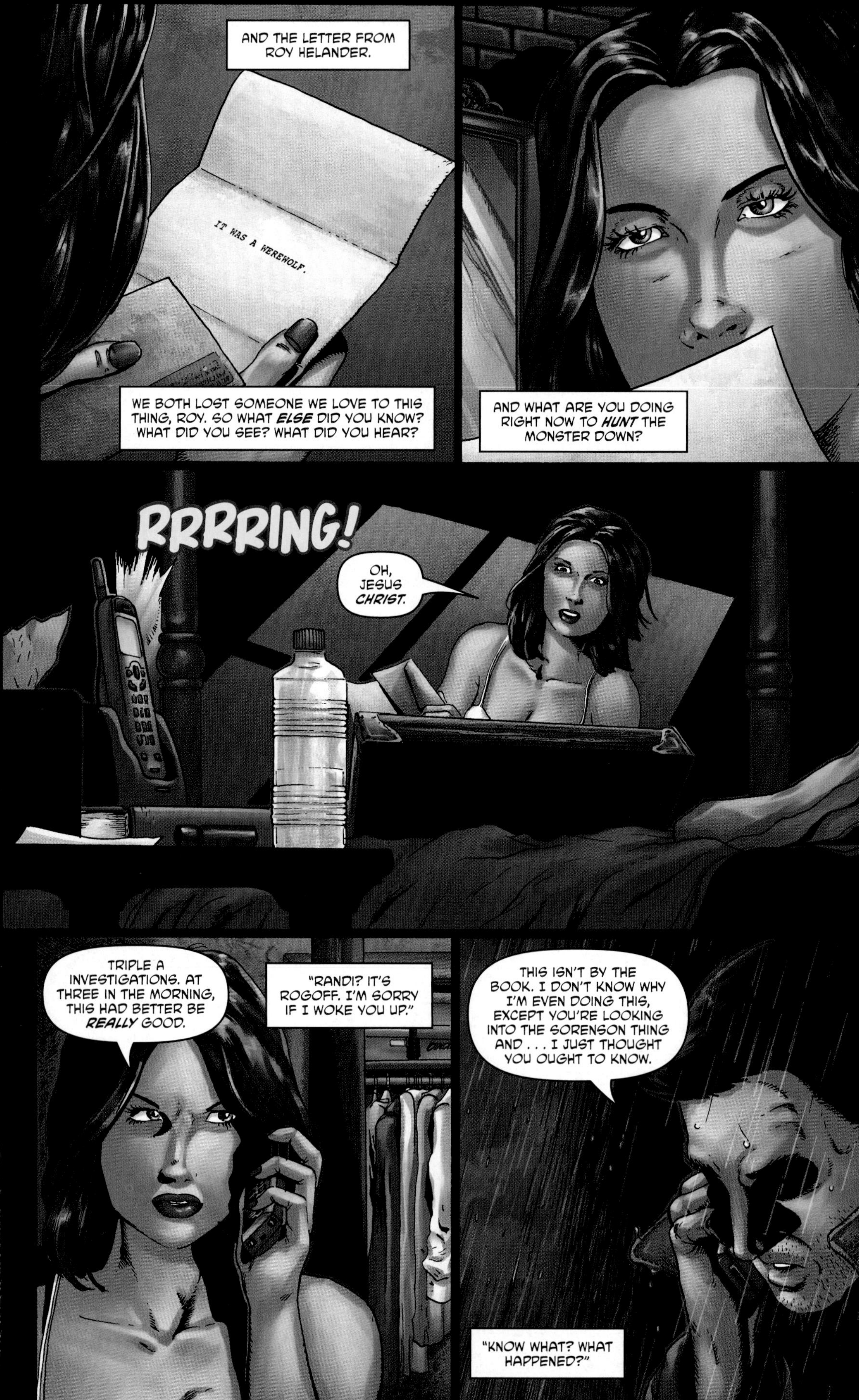
AND THE LETTER FROM ROY HELANDER.
IT WAS A WEREWOLF.
WE BOTH LOST SOMEONE WE LOVE TO THIS THING, ROY. SO WHAT ELSE DID YOU KNOW? WHAT DID YOU SEE? WHAT DID YOU HEAR?
AND WHAT ARE YOU DOING RIGHT NOW TO HUNT THE MONSTER DOWN?
RRRRING!
OH, JESUS CHRIST.
TRIPLE A INVESTIGATIONS. AT THREE IN THE MORNING, THIS HAD BETTER BE REALLY GOOD.
"RANDI? IT'S ROGOFF. I'M SORRY IF I WOKE YOU UP."
THIS ISN'T BY THE BOOK. I DON'T KNOW WHY I'M EVEN DOING THIS, EXCEPT YOU'RE LOOKING INTO THE SORENSON THING AND . . . I JUST THOUGHT YOU OUGHT TO KNOW.
"KNOW WHAT? WHAT HAPPENED?"

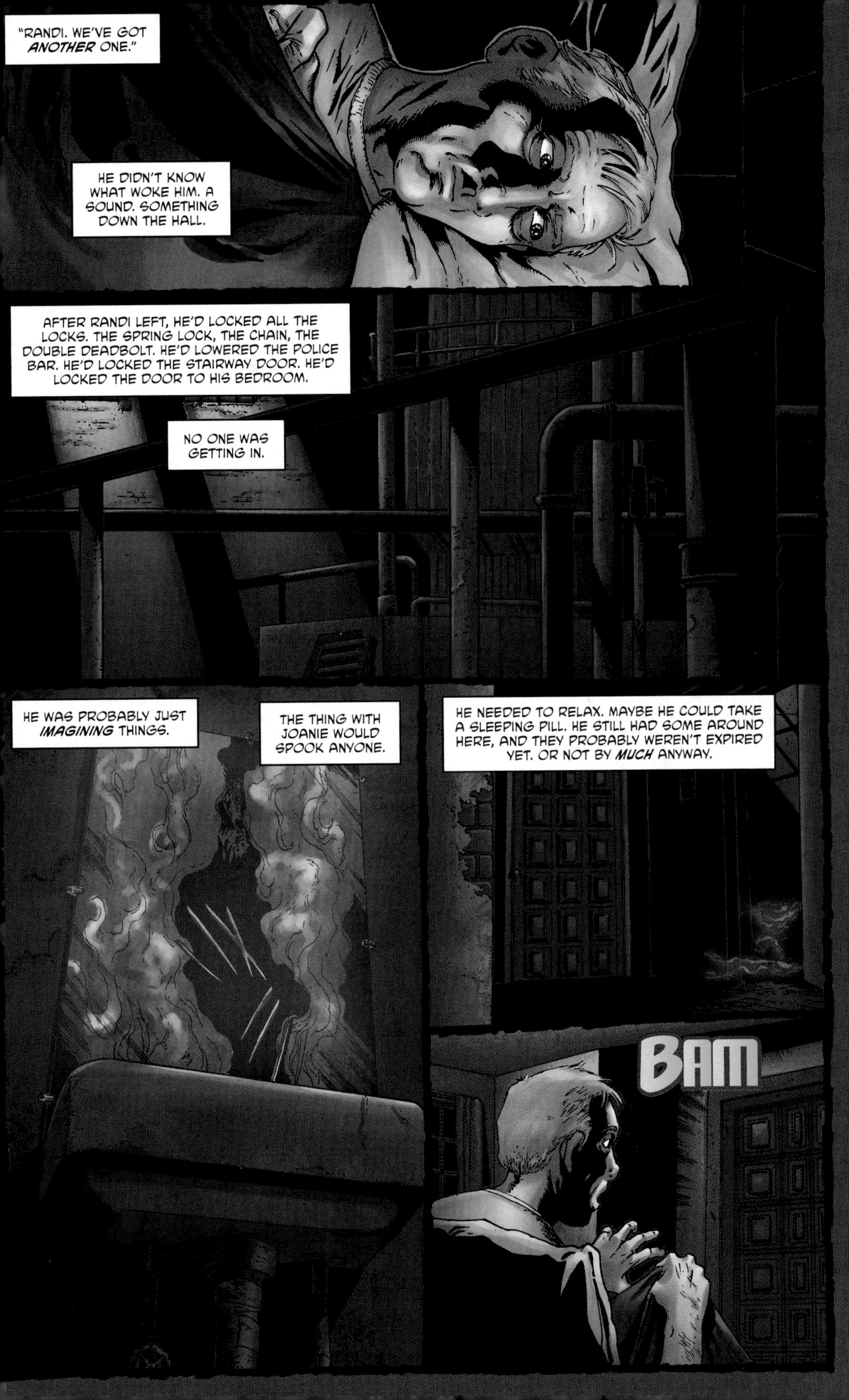
"RANDI. WE'VE GOT *ANOTHER* ONE."
HE DIDN'T KNOW WHAT WOKE HIM. A SOUND. SOMETHING DOWN THE HALL.
AFTER RANDI LEFT, HE'D LOCKED ALL THE LOCKS. THE SPRING LOCK, THE CHAIN, THE DOUBLE DEADBOLT. HE'D LOWERED THE POLICE BAR. HE'D LOCKED THE STAIRWAY DOOR. HE'D LOCKED THE DOOR TO HIS BEDROOM.
NO ONE WAS GETTING IN.
HE WAS PROBABLY JUST *IMAGINING* THINGS.
THE THING WITH JOANIE WOULD SPOOK ANYONE.
HE NEEDED TO RELAX. MAYBE HE COULD TAKE A SLEEPING PILL. HE STILL HAD SOME AROUND HERE, AND THEY PROBABLY WEREN'T EXPIRED YET. OR NOT BY *MUCH* ANYWAY.
BAM

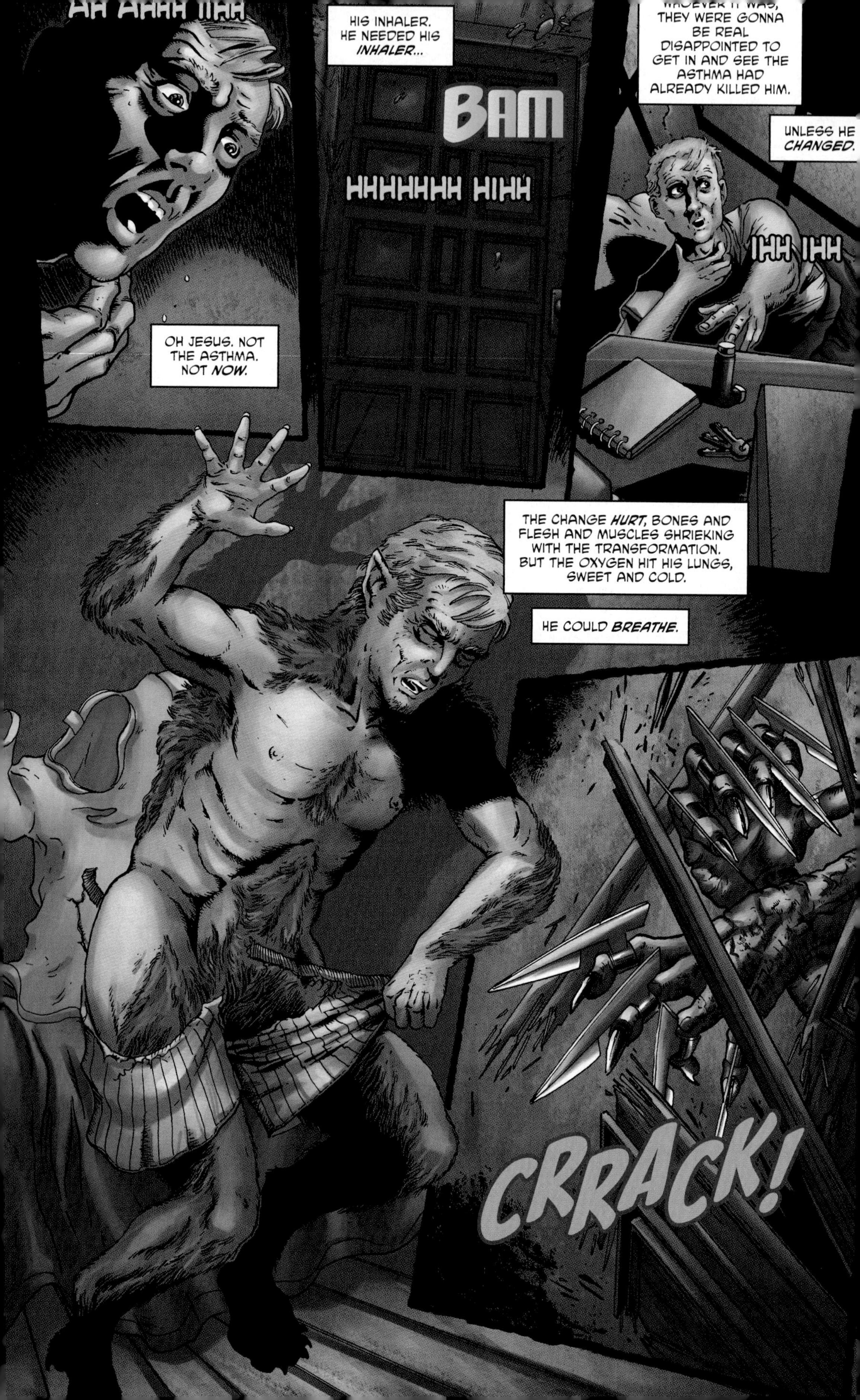
OH JESUS. NOT THE ASTHMA. NOT *NOW.*
HIS INHALER. HE NEEDED HIS *INHALER...*
BAM
HHHHHHH HIHH
THEY WERE GONNA BE REAL DISAPPOINTED TO GET IN AND SEE THE ASTHMA HAD ALREADY KILLED HIM.
UNLESS HE *CHANGED.*
IHH IHH
THE CHANGE *HURT,* BONES AND FLESH AND MUSCLES SHRIEKING WITH THE TRANSFORMATION. BUT THE OXYGEN HIT HIS LUNGS, SWEET AND COLD.
HE COULD *BREATHE.*
CRRACK!

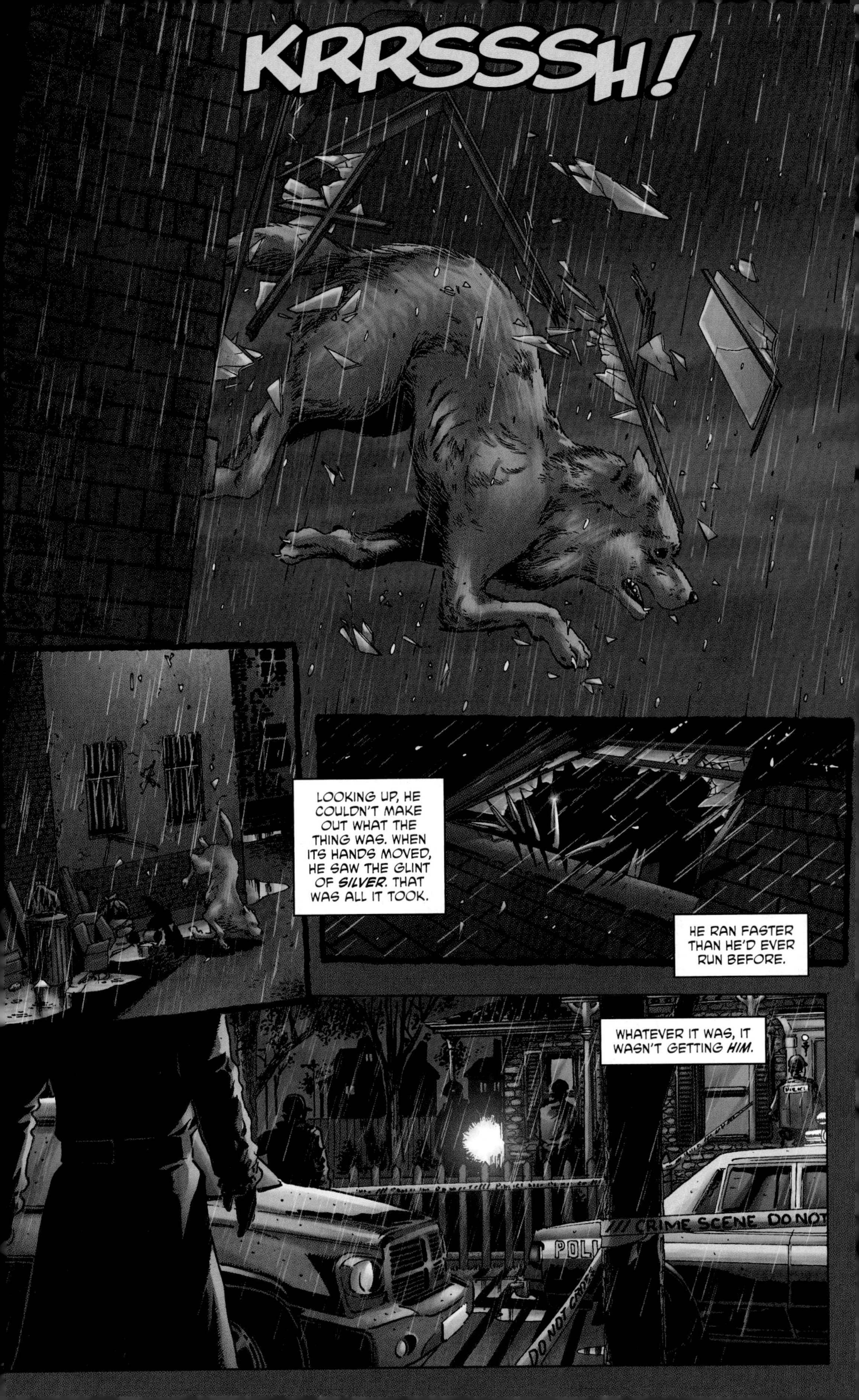
KRRSSSH!
LOOKING UP, HE COULDN'T MAKE OUT WHAT THE THING WAS. WHEN ITS HANDS MOVED, HE SAW THE GLINT OF *SILVER*. THAT WAS ALL IT TOOK.
HE RAN FASTER THAN HE'D EVER RUN BEFORE.
WHATEVER IT WAS, IT WASN'T GETTING *HIM*.
CRIME SCENE DO NOT
POLI

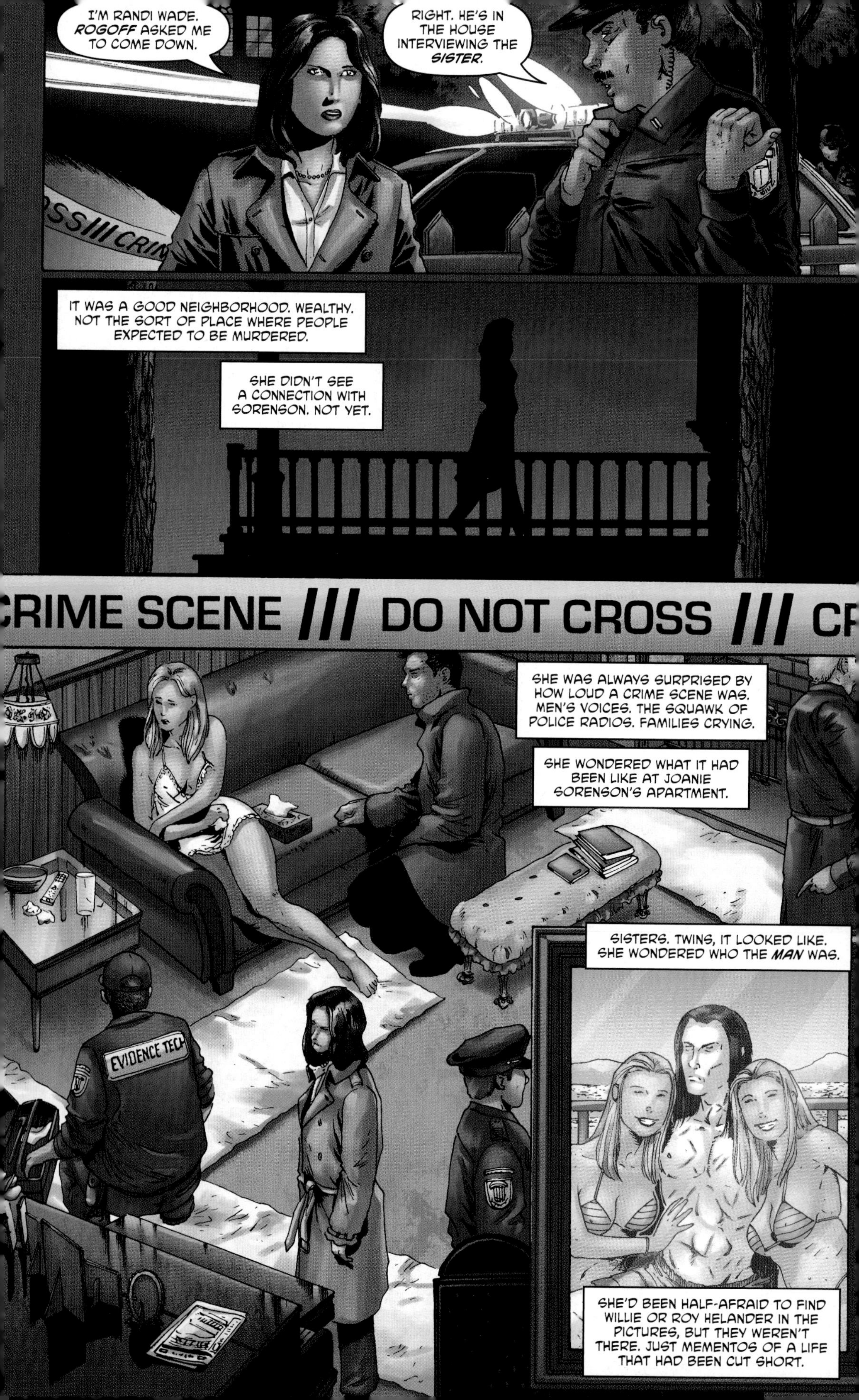
I'M RANDI WADE. ROGOFF ASKED ME TO COME DOWN.
RIGHT. HE'S IN THE HOUSE INTERVIEWING THE SISTER.
IT WAS A GOOD NEIGHBORHOOD. WEALTHY. NOT THE SORT OF PLACE WHERE PEOPLE EXPECTED TO BE MURDERED.
SHE DIDN'T SEE A CONNECTION WITH SORENSON. NOT YET.
CRIME SCENE /// DO NOT CROSS /// CR
SHE WAS ALWAYS SURPRISED BY HOW LOUD A CRIME SCENE WAS. MEN'S VOICES. THE SQUAWK OF POLICE RADIOS. FAMILIES CRYING.
SHE WONDERED WHAT IT HAD BEEN LIKE AT JOANIE SORENSON'S APARTMENT.
SISTERS. TWINS, IT LOOKED LIKE. SHE WONDERED WHO THE MAN WAS.
EVIDENCE TECH
SHE'D BEEN HALF-AFRAID TO FIND WILLIE OR ROY HELANDER IN THE PICTURES, BUT THEY WEREN'T THERE. JUST MEMENTOS OF A LIFE THAT HAD BEEN CUT SHORT.

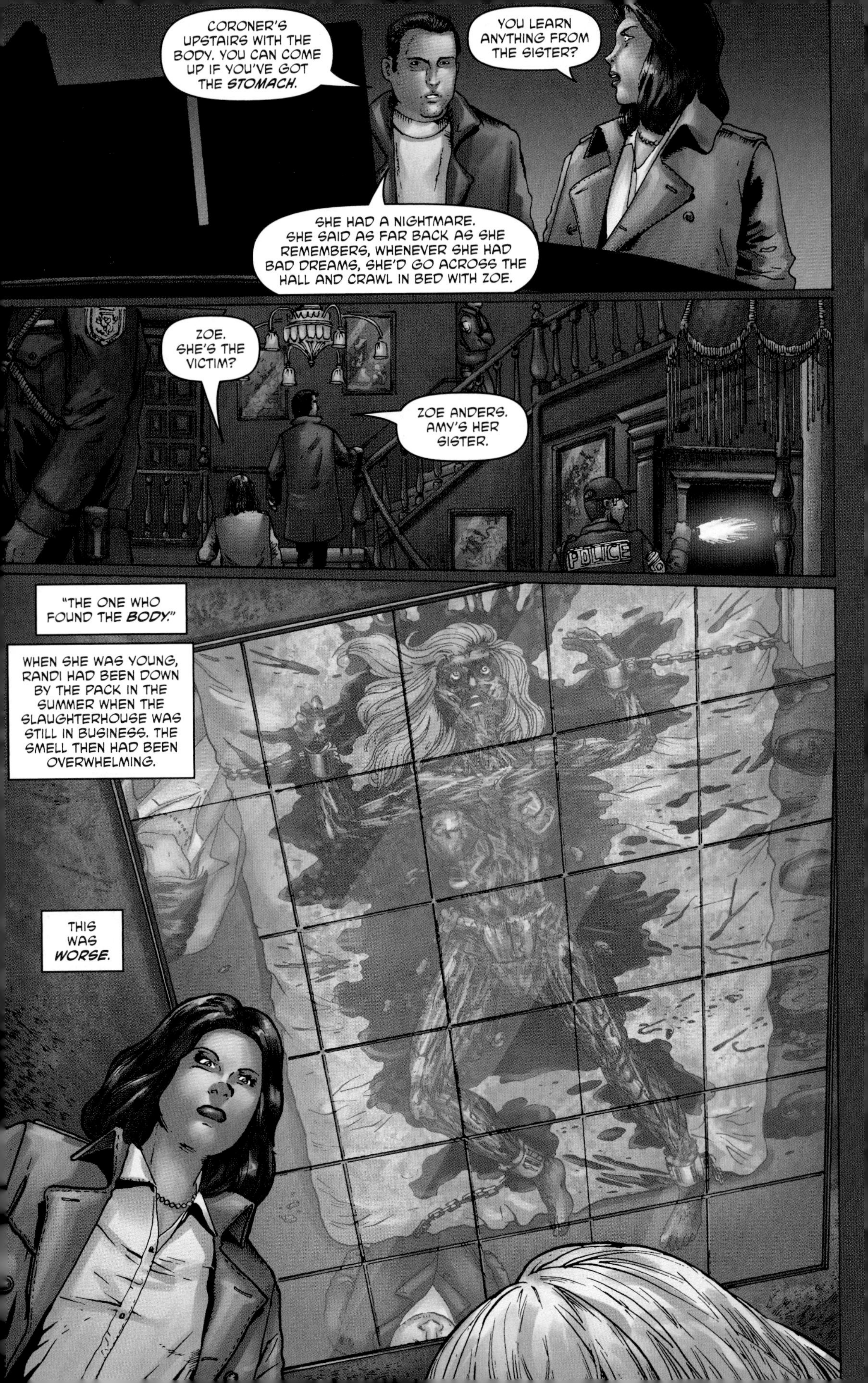
CORONER'S UPSTAIRS WITH THE BODY. YOU CAN COME UP IF YOU'VE GOT THE STOMACH.
YOU LEARN ANYTHING FROM THE SISTER?
SHE HAD A NIGHTMARE. SHE SAID AS FAR BACK AS SHE REMEMBERS, WHENEVER SHE HAD BAD DREAMS, SHE'D GO ACROSS THE HALL AND CRAWL IN BED WITH ZOE.
ZOE. SHE'S THE VICTIM?
ZOE ANDERS. AMY'S HER SISTER.
POLICE
"THE ONE WHO FOUND THE BODY."
WHEN SHE WAS YOUNG, RANDI HAD BEEN DOWN BY THE PACK IN THE SUMMER WHEN THE SLAUGHTERHOUSE WAS STILL IN BUSINESS. THE SMELL THEN HAD BEEN OVERWHELMING.
THIS WAS WORSE.

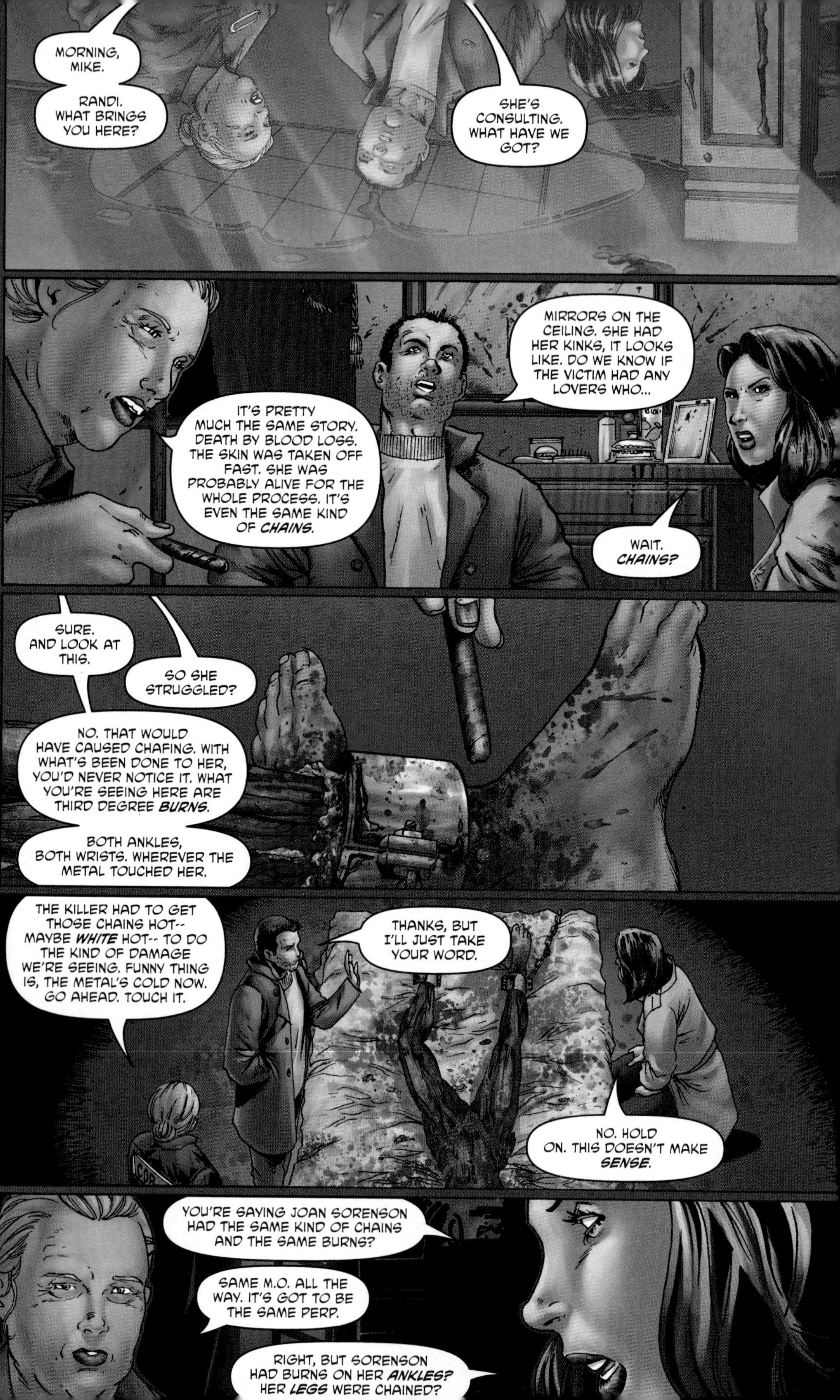
MORNING, MIKE.
RANDI. WHAT BRINGS YOU HERE?
SHE'S CONSULTING. WHAT HAVE WE GOT?
MIRRORS ON THE CEILING. SHE HAD HER KINKS, IT LOOKS LIKE. DO WE KNOW IF THE VICTIM HAD ANY LOVERS WHO...
IT'S PRETTY MUCH THE SAME STORY. DEATH BY BLOOD LOSS. THE SKIN WAS TAKEN OFF FAST. SHE WAS PROBABLY ALIVE FOR THE WHOLE PROCESS. IT'S EVEN THE SAME KIND OF *CHAINS*.
WAIT. *CHAINS?*
SURE. AND LOOK AT THIS.
SO SHE STRUGGLED?
NO. THAT WOULD HAVE CAUSED CHAFING. WITH WHAT'S BEEN DONE TO HER, YOU'D NEVER NOTICE IT. WHAT YOU'RE SEEING HERE ARE THIRD DEGREE *BURNS*.
BOTH ANKLES, BOTH WRISTS. WHEREVER THE METAL TOUCHED HER.
THE KILLER HAD TO GET THOSE CHAINS HOT-- MAYBE *WHITE* HOT-- TO DO THE KIND OF DAMAGE WE'RE SEEING. FUNNY THING IS, THE METAL'S COLD NOW. GO AHEAD. TOUCH IT.
THANKS, BUT I'LL JUST TAKE YOUR WORD.
NO. HOLD ON. THIS DOESN'T MAKE *SENSE*.
YOU'RE SAYING JOAN SORENSON HAD THE SAME KIND OF CHAINS AND THE SAME BURNS?
SAME M.O. ALL THE WAY. IT'S GOT TO BE THE SAME PERP.
RIGHT, BUT SORENSON HAD BURNS ON HER *ANKLES?* HER *LEGS* WERE CHAINED?

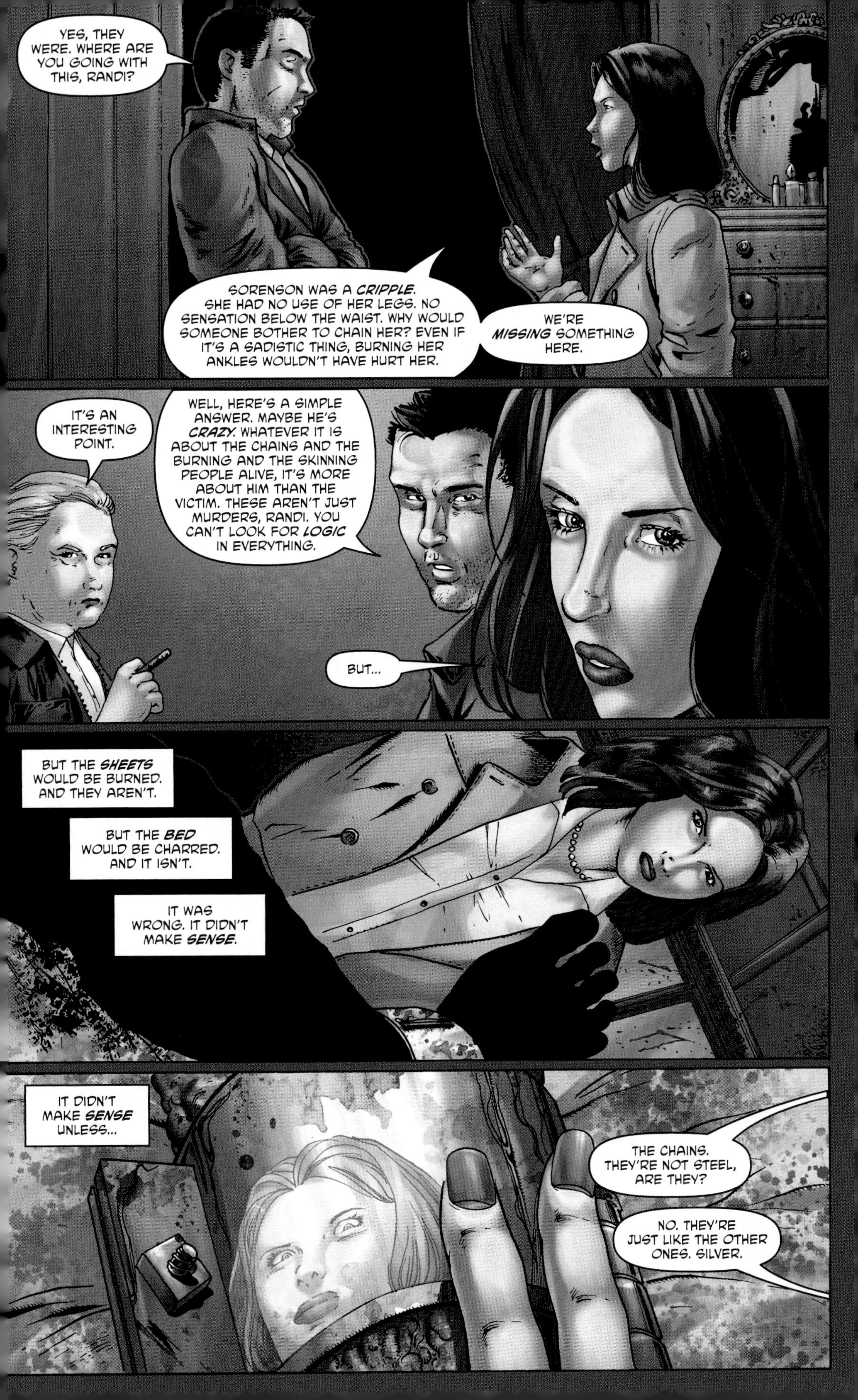
YES, THEY WERE. WHERE ARE YOU GOING WITH THIS, RANDI?
SORENSON WAS A CRIPPLE. SHE HAD NO USE OF HER LEGS. NO SENSATION BELOW THE WAIST. WHY WOULD SOMEONE BOTHER TO CHAIN HER? EVEN IF IT'S A SADISTIC THING, BURNING HER ANKLES WOULDN'T HAVE HURT HER.
WE'RE MISSING SOMETHING HERE.
IT'S AN INTERESTING POINT.
WELL, HERE'S A SIMPLE ANSWER. MAYBE HE'S CRAZY. WHATEVER IT IS ABOUT THE CHAINS AND THE BURNING AND THE SKINNING PEOPLE ALIVE, IT'S MORE ABOUT HIM THAN THE VICTIM. THESE AREN'T JUST MURDERS, RANDI. YOU CAN'T LOOK FOR LOGIC IN EVERYTHING.
BUT...
BUT THE SHEETS WOULD BE BURNED. AND THEY AREN'T.
BUT THE BED WOULD BE CHARRED. AND IT ISN'T.
IT WAS WRONG. IT DIDN'T MAKE SENSE.
IT DIDN'T MAKE SENSE UNLESS...
THE CHAINS. THEY'RE NOT STEEL, ARE THEY?
NO. THEY'RE JUST LIKE THE OTHER ONES. SILVER.

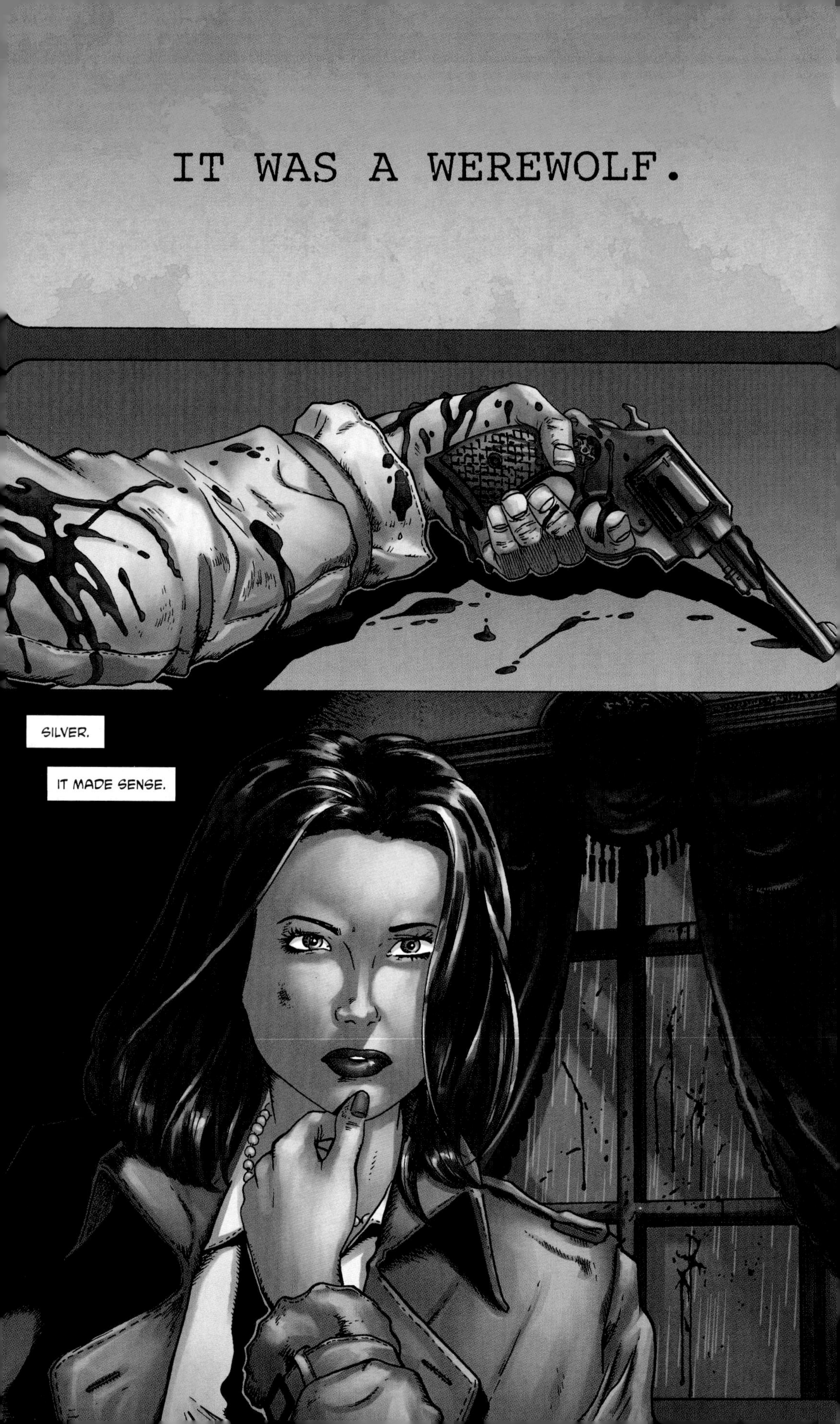
IT WAS A WEREWOLF.
SILVER.
IT MADE SENSE.

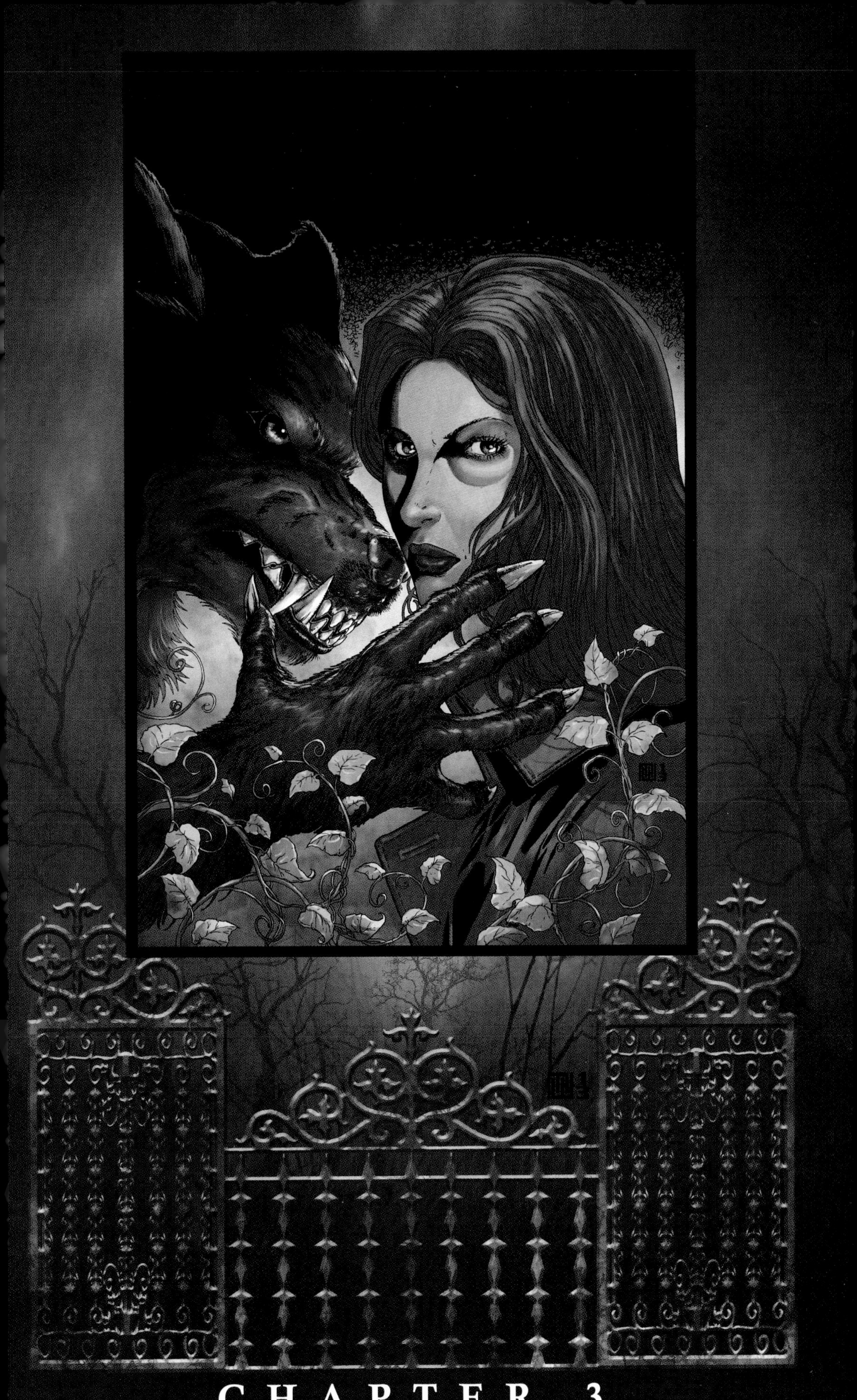

CHAPTER 3

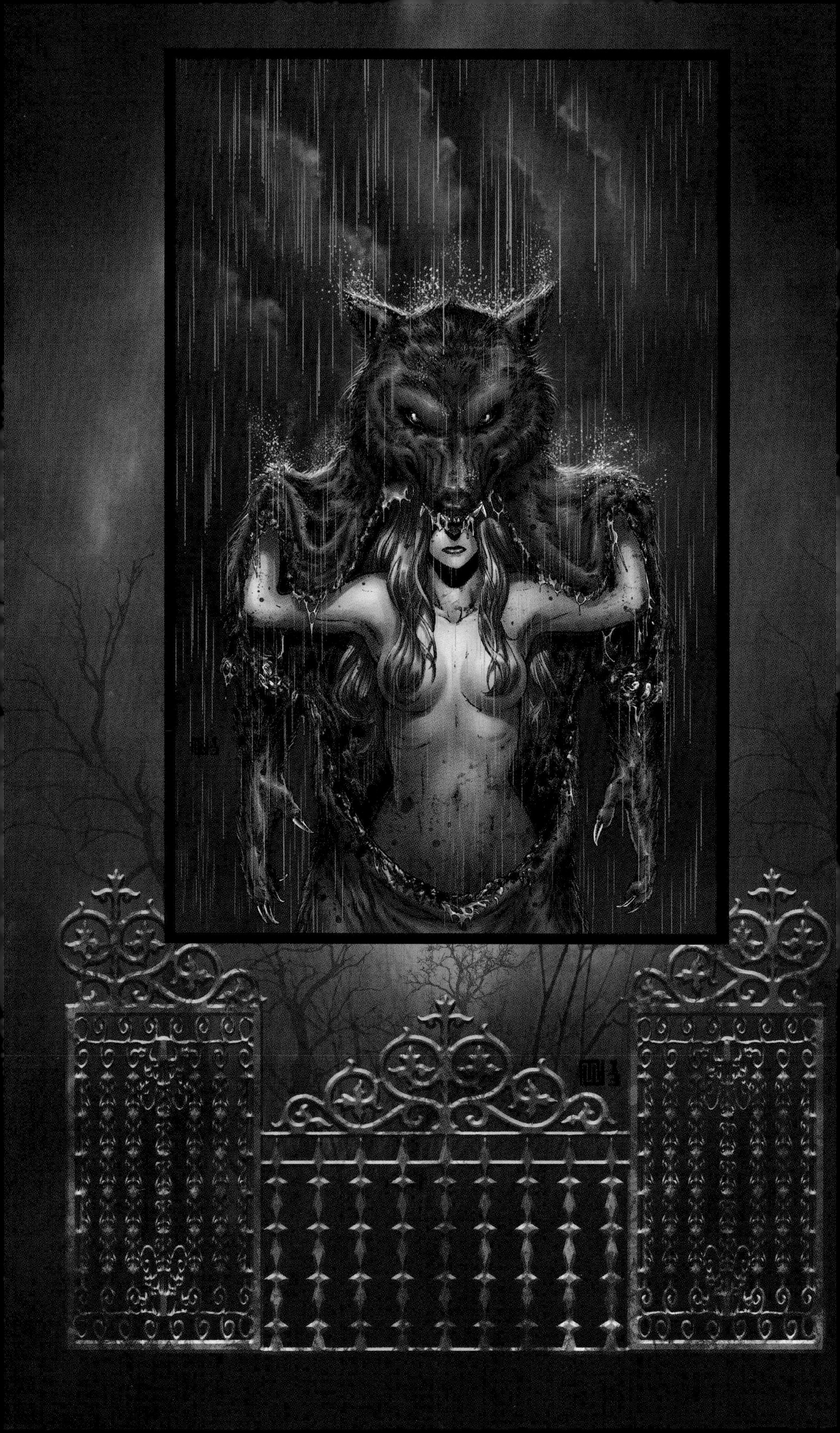

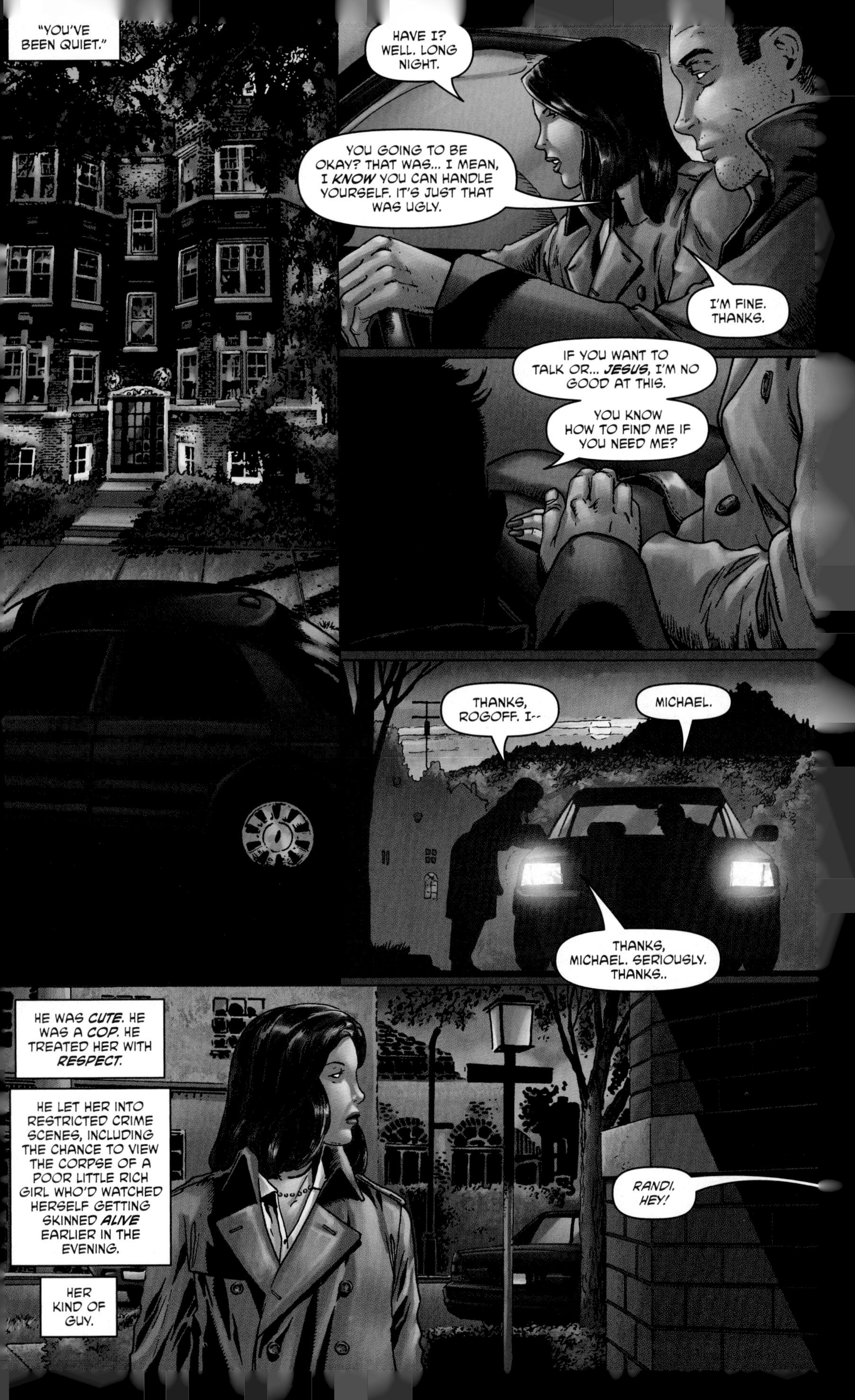
"YOU'VE BEEN QUIET."
HAVE I? WELL. LONG NIGHT.
YOU GOING TO BE OKAY? THAT WAS... I MEAN, I KNOW YOU CAN HANDLE YOURSELF. IT'S JUST THAT WAS UGLY.
I'M FINE. THANKS.
IF YOU WANT TO TALK OR... JESUS, I'M NO GOOD AT THIS.
YOU KNOW HOW TO FIND ME IF YOU NEED ME?
THANKS, ROGOFF. I--
MICHAEL.
THANKS, MICHAEL. SERIOUSLY. THANKS..
HE WAS CUTE. HE WAS A COP. HE TREATED HER WITH RESPECT.
HE LET HER INTO RESTRICTED CRIME SCENES, INCLUDING THE CHANCE TO VIEW THE CORPSE OF A POOR LITTLE RICH GIRL WHO'D WATCHED HERSELF GETTING SKINNED ALIVE EARLIER IN THE EVENING.
HER KIND OF GUY.
RANDI. HEY!

WILLIE? WHAT ARE YOU DOING HERE?

AND WHY ARE YOU *NAKED?*

SOMEONE TRIED TO KILL ME LAST NIGHT. I MADE IT OUT, MY CLOTHES DIDN'T. I'VE BEEN HERE OVER AN HOUR, NOT THAT I'M COMPLAINING, MIND YOU, BUT I THINK I HAVE PNEUMONIA AND MY BALLS ARE FROZEN SOLID. WHERE THE *FUCK* HAVE YOU BEEN?

THERE WAS ANOTHER MURDER. SAME M.O. I WAS AT THE SCENE.

AH, JESUS. WHO?

ZOE ANDERS.

FUCK, FUCK, *FUCK.* JESUS. WHAT ABOUT AMY?

IN SHOCK. SHE'LL BE FINE. SO YOU KNEW ZOE ANDERS TOO? THE WAY YOU KNEW JOAN SORENSON?

NOT THE *SAME* WAY, BUT I KNEW HER, YEAH.

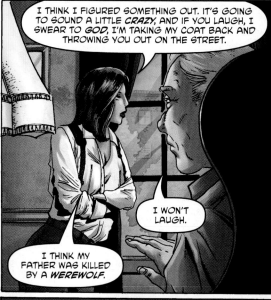

I THINK I FIGURED SOMETHING OUT. IT'S GOING TO SOUND A LITTLE *CRAZY,* AND IF YOU LAUGH, I SWEAR TO *GOD,* I'M TAKING MY COAT BACK AND THROWING YOU OUT ON THE STREET.

I WON'T LAUGH.

I THINK MY FATHER WAS KILLED BY A *WEREWOLF.*

A *WEREWOL...*

AHH

OH JEEZ. *ASTH*

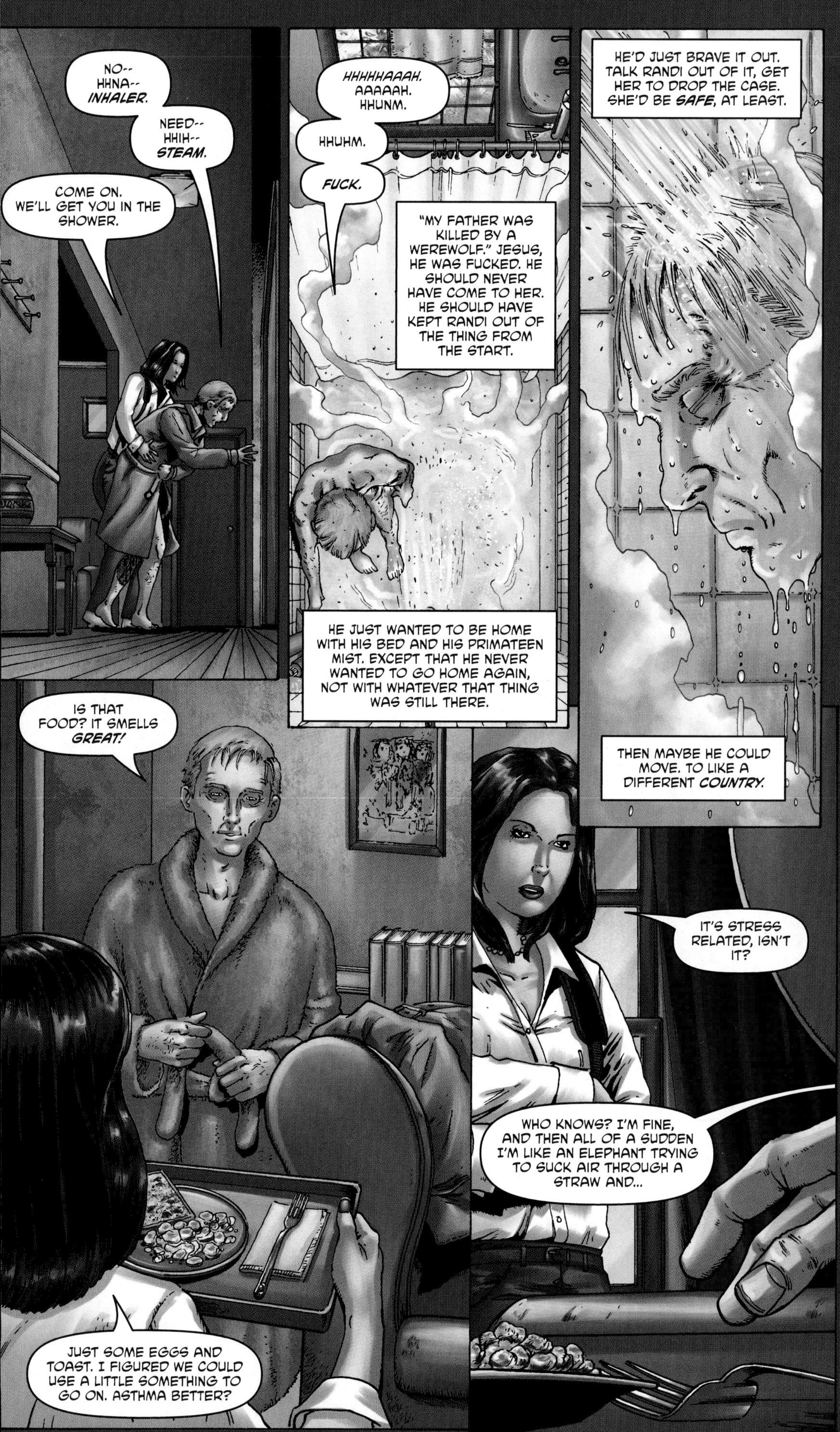
NO-- HHNA-- INHALER.
NEED-- HHIH-- STEAM.
COME ON. WE'LL GET YOU IN THE SHOWER.
HHHHHAAAH. AAAAAH. HHUNM.
HHUHM.
FUCK.
"MY FATHER WAS KILLED BY A WEREWOLF." JESUS, HE WAS FUCKED. HE SHOULD NEVER HAVE COME TO HER. HE SHOULD HAVE KEPT RANDI OUT OF THE THING FROM THE START.
HE JUST WANTED TO BE HOME WITH HIS BED AND HIS PRIMATEEN MIST. EXCEPT THAT HE NEVER WANTED TO GO HOME AGAIN, NOT WITH WHATEVER THAT THING WAS STILL THERE.
HE'D JUST BRAVE IT OUT. TALK RANDI OUT OF IT, GET HER TO DROP THE CASE. SHE'D BE SAFE, AT LEAST.
THEN MAYBE HE COULD MOVE. TO LIKE A DIFFERENT COUNTRY.
IS THAT FOOD? IT SMELLS GREAT!
JUST SOME EGGS AND TOAST. I FIGURED WE COULD USE A LITTLE SOMETHING TO GO ON. ASTHMA BETTER?
IT'S STRESS RELATED, ISN'T IT?
WHO KNOWS? I'M FINE, AND THEN ALL OF A SUDDEN I'M LIKE AN ELEPHANT TRYING TO SUCK AIR THROUGH A STRAW AND...

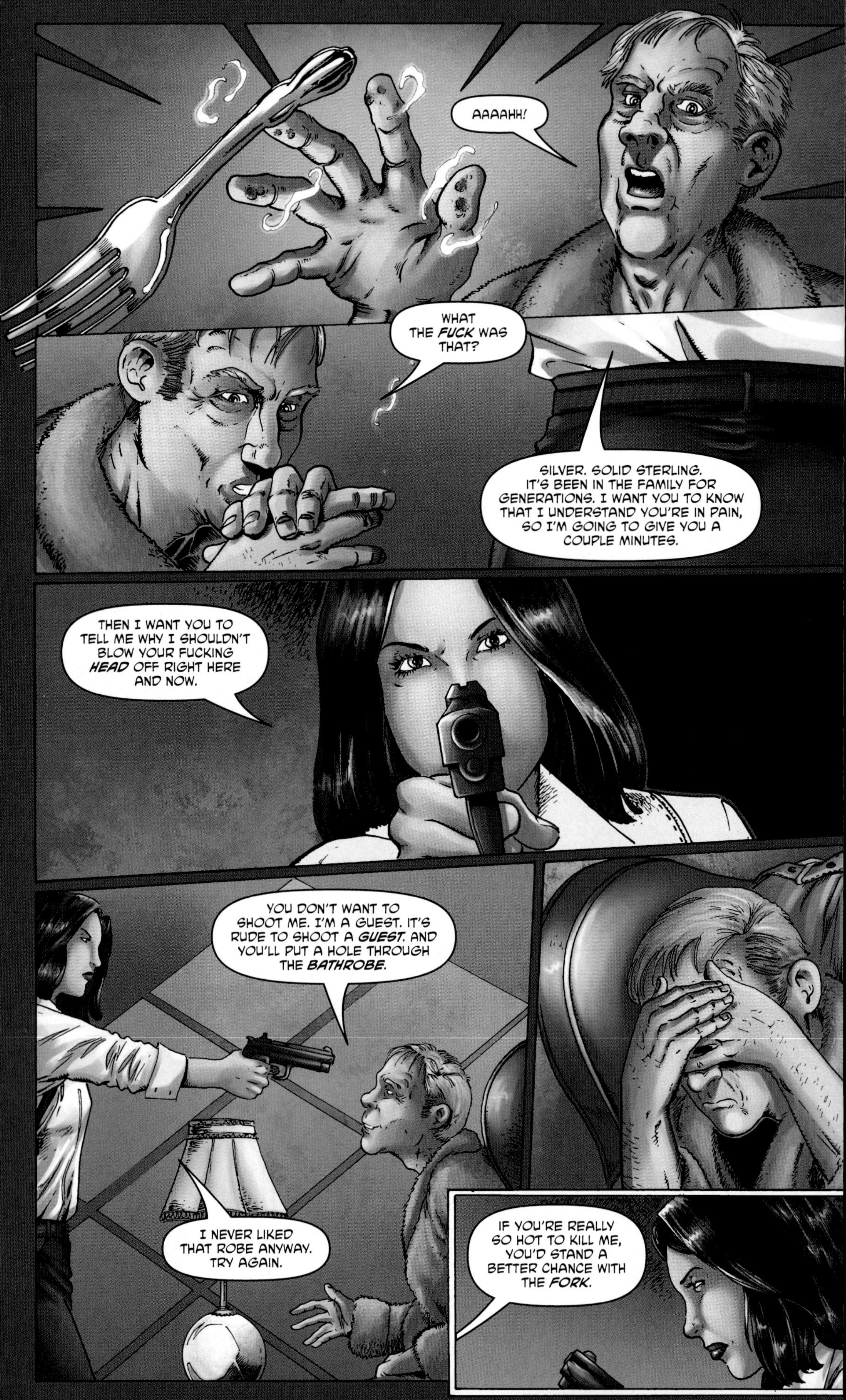
AAAAHH!
WHAT THE FUCK WAS THAT?
SILVER. SOLID STERLING. IT'S BEEN IN THE FAMILY FOR GENERATIONS. I WANT YOU TO KNOW THAT I UNDERSTAND YOU'RE IN PAIN, SO I'M GOING TO GIVE YOU A COUPLE MINUTES.
THEN I WANT YOU TO TELL ME WHY I SHOULDN'T BLOW YOUR FUCKING HEAD OFF RIGHT HERE AND NOW.
YOU DON'T WANT TO SHOOT ME. I'M A GUEST. IT'S RUDE TO SHOOT A GUEST. AND YOU'LL PUT A HOLE THROUGH THE BATHROBE.
I NEVER LIKED THAT ROBE ANYWAY. TRY AGAIN.
IF YOU'RE REALLY SO HOT TO KILL ME, YOU'D STAND A BETTER CHANCE WITH THE FORK.

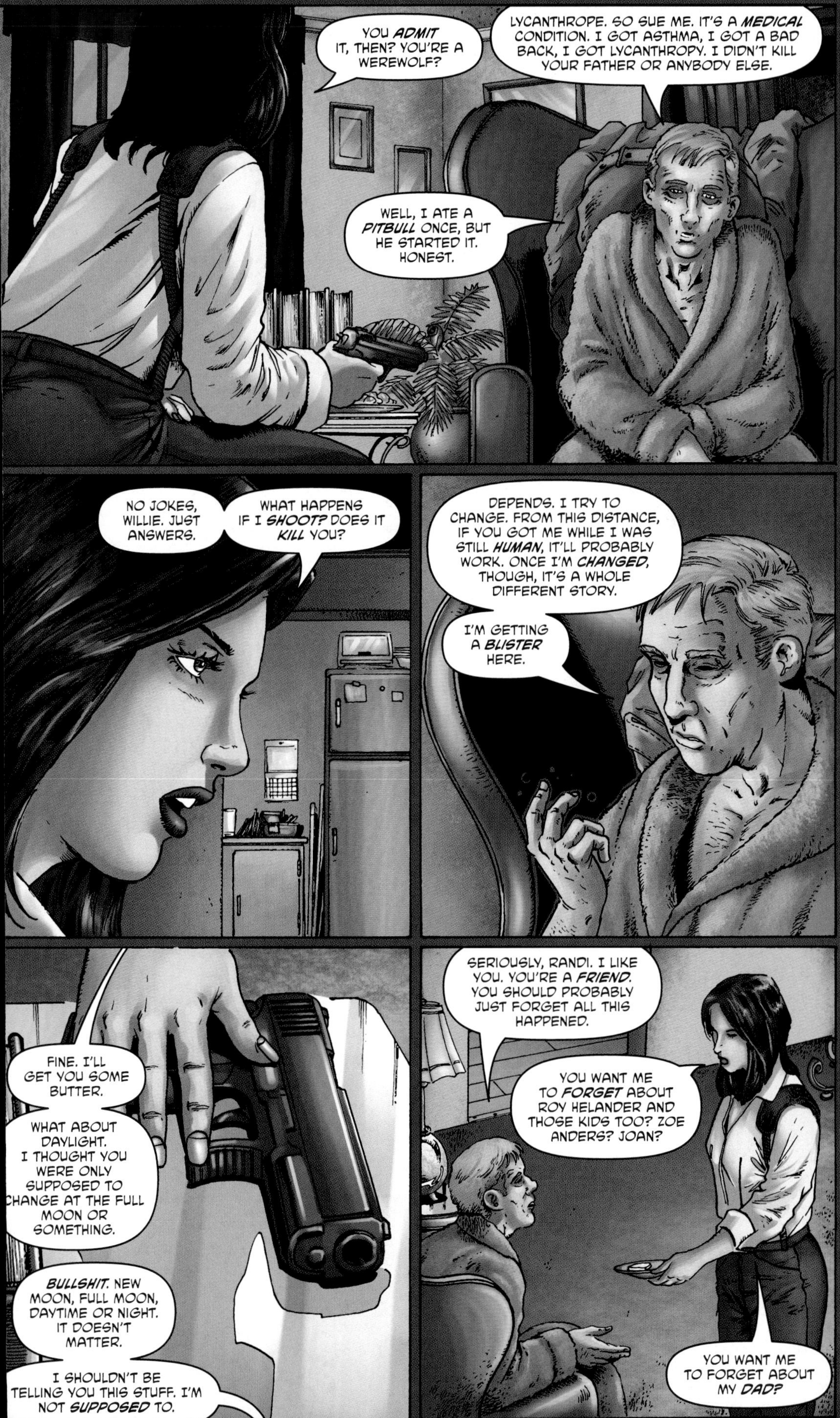
YOU *ADMIT* IT, THEN? YOU'RE A WEREWOLF?
LYCANTHROPE. SO SUE ME. IT'S A *MEDICAL* CONDITION. I GOT ASTHMA, I GOT A BAD BACK, I GOT LYCANTHROPY. I DIDN'T KILL YOUR FATHER OR ANYBODY ELSE.
WELL, I ATE A *PITBULL* ONCE, BUT HE STARTED IT. HONEST.
NO JOKES, WILLIE. JUST ANSWERS.
WHAT HAPPENS IF I *SHOOT?* DOES IT *KILL* YOU?
DEPENDS. I TRY TO CHANGE. FROM THIS DISTANCE, IF YOU GOT ME WHILE I WAS STILL *HUMAN*, IT'LL PROBABLY WORK. ONCE I'M *CHANGED*, THOUGH, IT'S A WHOLE DIFFERENT STORY.
I'M GETTING A *BLISTER* HERE.
FINE. I'LL GET YOU SOME BUTTER.
WHAT ABOUT DAYLIGHT. I THOUGHT YOU WERE ONLY SUPPOSED TO CHANGE AT THE FULL MOON OR SOMETHING.
BULLSHIT. NEW MOON, FULL MOON, DAYTIME OR NIGHT. IT DOESN'T MATTER.
I SHOULDN'T BE TELLING YOU THIS STUFF. I'M NOT *SUPPOSED* TO.
SERIOUSLY, RANDI. I LIKE YOU. YOU'RE A *FRIEND*. YOU SHOULD PROBABLY JUST FORGET ALL THIS HAPPENED.
YOU WANT ME TO *FORGET* ABOUT ROY HELANDER AND THOSE KIDS TOO? ZOE ANDERS? JOAN?
YOU WANT ME TO FORGET ABOUT MY *DAD?*

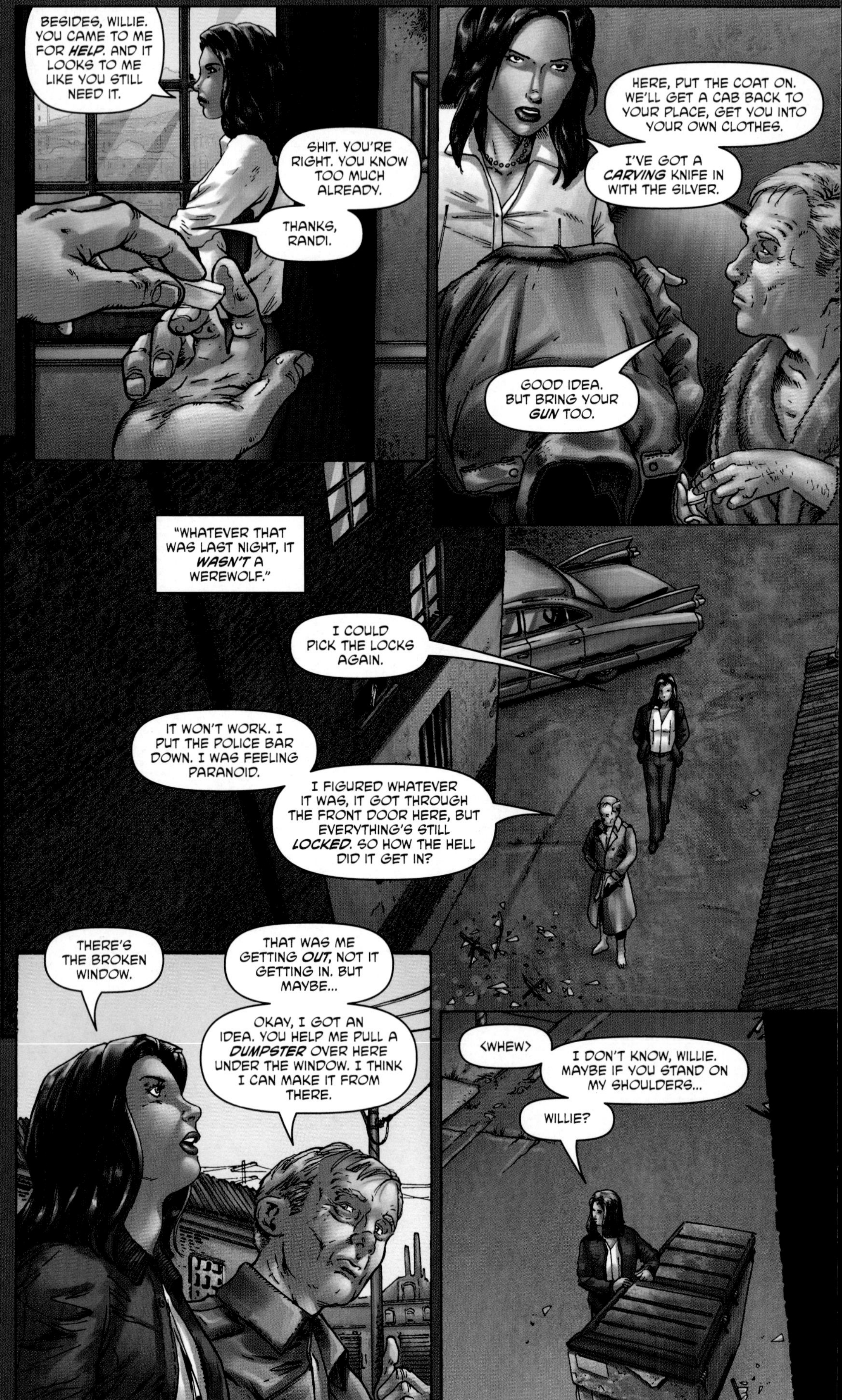
BESIDES, WILLIE. YOU CAME TO ME FOR HELP. AND IT LOOKS TO ME LIKE YOU STILL NEED IT.
SHIT. YOU'RE RIGHT. YOU KNOW TOO MUCH ALREADY.
THANKS, RANDI.
HERE, PUT THE COAT ON. WE'LL GET A CAB BACK TO YOUR PLACE, GET YOU INTO YOUR OWN CLOTHES.
I'VE GOT A CARVING KNIFE IN WITH THE SILVER.
GOOD IDEA. BUT BRING YOUR GUN TOO.
"WHATEVER THAT WAS LAST NIGHT, IT WASN'T A WEREWOLF."
I COULD PICK THE LOCKS AGAIN.
IT WON'T WORK. I PUT THE POLICE BAR DOWN. I WAS FEELING PARANOID.
I FIGURED WHATEVER IT WAS, IT GOT THROUGH THE FRONT DOOR HERE, BUT EVERYTHING'S STILL LOCKED. SO HOW THE HELL DID IT GET IN?
THERE'S THE BROKEN WINDOW.
THAT WAS ME GETTING OUT, NOT IT GETTING IN. BUT MAYBE...
OKAY, I GOT AN IDEA. YOU HELP ME PULL A DUMPSTER OVER HERE UNDER THE WINDOW. I THINK I CAN MAKE IT FROM THERE.
<WHEW>
I DON'T KNOW, WILLIE. MAYBE IF YOU STAND ON MY SHOULDERS...
WILLIE?

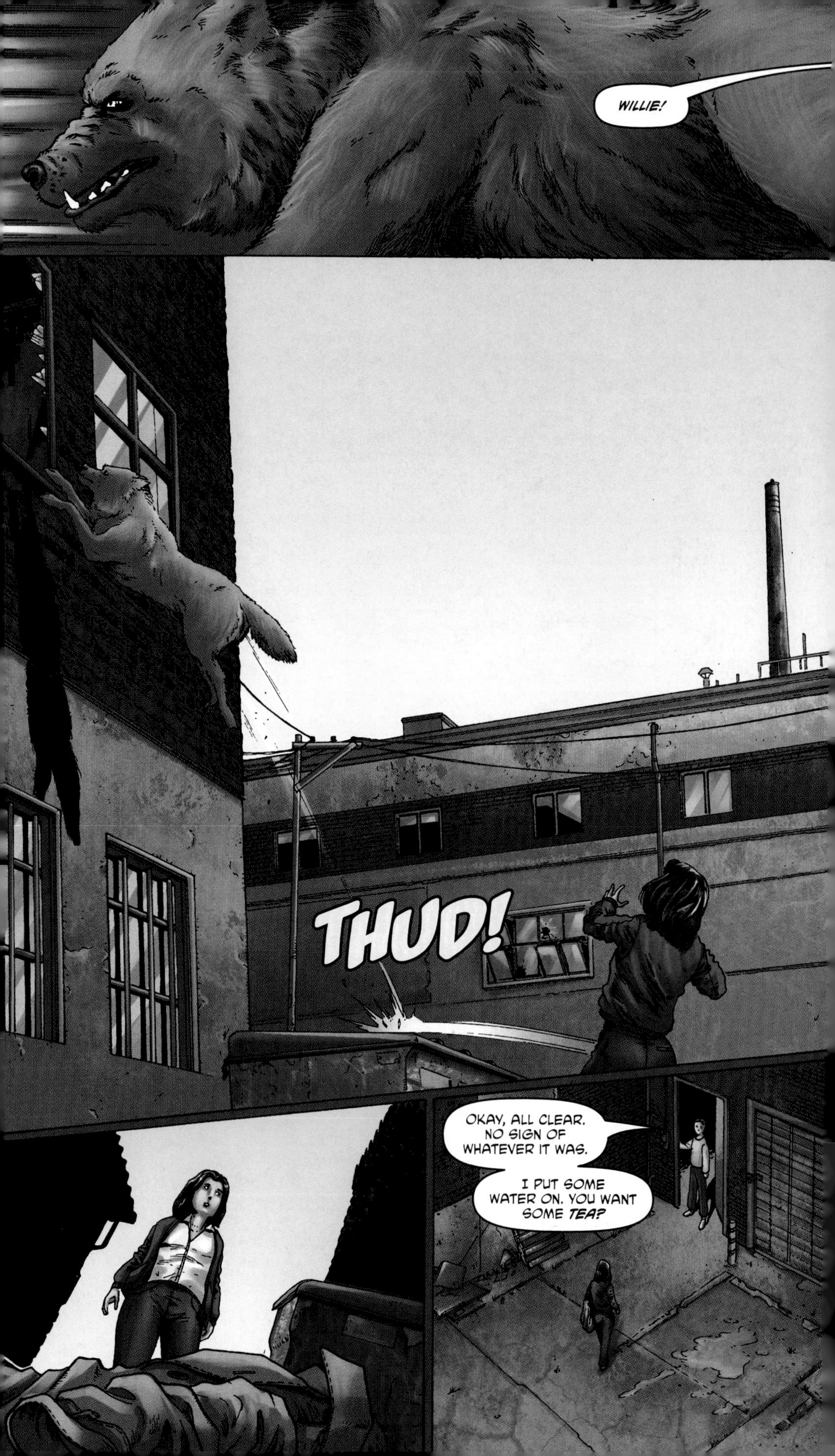
WILLIE!
THUD!
OKAY, ALL CLEAR. NO SIGN OF WHATEVER IT WAS.
I PUT SOME WATER ON. YOU WANT SOME TEA?

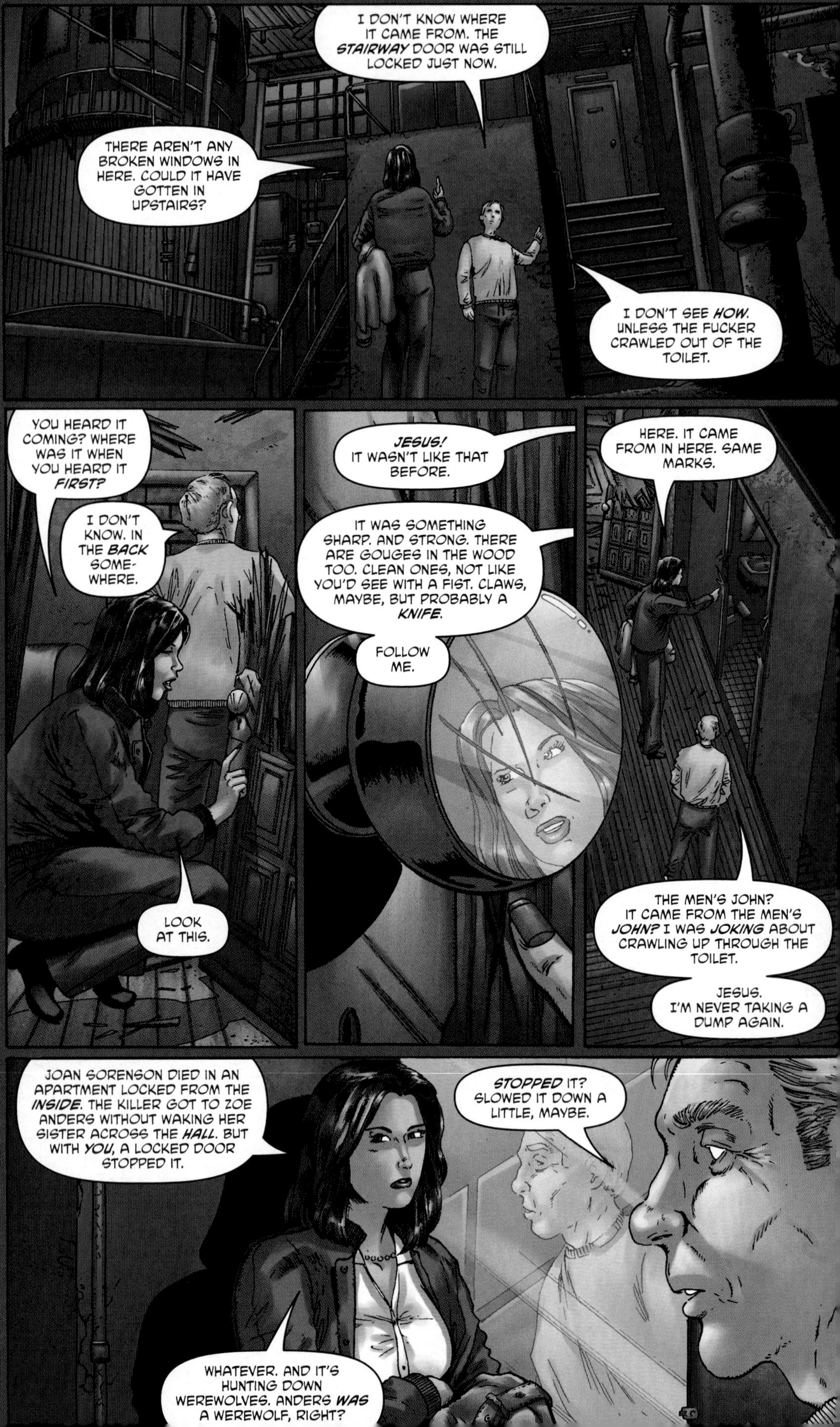
I DON'T KNOW WHERE IT CAME FROM. THE *STAIRWAY* DOOR WAS STILL LOCKED JUST NOW.
THERE AREN'T ANY BROKEN WINDOWS IN HERE. COULD IT HAVE GOTTEN IN UPSTAIRS?
I DON'T SEE *HOW*. UNLESS THE FUCKER CRAWLED OUT OF THE TOILET.
YOU HEARD IT COMING? WHERE WAS IT WHEN YOU HEARD IT *FIRST?*
I DON'T KNOW. IN THE *BACK* SOME-WHERE.
LOOK AT THIS.
JESUS! IT WASN'T LIKE THAT BEFORE.
IT WAS SOMETHING SHARP. AND STRONG. THERE ARE GOUGES IN THE WOOD TOO. CLEAN ONES, NOT LIKE YOU'D SEE WITH A FIST. CLAWS, MAYBE, BUT PROBABLY A *KNIFE*.
FOLLOW ME.
HERE. IT CAME FROM IN HERE. SAME MARKS.
THE MEN'S JOHN? IT CAME FROM THE MEN'S *JOHN?* I WAS *JOKING* ABOUT CRAWLING UP THROUGH THE TOILET.
JESUS. I'M NEVER TAKING A DUMP AGAIN.
JOAN SORENSON DIED IN AN APARTMENT LOCKED FROM THE *INSIDE*. THE KILLER GOT TO ZOE ANDERS WITHOUT WAKING HER SISTER ACROSS THE *HALL*. BUT WITH *YOU*, A LOCKED DOOR STOPPED IT.
STOPPED IT? SLOWED IT DOWN A LITTLE, MAYBE.
WHATEVER. AND IT'S HUNTING DOWN WEREWOLVES. ANDERS *WAS* A WEREWOLF, RIGHT?

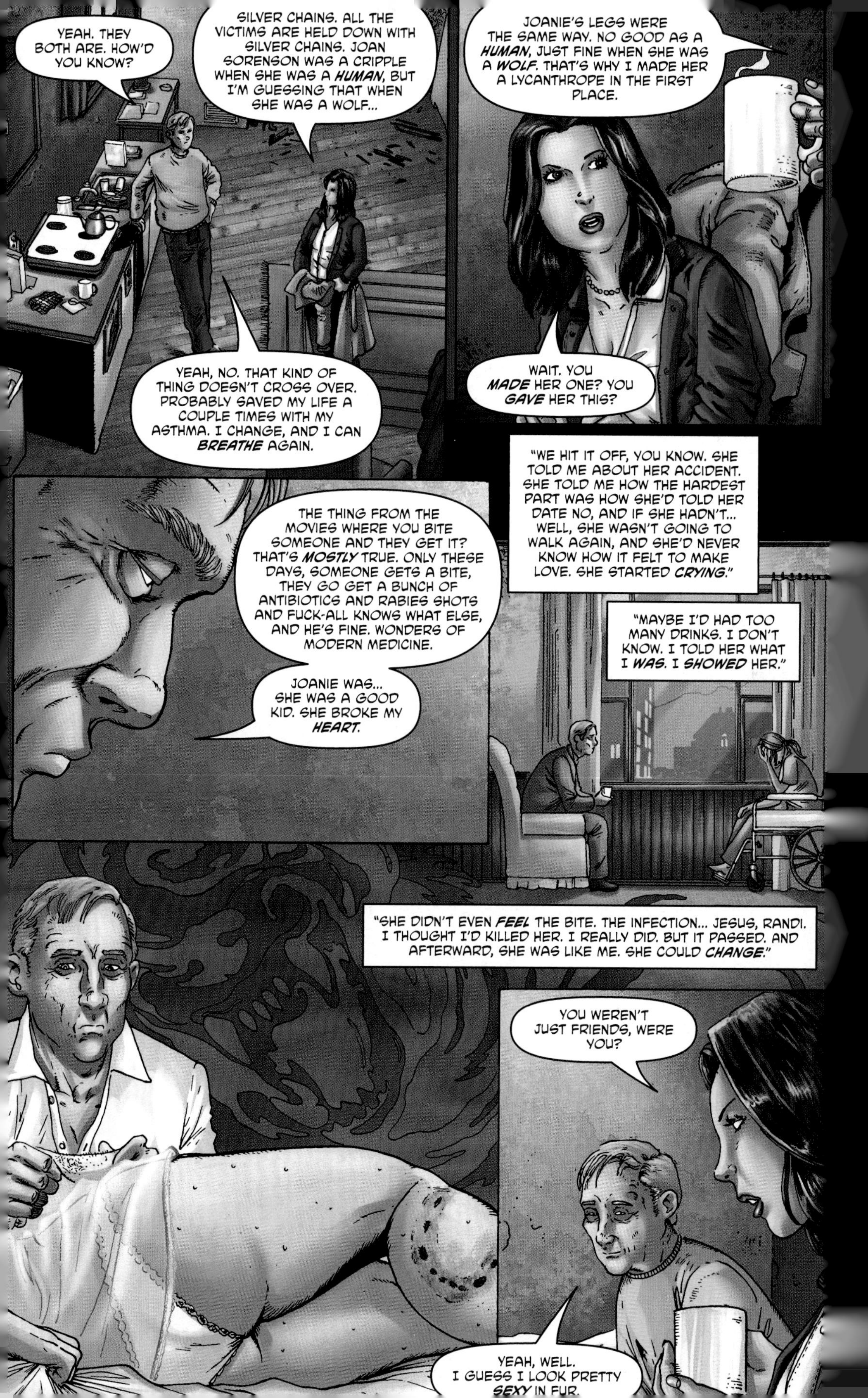
YEAH. THEY BOTH ARE. HOW'D YOU KNOW?
SILVER CHAINS. ALL THE VICTIMS ARE HELD DOWN WITH SILVER CHAINS. JOAN SORENSON WAS A CRIPPLE WHEN SHE WAS A HUMAN, BUT I'M GUESSING THAT WHEN SHE WAS A WOLF...
YEAH, NO. THAT KIND OF THING DOESN'T CROSS OVER. PROBABLY SAVED MY LIFE A COUPLE TIMES WITH MY ASTHMA. I CHANGE, AND I CAN BREATHE AGAIN.
JOANIE'S LEGS WERE THE SAME WAY. NO GOOD AS A HUMAN, JUST FINE WHEN SHE WAS A WOLF. THAT'S WHY I MADE HER A LYCANTHROPE IN THE FIRST PLACE.
WAIT. YOU MADE HER ONE? YOU GAVE HER THIS?
THE THING FROM THE MOVIES WHERE YOU BITE SOMEONE AND THEY GET IT? THAT'S MOSTLY TRUE. ONLY THESE DAYS, SOMEONE GETS A BITE, THEY GO GET A BUNCH OF ANTIBIOTICS AND RABIES SHOTS AND FUCK-ALL KNOWS WHAT ELSE, AND HE'S FINE. WONDERS OF MODERN MEDICINE.
JOANIE WAS... SHE WAS A GOOD KID. SHE BROKE MY HEART.
"WE HIT IT OFF, YOU KNOW. SHE TOLD ME ABOUT HER ACCIDENT. SHE TOLD ME HOW THE HARDEST PART WAS HOW SHE'D TOLD HER DATE NO, AND IF SHE HADN'T... WELL, SHE WASN'T GOING TO WALK AGAIN, AND SHE'D NEVER KNOW HOW IT FELT TO MAKE LOVE. SHE STARTED CRYING."
"MAYBE I'D HAD TOO MANY DRINKS. I DON'T KNOW. I TOLD HER WHAT I WAS. I SHOWED HER."
"SHE DIDN'T EVEN FEEL THE BITE. THE INFECTION... JESUS, RANDI. I THOUGHT I'D KILLED HER. I REALLY DID. BUT IT PASSED. AND AFTERWARD, SHE WAS LIKE ME. SHE COULD CHANGE."
YOU WEREN'T JUST FRIENDS, WERE YOU?
YEAH, WELL. I GUESS I LOOK PRETTY SEXY IN FUR.

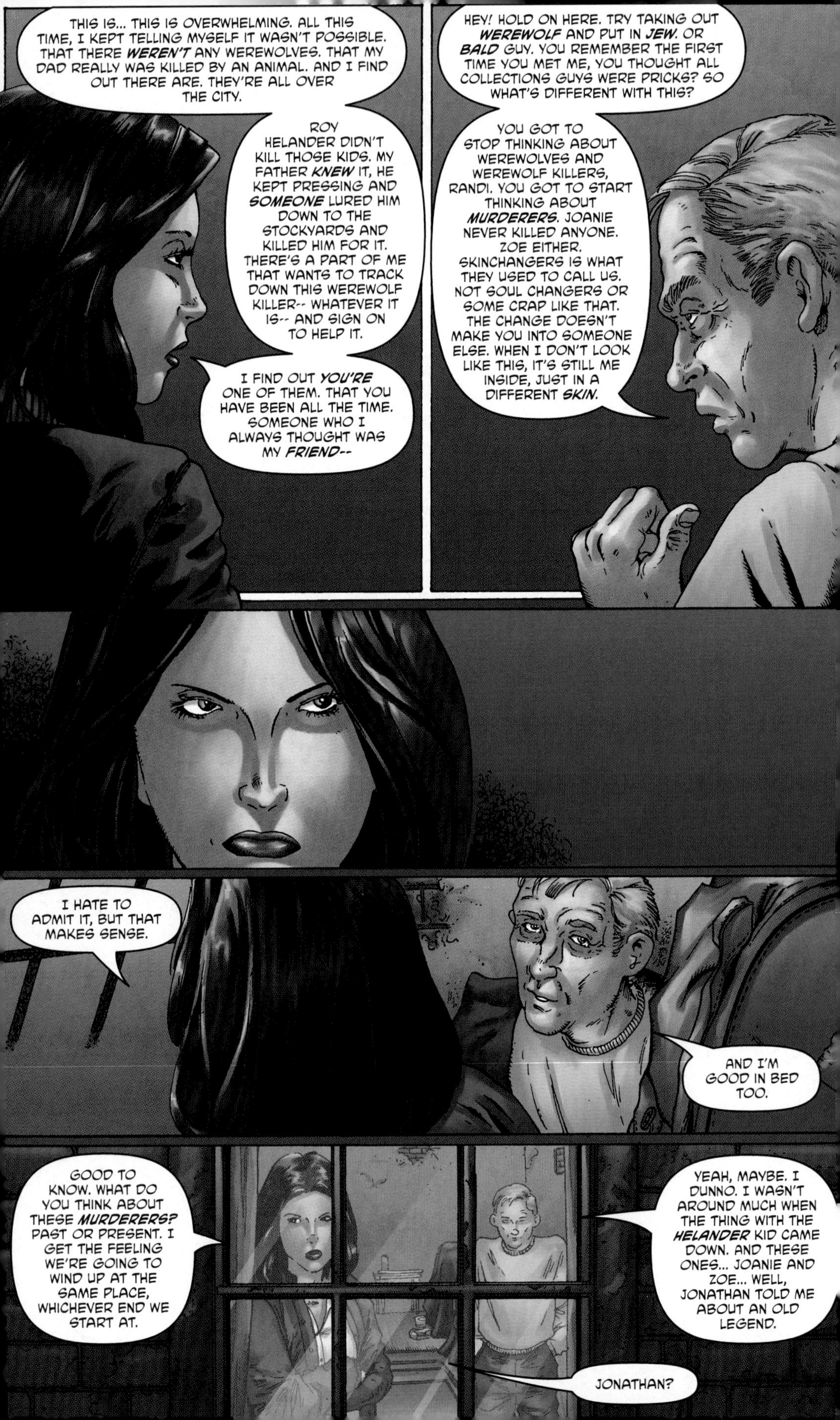
THIS IS... THIS IS OVERWHELMING. ALL THIS TIME, I KEPT TELLING MYSELF IT WASN'T POSSIBLE. THAT THERE WEREN'T ANY WEREWOLVES. THAT MY DAD REALLY WAS KILLED BY AN ANIMAL. AND I FIND OUT THERE ARE. THEY'RE ALL OVER THE CITY.
ROY HELANDER DIDN'T KILL THOSE KIDS. MY FATHER KNEW IT, HE KEPT PRESSING AND SOMEONE LURED HIM DOWN TO THE STOCKYARDS AND KILLED HIM FOR IT. THERE'S A PART OF ME THAT WANTS TO TRACK DOWN THIS WEREWOLF KILLER-- WHATEVER IT IS-- AND SIGN ON TO HELP IT.
I FIND OUT YOU'RE ONE OF THEM. THAT YOU HAVE BEEN ALL THE TIME. SOMEONE WHO I ALWAYS THOUGHT WAS MY FRIEND--
HEY! HOLD ON HERE. TRY TAKING OUT WEREWOLF AND PUT IN JEW. OR BALD GUY. YOU REMEMBER THE FIRST TIME YOU MET ME, YOU THOUGHT ALL COLLECTIONS GUYS WERE PRICKS? SO WHAT'S DIFFERENT WITH THIS?
YOU GOT TO STOP THINKING ABOUT WEREWOLVES AND WEREWOLF KILLERS, RANDI. YOU GOT TO START THINKING ABOUT MURDERERS. JOANIE NEVER KILLED ANYONE. ZOE EITHER. SKINCHANGERS IS WHAT THEY USED TO CALL US. NOT SOUL CHANGERS OR SOME CRAP LIKE THAT. THE CHANGE DOESN'T MAKE YOU INTO SOMEONE ELSE. WHEN I DON'T LOOK LIKE THIS, IT'S STILL ME INSIDE, JUST IN A DIFFERENT SKIN.
I HATE TO ADMIT IT, BUT THAT MAKES SENSE.
AND I'M GOOD IN BED TOO.
GOOD TO KNOW. WHAT DO YOU THINK ABOUT THESE MURDERERS? PAST OR PRESENT. I GET THE FEELING WE'RE GOING TO WIND UP AT THE SAME PLACE, WHICHEVER END WE START AT.
YEAH, MAYBE. I DUNNO. I WASN'T AROUND MUCH WHEN THE THING WITH THE HELANDER KID CAME DOWN. AND THESE ONES... JOANIE AND ZOE... WELL, JONATHAN TOLD ME ABOUT AN OLD LEGEND.
JONATHAN?

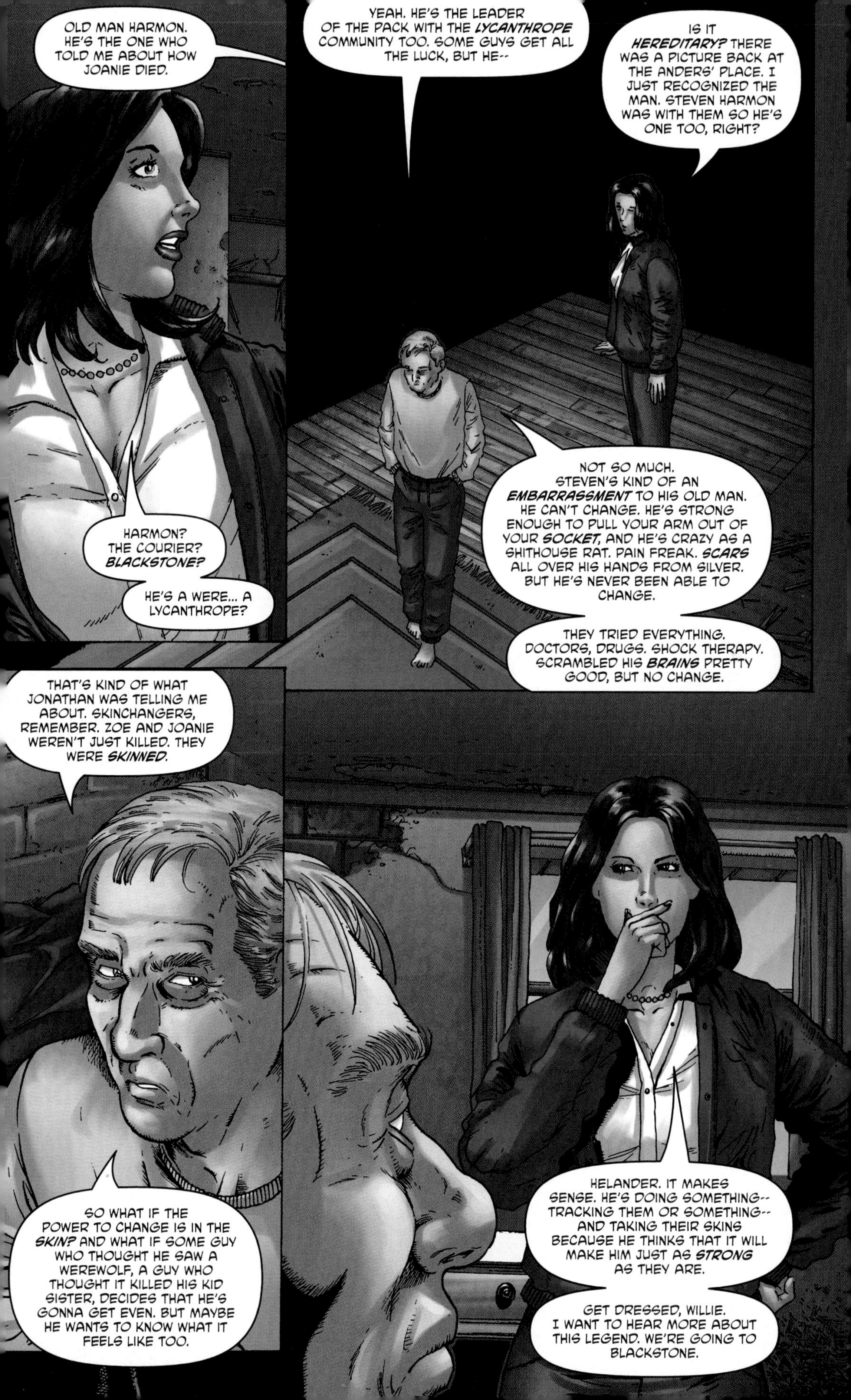
OLD MAN HARMON. HE'S THE ONE WHO TOLD ME ABOUT HOW JOANIE DIED.
YEAH. HE'S THE LEADER OF THE PACK WITH THE *LYCANTHROPE* COMMUNITY TOO. SOME GUYS GET ALL THE LUCK, BUT HE--
IS IT *HEREDITARY?* THERE WAS A PICTURE BACK AT THE ANDERS' PLACE. I JUST RECOGNIZED THE MAN. STEVEN HARMON WAS WITH THEM SO HE'S ONE TOO, RIGHT?
NOT SO MUCH. STEVEN'S KIND OF AN *EMBARRASSMENT* TO HIS OLD MAN. HE CAN'T CHANGE. HE'S STRONG ENOUGH TO PULL YOUR ARM OUT OF YOUR *SOCKET,* AND HE'S CRAZY AS A SHITHOUSE RAT. PAIN FREAK. *SCARS* ALL OVER HIS HANDS FROM SILVER. BUT HE'S NEVER BEEN ABLE TO CHANGE.
THEY TRIED EVERYTHING. DOCTORS, DRUGS. SHOCK THERAPY. SCRAMBLED HIS *BRAINS* PRETTY GOOD, BUT NO CHANGE.
HARMON? THE COURIER? *BLACKSTONE?*
HE'S A WERE... A LYCANTHROPE?
THAT'S KIND OF WHAT JONATHAN WAS TELLING ME ABOUT. SKINCHANGERS, REMEMBER. ZOE AND JOANIE WEREN'T JUST KILLED. THEY WERE *SKINNED.*
SO WHAT IF THE POWER TO CHANGE IS IN THE *SKIN?* AND WHAT IF SOME GUY WHO THOUGHT HE SAW A WEREWOLF, A GUY WHO THOUGHT IT KILLED HIS KID SISTER, DECIDES THAT HE'S GONNA GET EVEN. BUT MAYBE HE WANTS TO KNOW WHAT IT FEELS LIKE TOO.
HELANDER. IT MAKES SENSE. HE'S DOING SOMETHING-- TRACKING THEM OR SOMETHING-- AND TAKING THEIR SKINS BECAUSE HE THINKS THAT IT WILL MAKE HIM JUST AS *STRONG* AS THEY ARE.
GET DRESSED, WILLIE. I WANT TO HEAR MORE ABOUT THIS LEGEND. WE'RE GOING TO BLACKSTONE.

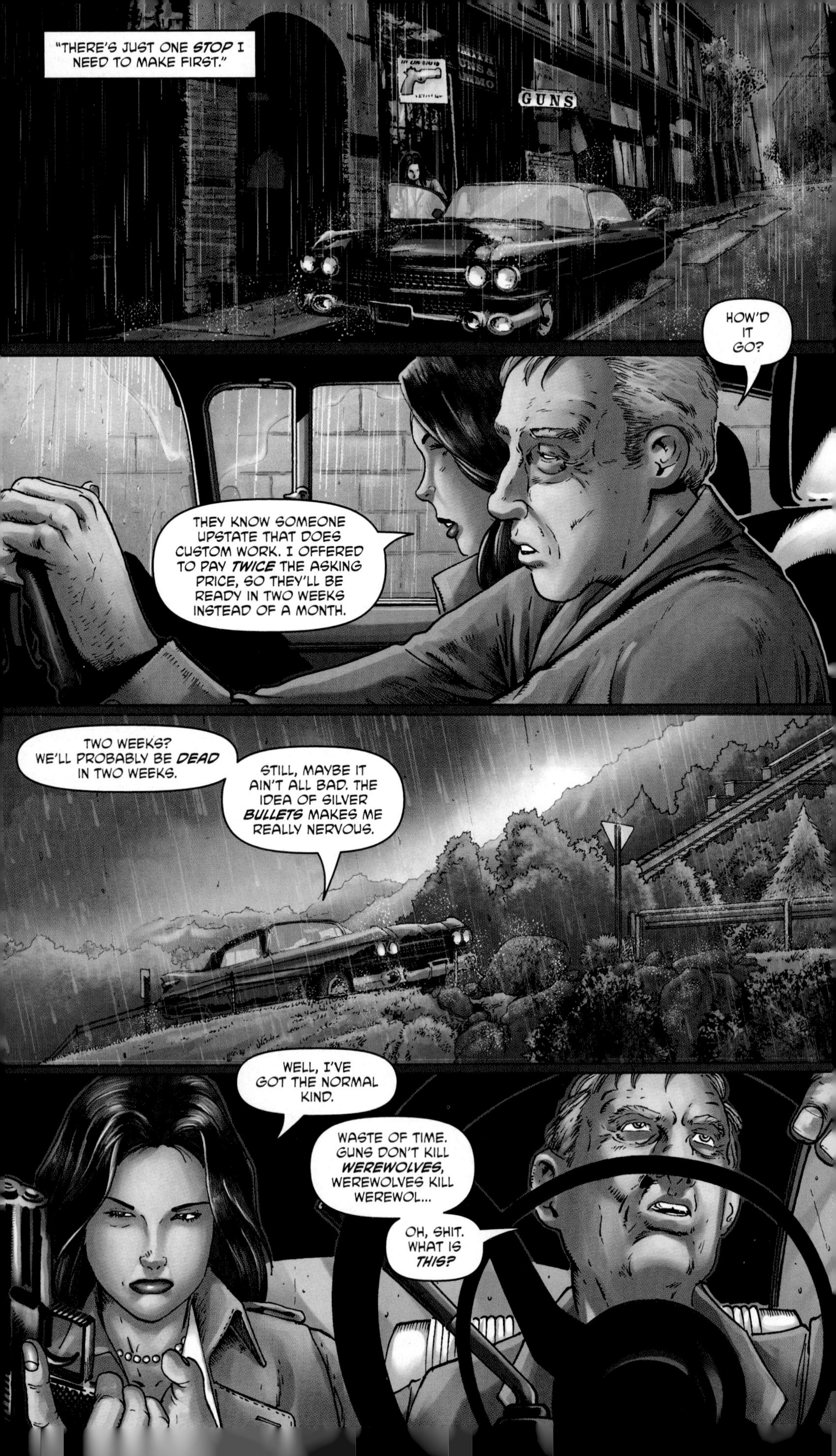
"THERE'S JUST ONE *STOP* I NEED TO MAKE FIRST."
GUNS
HOW'D IT GO?
THEY KNOW SOMEONE UPSTATE THAT DOES CUSTOM WORK. I OFFERED TO PAY *TWICE* THE ASKING PRICE, SO THEY'LL BE READY IN TWO WEEKS INSTEAD OF A MONTH.
TWO WEEKS? WE'LL PROBABLY BE *DEAD* IN TWO WEEKS.
STILL, MAYBE IT AIN'T ALL BAD. THE IDEA OF SILVER *BULLETS* MAKES ME REALLY NERVOUS.
WELL, I'VE GOT THE NORMAL KIND.
WASTE OF TIME. GUNS DON'T KILL *WEREWOLVES*, WEREWOLVES KILL WEREWOL...
OH, SHIT. WHAT IS *THIS?*

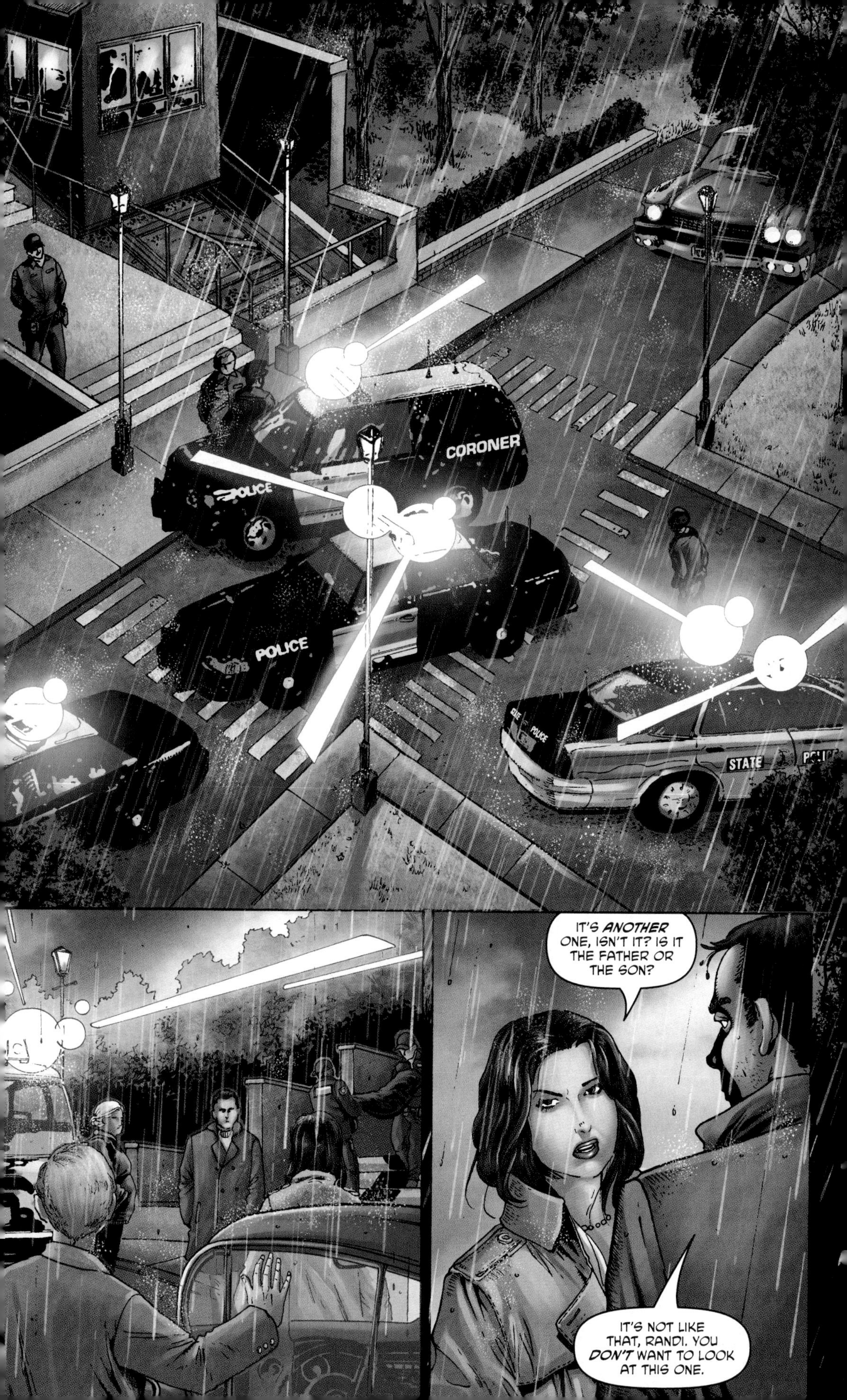
CORONER
POLICE
POLICE
STATE
IT'S *ANOTHER* ONE, ISN'T IT? IS IT THE FATHER OR THE SON?
IT'S NOT LIKE THAT, RANDI. YOU *DON'T* WANT TO LOOK AT THIS ONE.

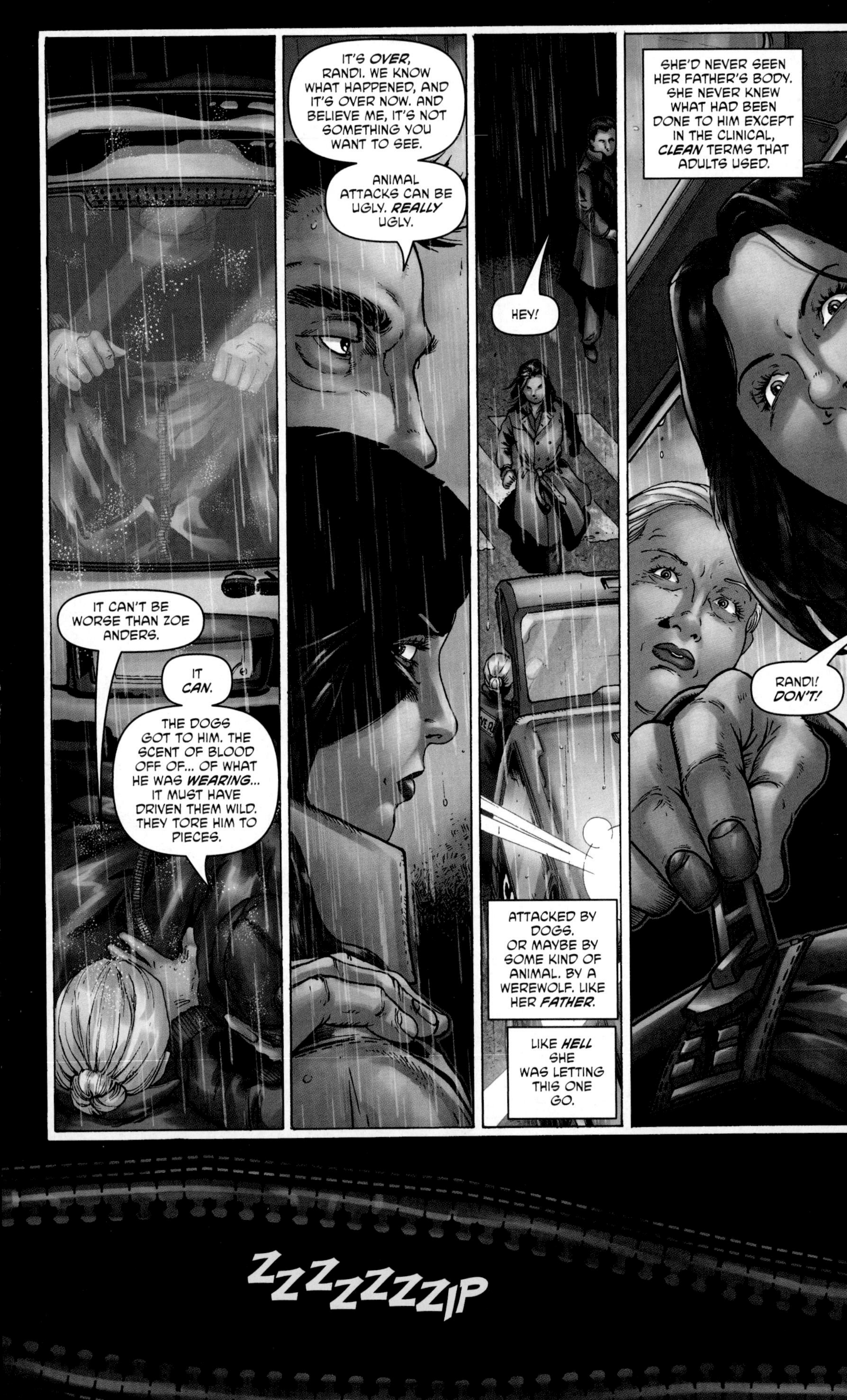
IT CAN'T BE WORSE THAN ZOE ANDERS.
IT CAN.
THE DOGS GOT TO HIM. THE SCENT OF BLOOD OFF OF... OF WHAT HE WAS WEARING... IT MUST HAVE DRIVEN THEM WILD. THEY TORE HIM TO PIECES.
IT'S OVER, RANDI. WE KNOW WHAT HAPPENED, AND IT'S OVER NOW. AND BELIEVE ME, IT'S NOT SOMETHING YOU WANT TO SEE.
ANIMAL ATTACKS CAN BE UGLY. REALLY UGLY.
HEY!
ATTACKED BY DOGS. OR MAYBE BY SOME KIND OF ANIMAL. BY A WEREWOLF. LIKE HER FATHER.
LIKE HELL SHE WAS LETTING THIS ONE GO.
SHE'D NEVER SEEN HER FATHER'S BODY. SHE NEVER KNEW WHAT HAD BEEN DONE TO HIM EXCEPT IN THE CLINICAL, CLEAN TERMS THAT ADULTS USED.
RANDI! DON'T!
ZZZZZZZZIP

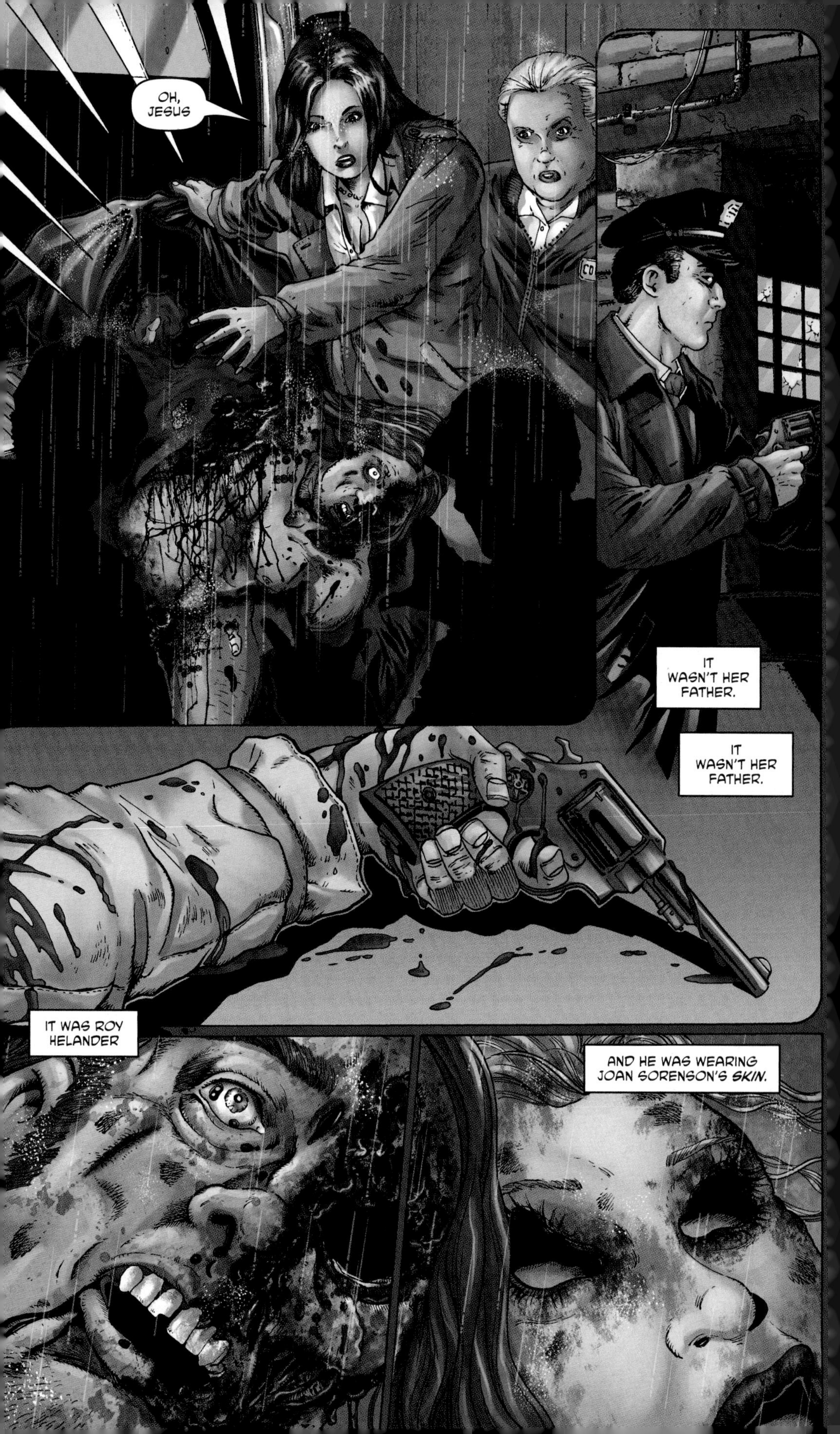
OH, JESUS
IT WASN'T HER FATHER.
IT WASN'T HER FATHER.
IT WAS ROY HELANDER
AND HE WAS WEARING JOAN SORENSON'S *SKIN*.

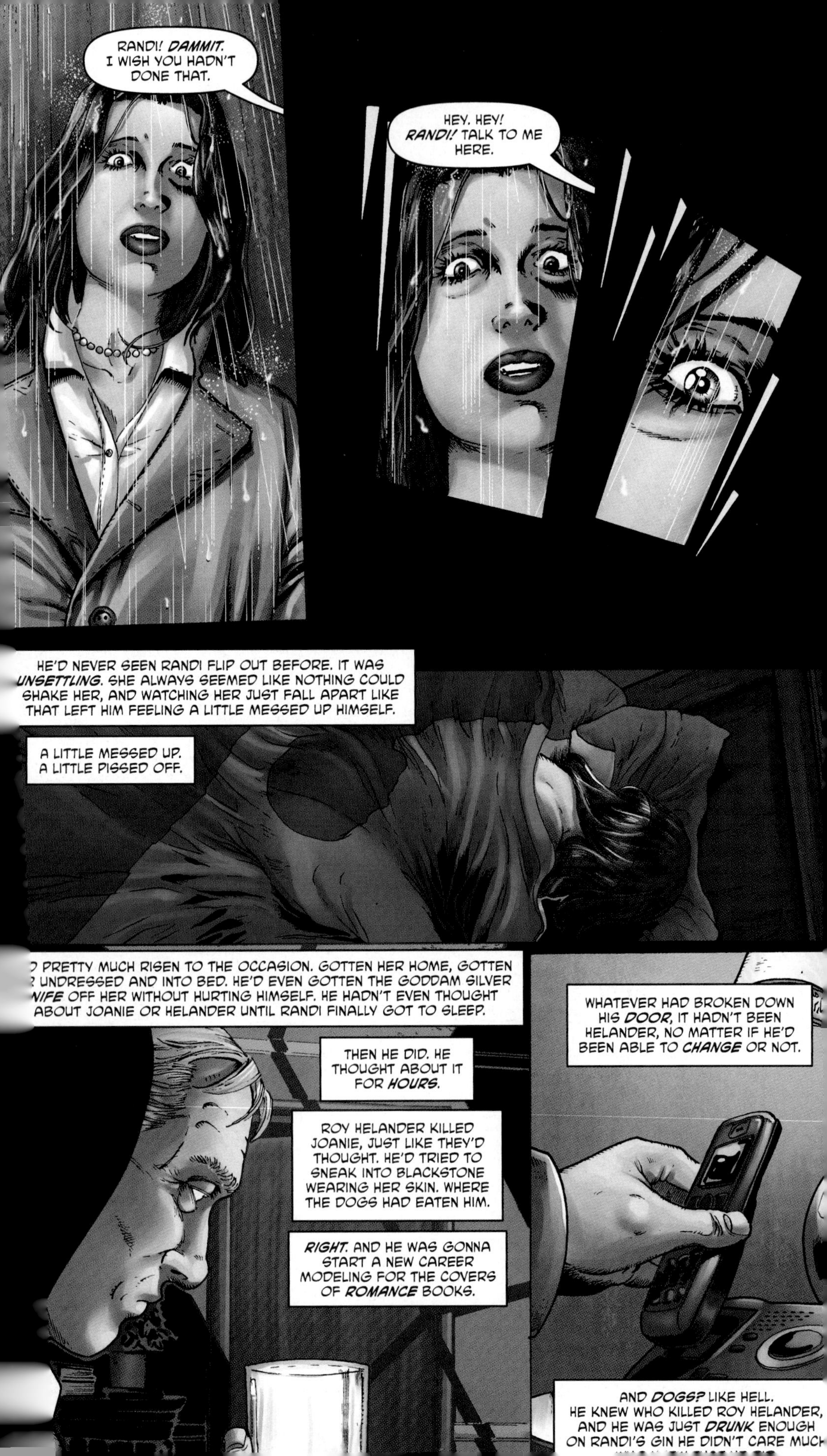

RANDI! DAMMIT. I WISH YOU HADN'T DONE THAT.
HEY. HEY! RANDI! TALK TO ME HERE.
HE'D NEVER SEEN RANDI FLIP OUT BEFORE. IT WAS UNSETTLING. SHE ALWAYS SEEMED LIKE NOTHING COULD SHAKE HER, AND WATCHING HER JUST FALL APART LIKE THAT LEFT HIM FEELING A LITTLE MESSED UP HIMSELF.
A LITTLE MESSED UP. A LITTLE PISSED OFF.
PRETTY MUCH RISEN TO THE OCCASION. GOTTEN HER HOME, GOTTEN
UNDRESSED AND INTO BED. HE'D EVEN GOTTEN THE GODDAM SILVER
NIFE OFF HER WITHOUT HURTING HIMSELF. HE HADN'T EVEN THOUGHT
ABOUT JOANIE OR HELANDER UNTIL RANDI FINALLY GOT TO SLEEP.
THEN HE DID. HE THOUGHT ABOUT IT FOR HOURS.
ROY HELANDER KILLED JOANIE, JUST LIKE THEY'D THOUGHT. HE'D TRIED TO SNEAK INTO BLACKSTONE WEARING HER SKIN. WHERE THE DOGS HAD EATEN HIM.
RIGHT. AND HE WAS GONNA START A NEW CAREER MODELING FOR THE COVERS OF ROMANCE BOOKS.
WHATEVER HAD BROKEN DOWN HIS DOOR, IT HADN'T BEEN HELANDER, NO MATTER IF HE'D BEEN ABLE TO CHANGE OR NOT.
AND DOGS? LIKE HELL.
HE KNEW WHO KILLED ROY HELANDER,
AND HE WAS JUST DRUNK ENOUGH
ON RANDI'S GIN HE DIDN'T CARE MUCH

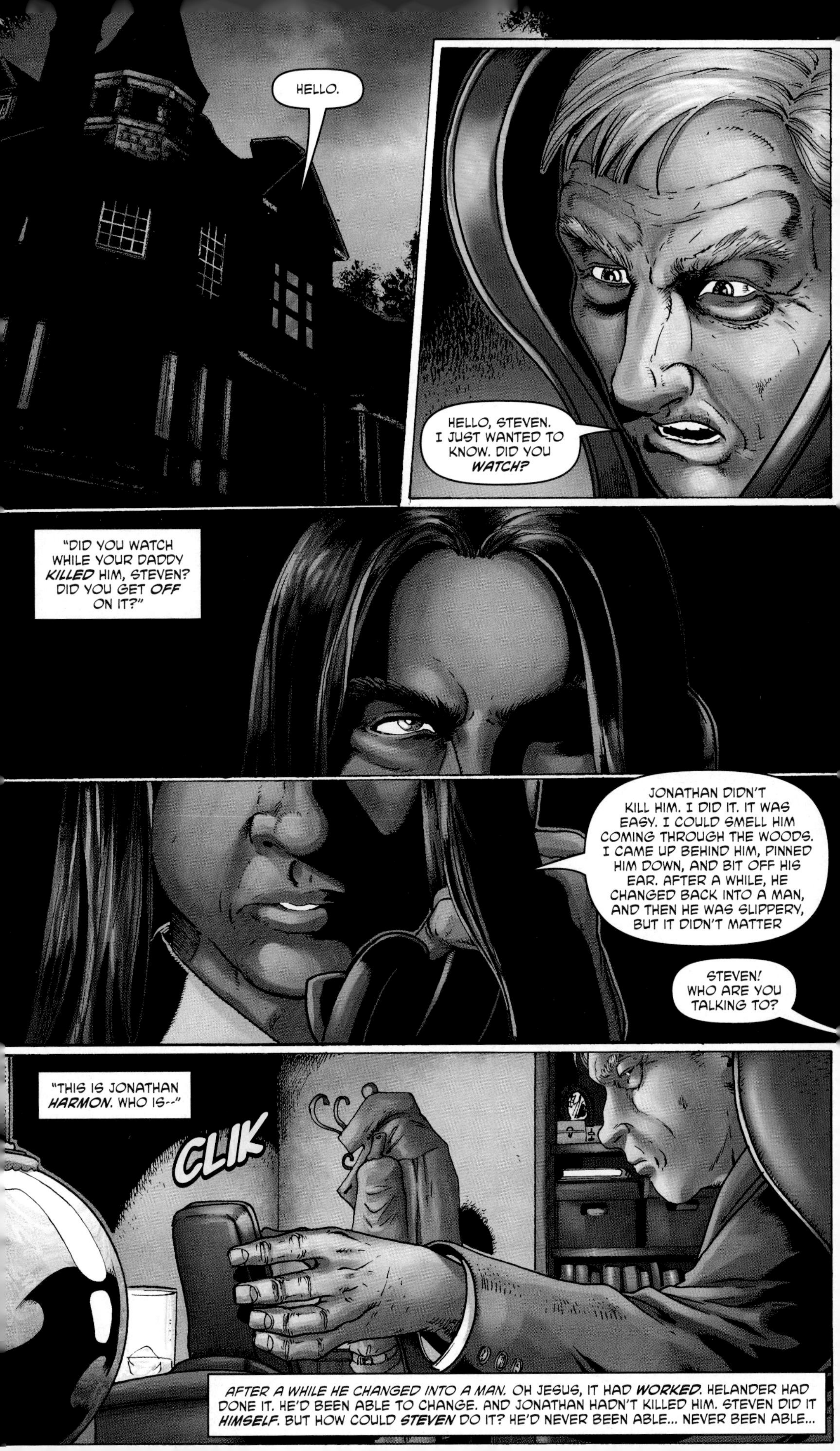
HELLO.
HELLO, STEVEN. I JUST WANTED TO KNOW. DID YOU *WATCH?*
"DID YOU WATCH WHILE YOUR DADDY *KILLED* HIM, STEVEN? DID YOU GET *OFF* ON IT?"
JONATHAN DIDN'T KILL HIM. I DID IT. IT WAS EASY. I COULD SMELL HIM COMING THROUGH THE WOODS. I CAME UP BEHIND HIM, PINNED HIM DOWN, AND BIT OFF HIS EAR. AFTER A WHILE, HE CHANGED BACK INTO A MAN, AND THEN HE WAS SLIPPERY, BUT IT DIDN'T MATTER
STEVEN! WHO ARE YOU TALKING TO?
"THIS IS JONATHAN *HARMON*. WHO IS--"
CLIK
AFTER A WHILE HE CHANGED INTO A MAN. OH JESUS, IT HAD *WORKED*. HELANDER HAD DONE IT. HE'D BEEN ABLE TO CHANGE. AND JONATHAN HADN'T KILLED HIM. STEVEN DID IT *HIMSELF*. BUT HOW COULD *STEVEN* DO IT? HE'D NEVER BEEN ABLE... NEVER BEEN ABLE...

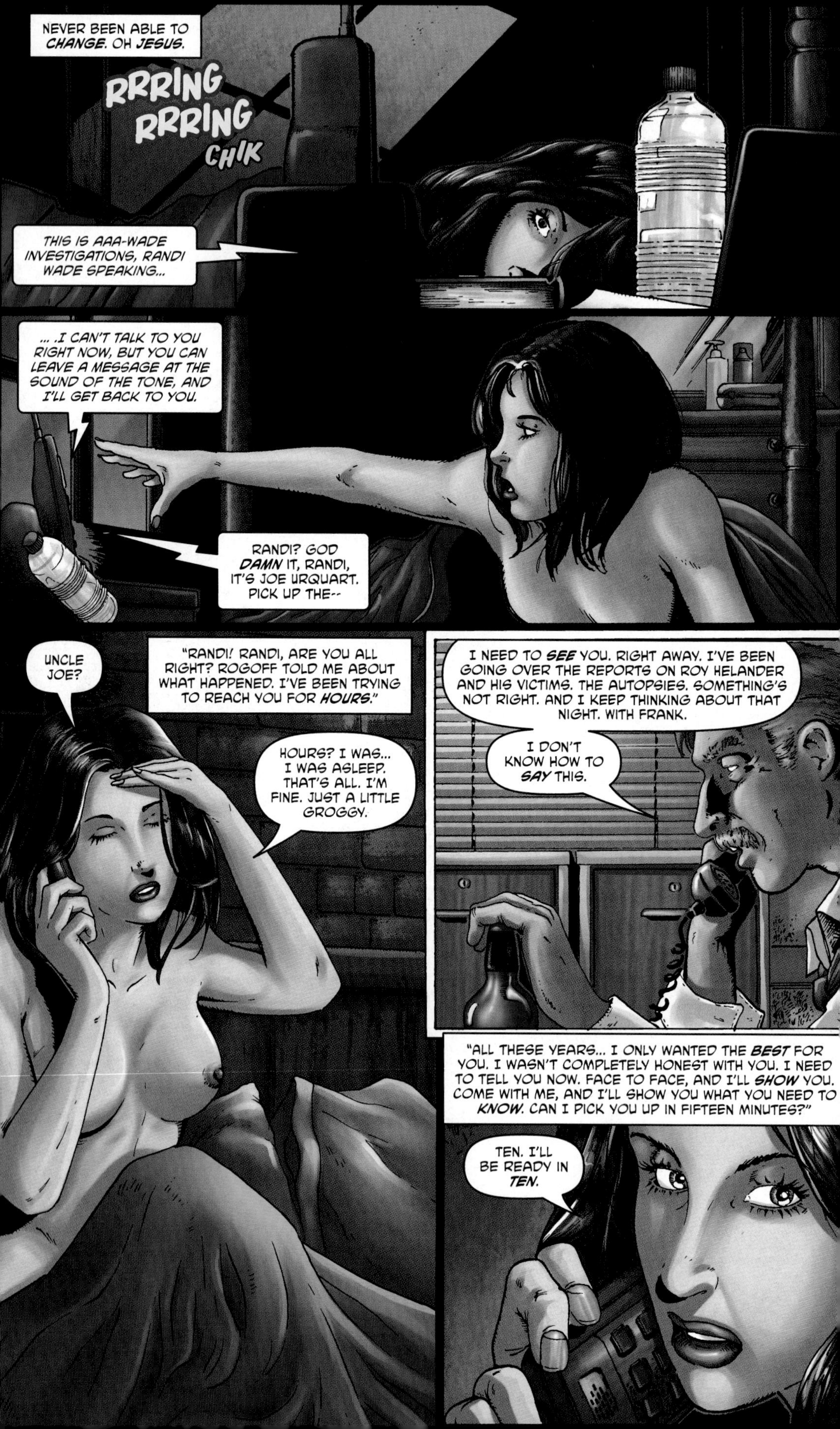

NEVER BEEN ABLE TO CHANGE. OH JESUS.
RRRING RRRING
CHIK
THIS IS AAA-WADE INVESTIGATIONS, RANDI WADE SPEAKING...
... .I CAN'T TALK TO YOU RIGHT NOW, BUT YOU CAN LEAVE A MESSAGE AT THE SOUND OF THE TONE, AND I'LL GET BACK TO YOU.
RANDI? GOD DAMN IT, RANDI, IT'S JOE URQUART. PICK UP THE--
UNCLE JOE?
"RANDI! RANDI, ARE YOU ALL RIGHT? ROGOFF TOLD ME ABOUT WHAT HAPPENED. I'VE BEEN TRYING TO REACH YOU FOR HOURS."
HOURS? I WAS... I WAS ASLEEP. THAT'S ALL. I'M FINE. JUST A LITTLE GROGGY.
I NEED TO SEE YOU. RIGHT AWAY. I'VE BEEN GOING OVER THE REPORTS ON ROY HELANDER AND HIS VICTIMS. THE AUTOPSIES. SOMETHING'S NOT RIGHT. AND I KEEP THINKING ABOUT THAT NIGHT. WITH FRANK.
I DON'T KNOW HOW TO SAY THIS.
"ALL THESE YEARS... I ONLY WANTED THE BEST FOR YOU. I WASN'T COMPLETELY HONEST WITH YOU. I NEED TO TELL YOU NOW. FACE TO FACE, AND I'LL SHOW YOU. COME WITH ME, AND I'LL SHOW YOU WHAT YOU NEED TO KNOW. CAN I PICK YOU UP IN FIFTEEN MINUTES?"
TEN. I'LL BE READY IN TEN.

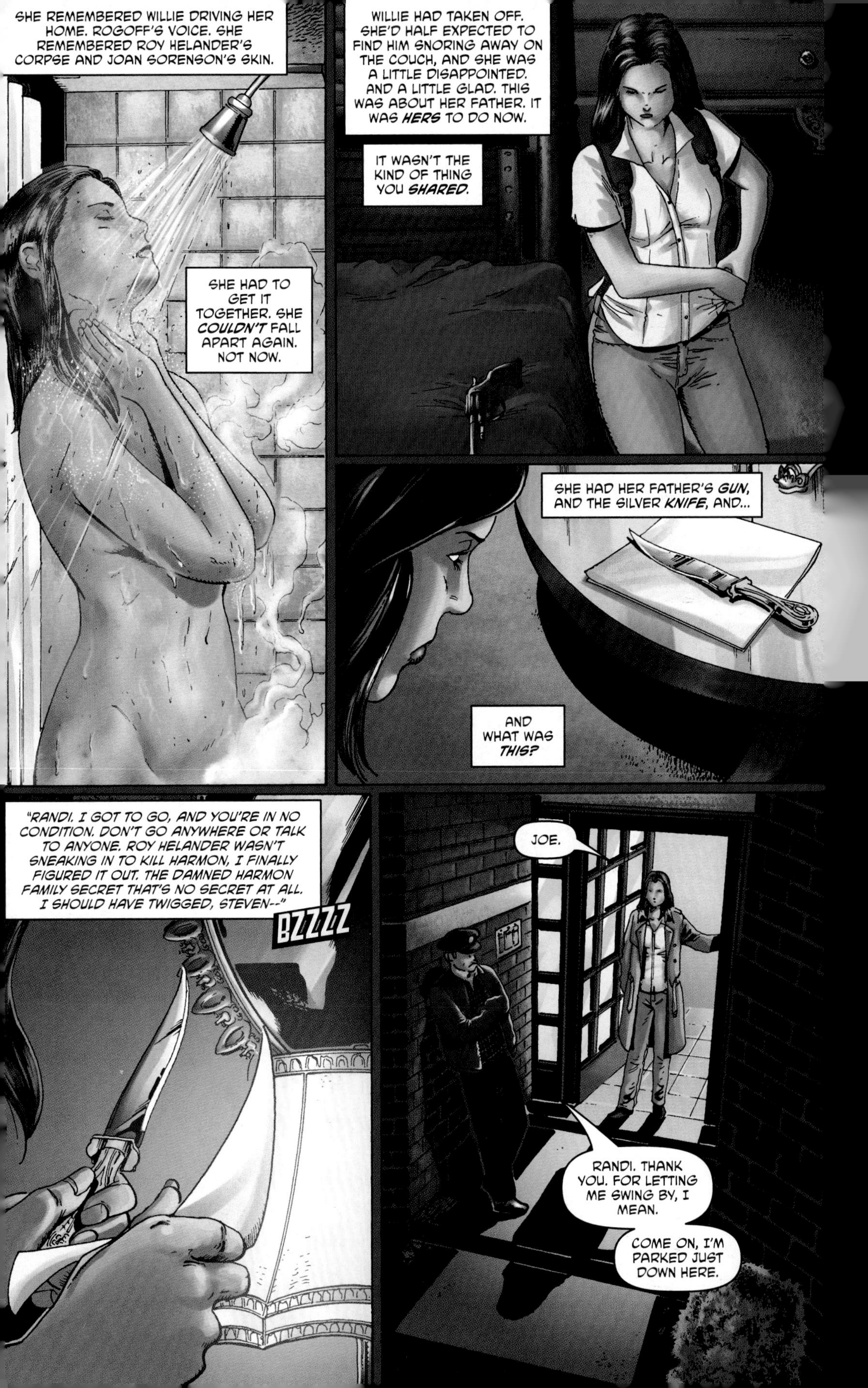
SHE REMEMBERED WILLIE DRIVING HER HOME. ROGOFF'S VOICE. SHE REMEMBERED ROY HELANDER'S CORPSE AND JOAN SORENSON'S SKIN.
SHE HAD TO GET IT TOGETHER. SHE *COULDN'T* FALL APART AGAIN. NOT NOW.
WILLIE HAD TAKEN OFF. SHE'D HALF EXPECTED TO FIND HIM SNORING AWAY ON THE COUCH, AND SHE WAS A LITTLE DISAPPOINTED. AND A LITTLE GLAD. THIS WAS ABOUT HER FATHER. IT WAS *HERS* TO DO NOW.
IT WASN'T THE KIND OF THING YOU *SHARED*.
SHE HAD HER FATHER'S *GUN*, AND THE SILVER *KNIFE*, AND...
AND WHAT WAS *THIS?*
"RANDI. I GOT TO GO, AND YOU'RE IN NO CONDITION. DON'T GO ANYWHERE OR TALK TO ANYONE. ROY HELANDER WASN'T SNEAKING IN TO KILL HARMON, I FINALLY FIGURED IT OUT. THE DAMNED HARMON FAMILY SECRET THAT'S NO SECRET AT ALL. I SHOULD HAVE TWIGGED, STEVEN--"
BZZZZ
JOE.
RANDI. THANK YOU. FOR LETTING ME SWING BY, I MEAN.
COME ON, I'M PARKED JUST DOWN HERE.

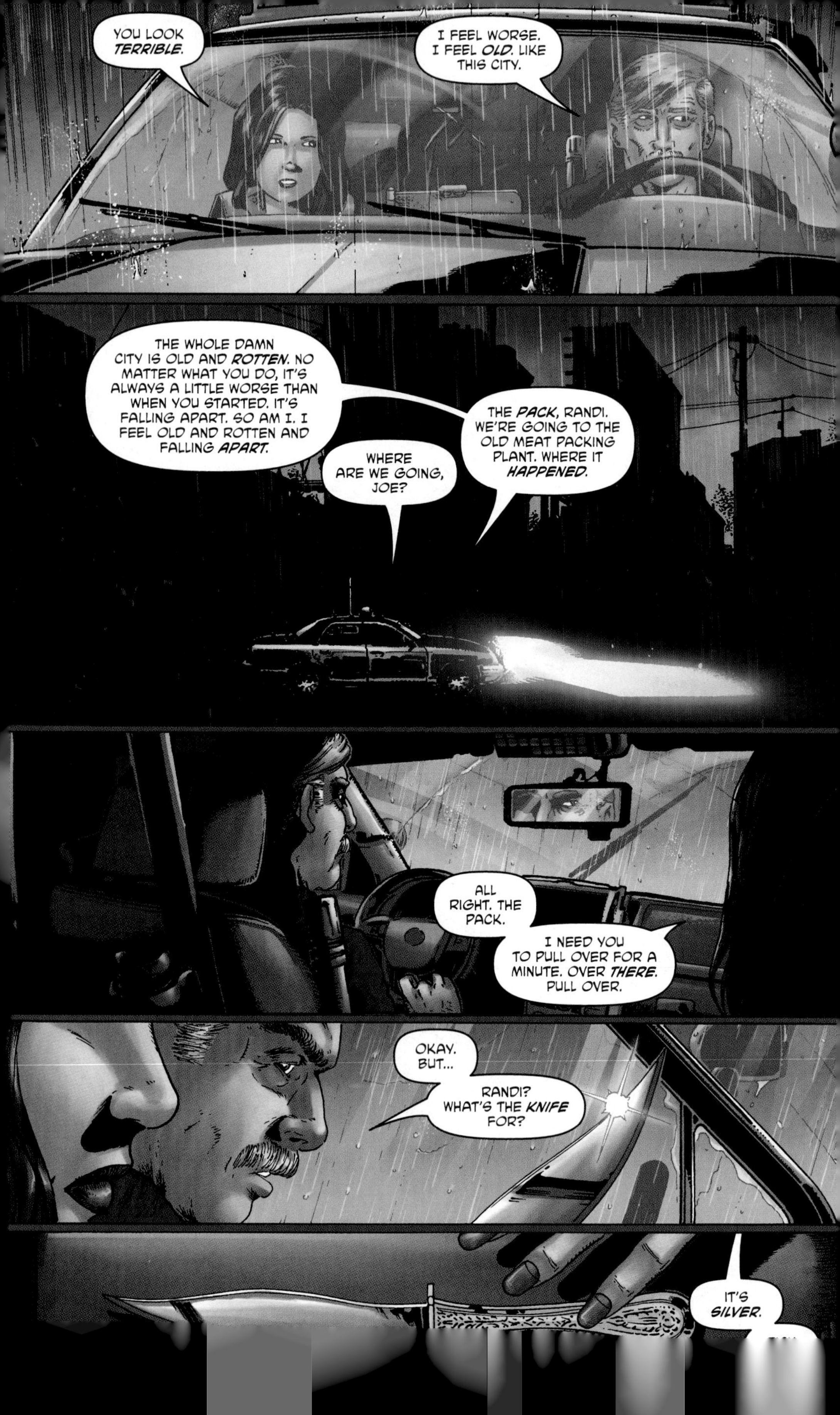
YOU LOOK TERRIBLE.
I FEEL WORSE. I FEEL OLD. LIKE THIS CITY.
THE WHOLE DAMN CITY IS OLD AND ROTTEN. NO MATTER WHAT YOU DO, IT'S ALWAYS A LITTLE WORSE THAN WHEN YOU STARTED. IT'S FALLING APART. SO AM I. I FEEL OLD AND ROTTEN AND FALLING APART.
WHERE ARE WE GOING, JOE?
THE PACK, RANDI. WE'RE GOING TO THE OLD MEAT PACKING PLANT. WHERE IT HAPPENED.
ALL RIGHT. THE PACK.
I NEED YOU TO PULL OVER FOR A MINUTE. OVER THERE. PULL OVER.
OKAY. BUT...
RANDI? WHAT'S THE KNIFE FOR?
IT'S SILVER.

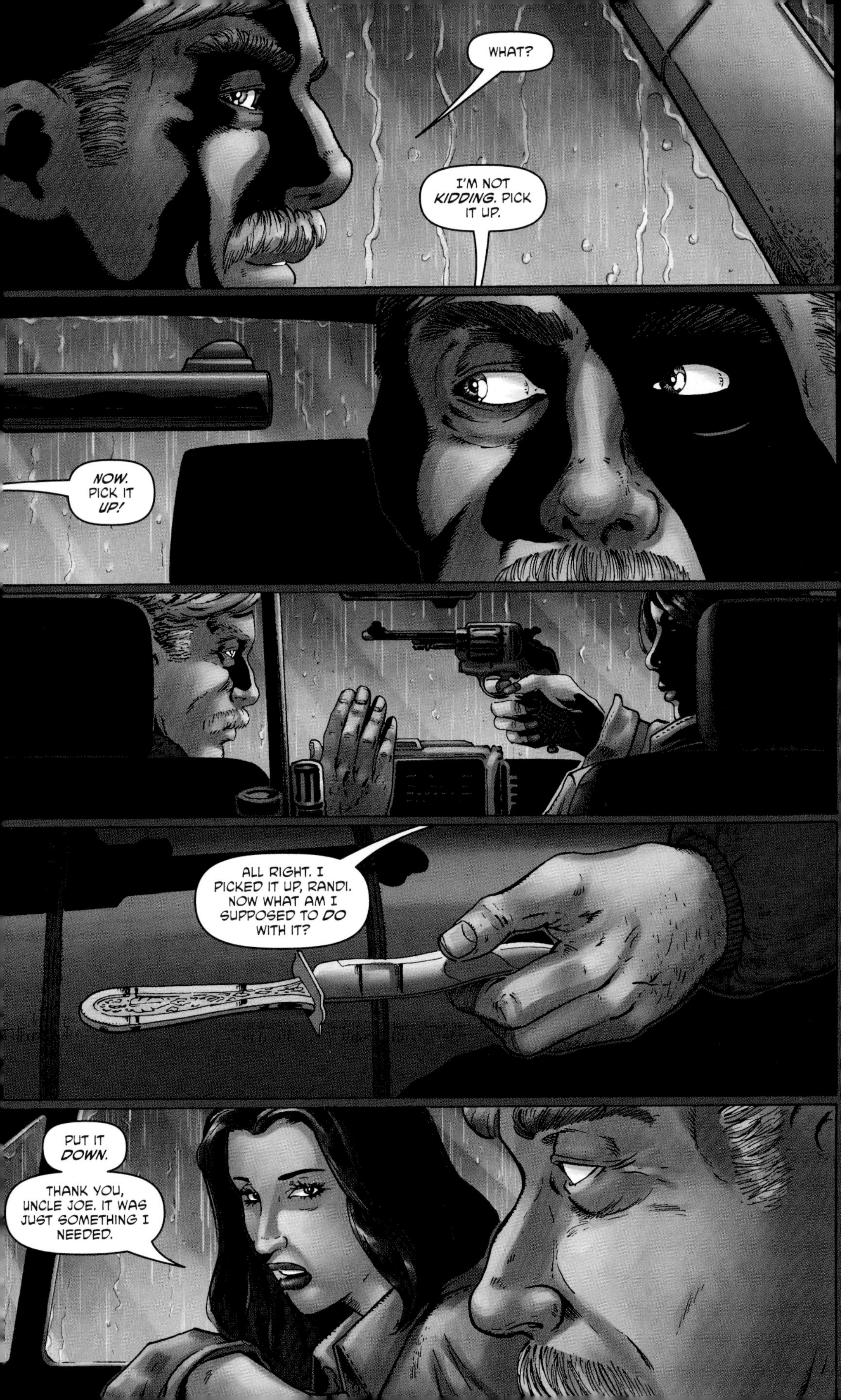
WHAT?
I'M NOT KIDDING. PICK IT UP.
NOW. PICK IT UP!
ALL RIGHT. I PICKED IT UP, RANDI. NOW WHAT AM I SUPPOSED TO DO WITH IT?
PUT IT DOWN.
THANK YOU, UNCLE JOE. IT WAS JUST SOMETHING I NEEDED.

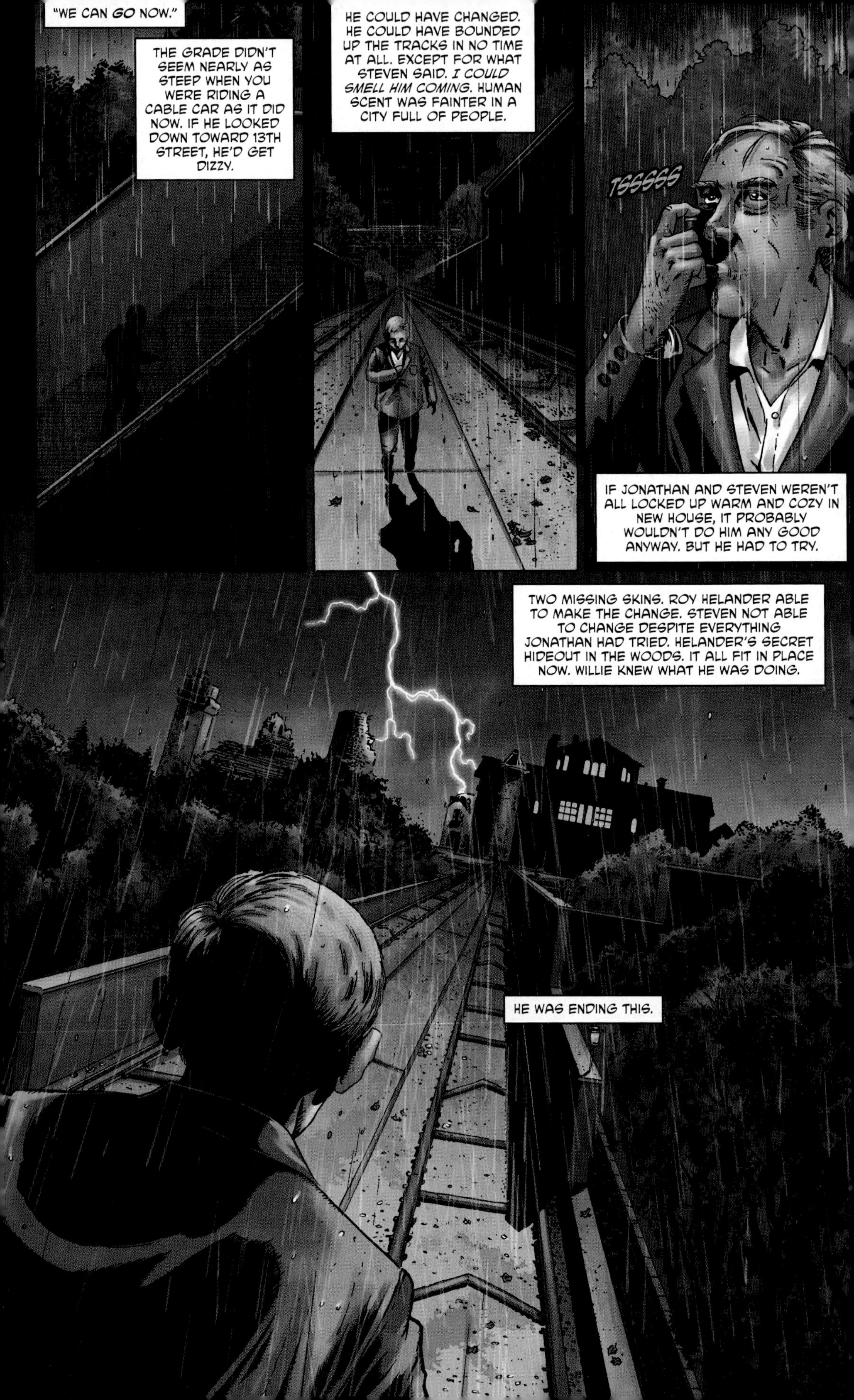
"WE CAN *GO* NOW."
THE GRADE DIDN'T SEEM NEARLY AS STEEP WHEN YOU WERE RIDING A CABLE CAR AS IT DID NOW. IF HE LOOKED DOWN TOWARD 13TH STREET, HE'D GET DIZZY.
HE COULD HAVE CHANGED. HE COULD HAVE BOUNDED UP THE TRACKS IN NO TIME AT ALL. EXCEPT FOR WHAT STEVEN SAID. *I COULD SMELL HIM COMING.* HUMAN SCENT WAS FAINTER IN A CITY FULL OF PEOPLE.
TSSSSS
IF JONATHAN AND STEVEN WEREN'T ALL LOCKED UP WARM AND COZY IN NEW HOUSE, IT PROBABLY WOULDN'T DO HIM ANY GOOD ANYWAY. BUT HE HAD TO TRY.
TWO MISSING SKINS. ROY HELANDER ABLE TO MAKE THE CHANGE. STEVEN NOT ABLE TO CHANGE DESPITE EVERYTHING JONATHAN HAD TRIED. HELANDER'S SECRET HIDEOUT IN THE WOODS. IT ALL FIT IN PLACE NOW. WILLIE KNEW WHAT HE WAS DOING.
HE WAS ENDING THIS.

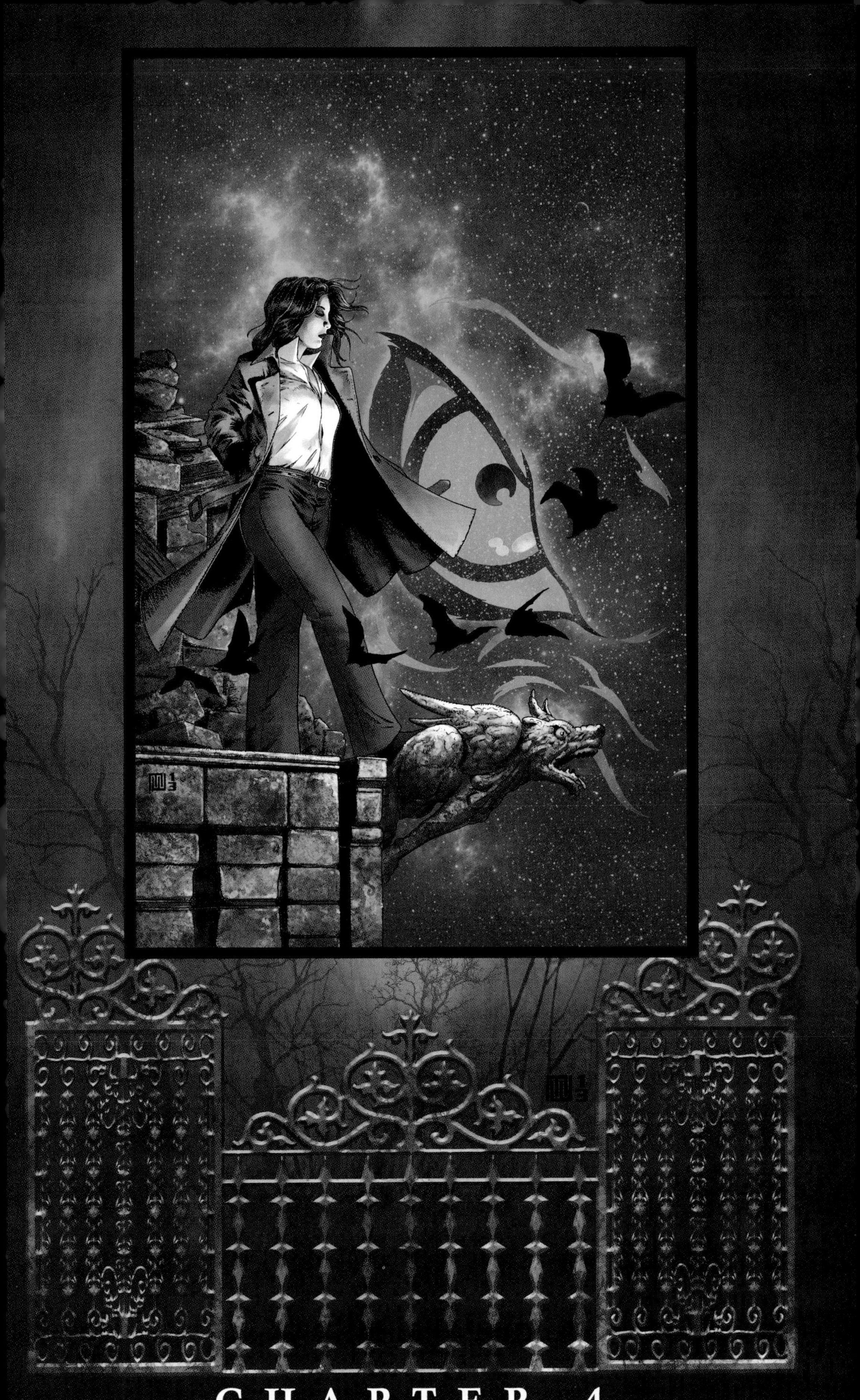

CHAPTER 4

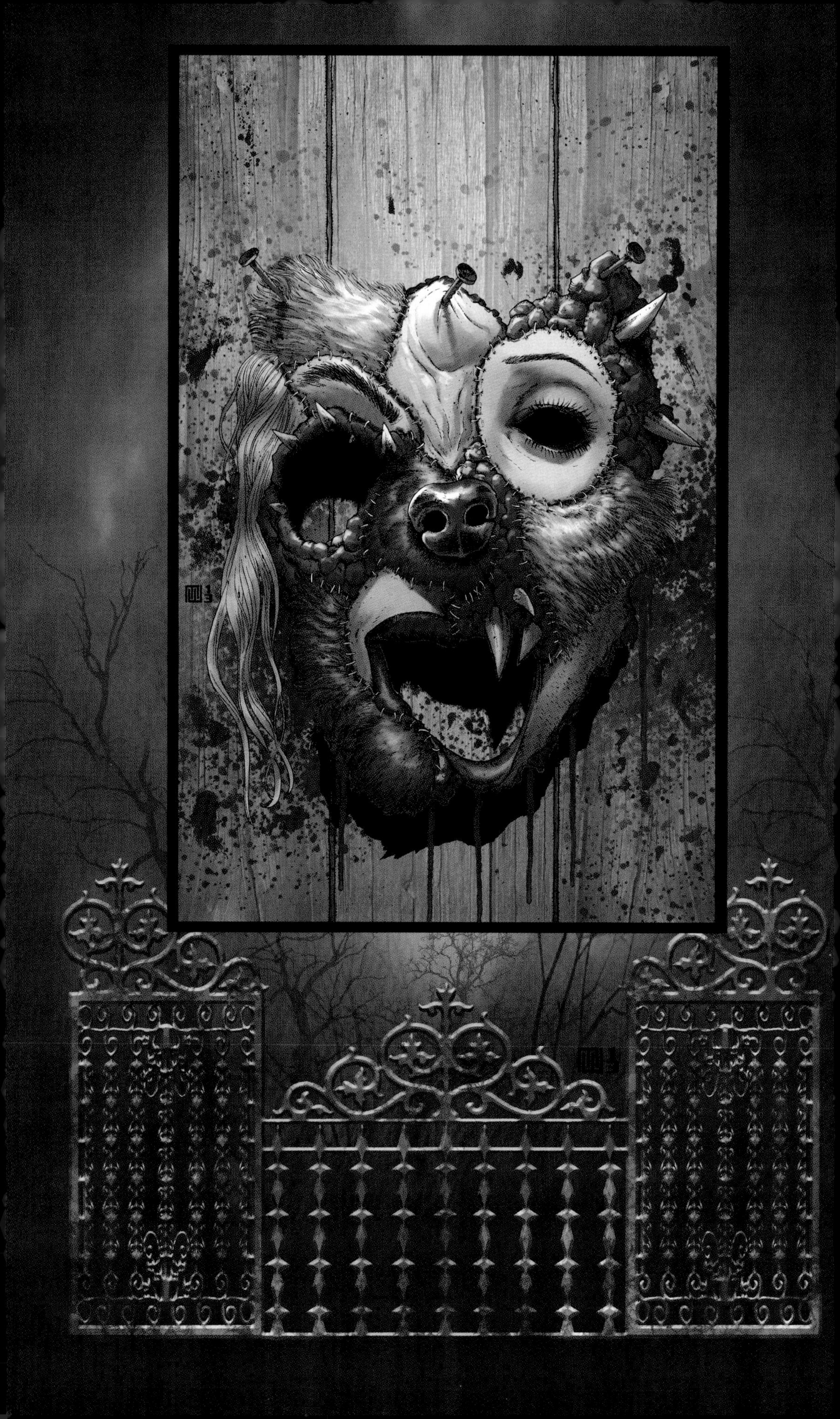

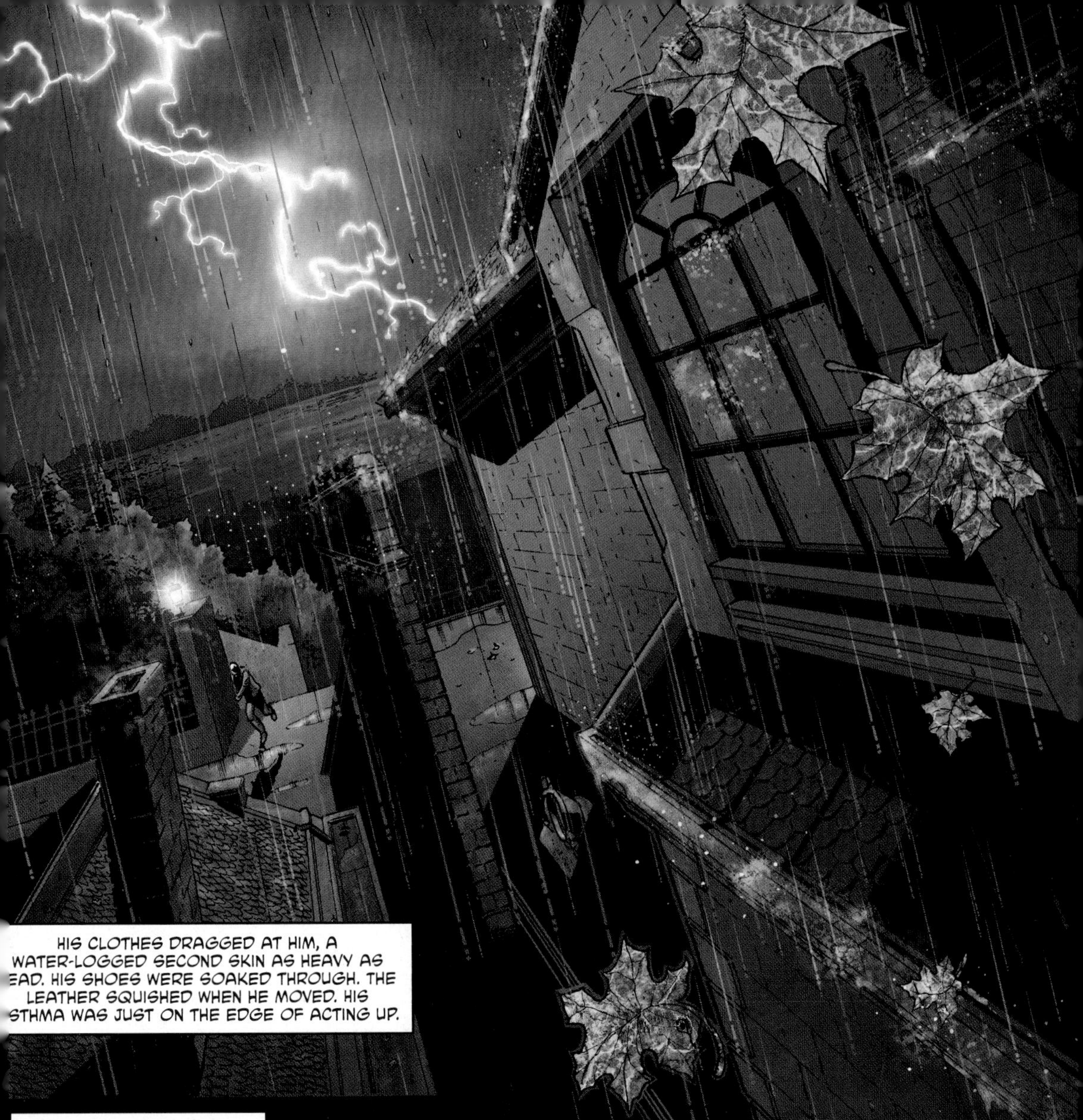
HIS CLOTHES DRAGGED AT HIM, A WATER-LOGGED SECOND SKIN AS HEAVY AS EAD. HIS SHOES WERE SOAKED THROUGH. THE LEATHER SQUISHED WHEN HE MOVED. HIS STHMA WAS JUST ON THE EDGE OF ACTING UP.

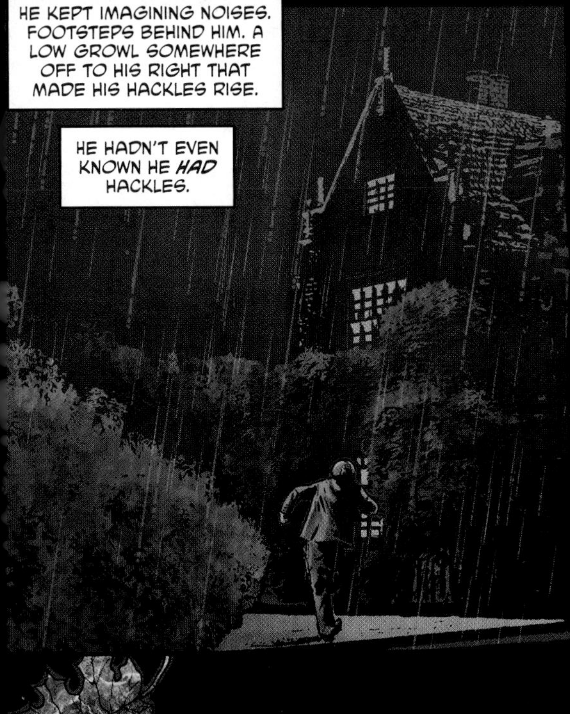
HE KEPT IMAGINING NOISES. FOOTSTEPS BEHIND HIM. A LOW GROWL SOMEWHERE OFF TO HIS RIGHT THAT MADE HIS HACKLES RISE.
HE HADN'T EVEN KNOWN HE *HAD* HACKLES.

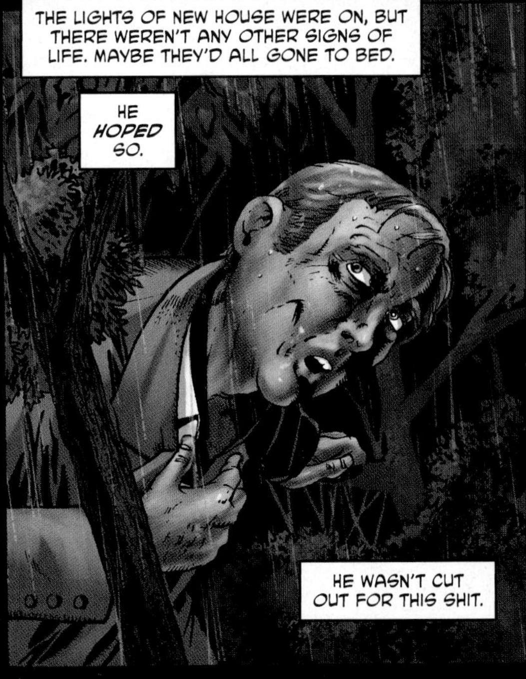
THE LIGHTS OF NEW HOUSE WERE ON, BUT THERE WEREN'T ANY OTHER SIGNS OF LIFE. MAYBE THEY'D ALL GONE TO BED.
HE *HOPED* SO.
HE WASN'T CUT OUT FOR THIS SHIT.

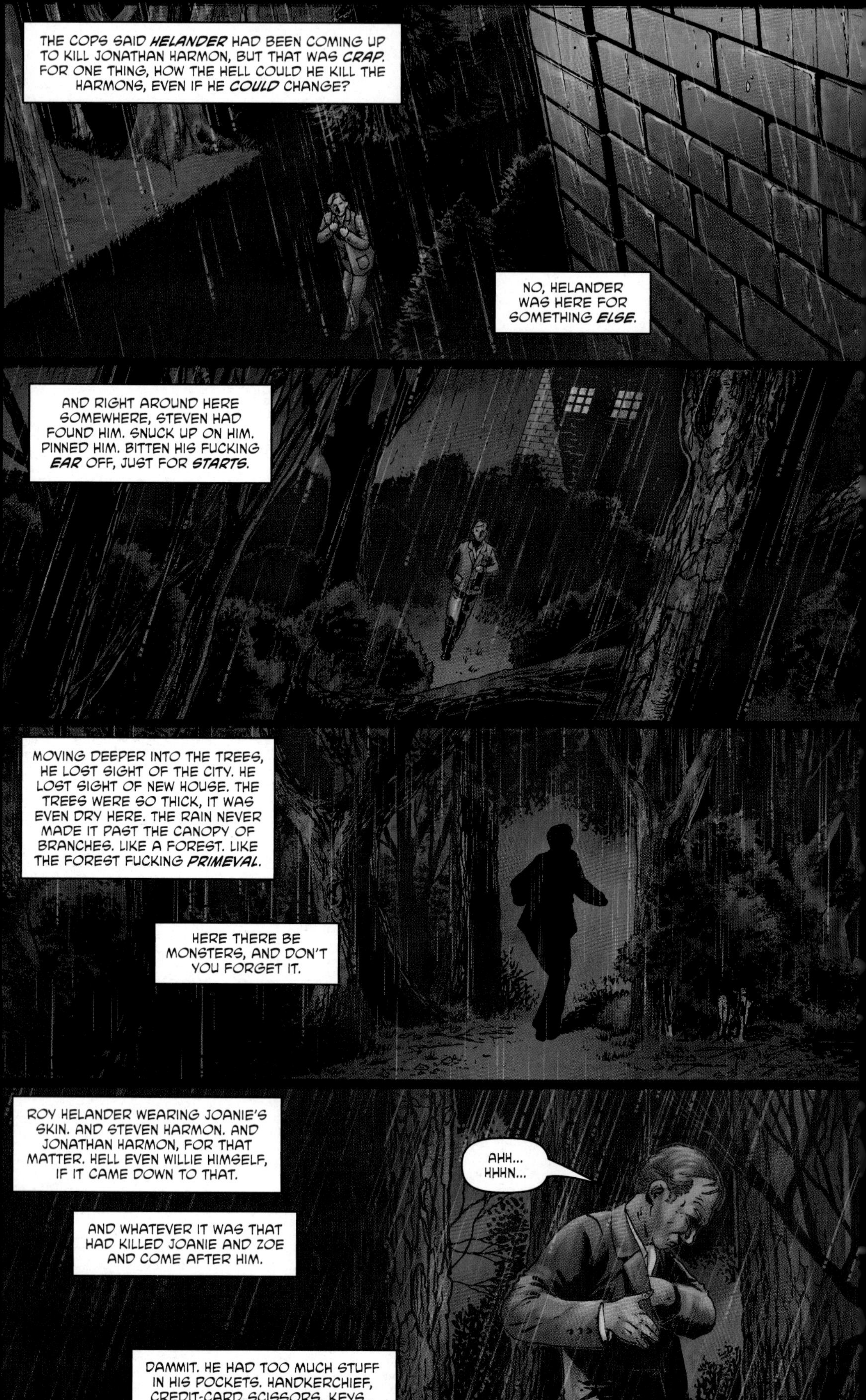
THE COPS SAID HELANDER HAD BEEN COMING UP TO KILL JONATHAN HARMON, BUT THAT WAS CRAP. FOR ONE THING, HOW THE HELL COULD HE KILL THE HARMONS, EVEN IF HE COULD CHANGE?
NO, HELANDER WAS HERE FOR SOMETHING ELSE.
AND RIGHT AROUND HERE SOMEWHERE, STEVEN HAD FOUND HIM. SNUCK UP ON HIM. PINNED HIM. BITTEN HIS FUCKING EAR OFF, JUST FOR STARTS.
MOVING DEEPER INTO THE TREES, HE LOST SIGHT OF THE CITY. HE LOST SIGHT OF NEW HOUSE. THE TREES WERE SO THICK, IT WAS EVEN DRY HERE. THE RAIN NEVER MADE IT PAST THE CANOPY OF BRANCHES. LIKE A FOREST. LIKE THE FOREST FUCKING PRIMEVAL.
HERE THERE BE MONSTERS, AND DON'T YOU FORGET IT.
ROY HELANDER WEARING JOANIE'S SKIN. AND STEVEN HARMON. AND JONATHAN HARMON, FOR THAT MATTER. HELL EVEN WILLIE HIMSELF, IF IT CAME DOWN TO THAT.
AHH... HHHN...
AND WHATEVER IT WAS THAT HAD KILLED JOANIE AND ZOE AND COME AFTER HIM.
DAMMIT. HE HAD TOO MUCH STUFF IN HIS POCKETS. HANDKERCHIEF, CREDIT-CARD SCISSORS, KEYS...

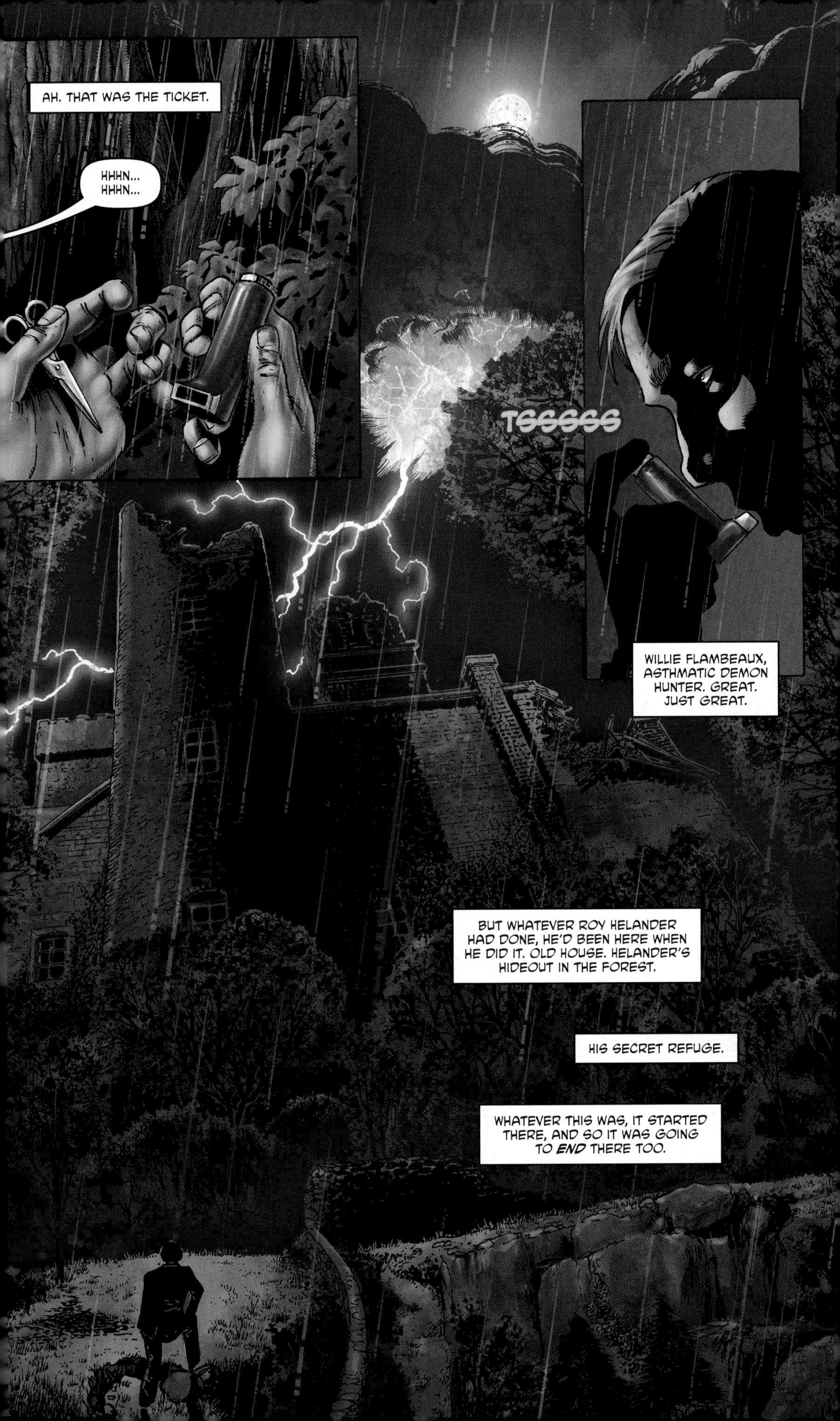

AH. THAT WAS THE TICKET.
HHHN... HHHN...
TSSSSS
WILLIE FLAMBEAUX, ASTHMATIC DEMON HUNTER. GREAT. JUST GREAT.
BUT WHATEVER ROY HELANDER HAD DONE, HE'D BEEN HERE WHEN HE DID IT. OLD HOUSE. HELANDER'S HIDEOUT IN THE FOREST.
HIS SECRET REFUGE.
WHATEVER THIS WAS, IT STARTED THERE, AND SO IT WAS GOING TO *END* THERE TOO.

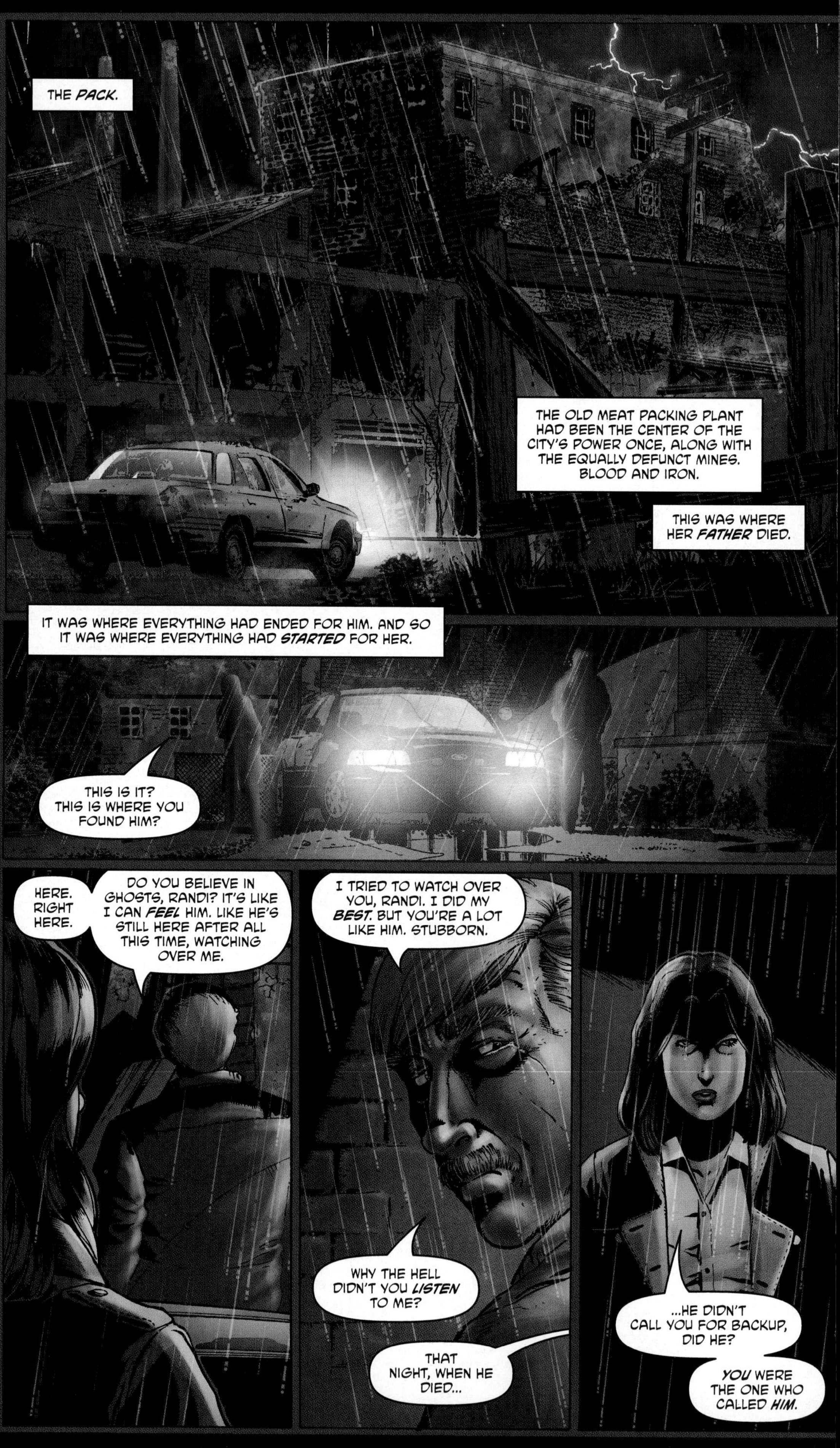
THE PACK.
THE OLD MEAT PACKING PLANT HAD BEEN THE CENTER OF THE CITY'S POWER ONCE, ALONG WITH THE EQUALLY DEFUNCT MINES. BLOOD AND IRON.
THIS WAS WHERE HER FATHER DIED.
IT WAS WHERE EVERYTHING HAD ENDED FOR HIM. AND SO IT WAS WHERE EVERYTHING HAD STARTED FOR HER.
THIS IS IT? THIS IS WHERE YOU FOUND HIM?
HERE. RIGHT HERE.
DO YOU BELIEVE IN GHOSTS, RANDI? IT'S LIKE I CAN FEEL HIM. LIKE HE'S STILL HERE AFTER ALL THIS TIME, WATCHING OVER ME.
I TRIED TO WATCH OVER YOU, RANDI. I DID MY BEST. BUT YOU'RE A LOT LIKE HIM. STUBBORN.
WHY THE HELL DIDN'T YOU LISTEN TO ME?
THAT NIGHT, WHEN HE DIED...
...HE DIDN'T CALL YOU FOR BACKUP, DID HE?
YOU WERE THE ONE WHO CALLED HIM.

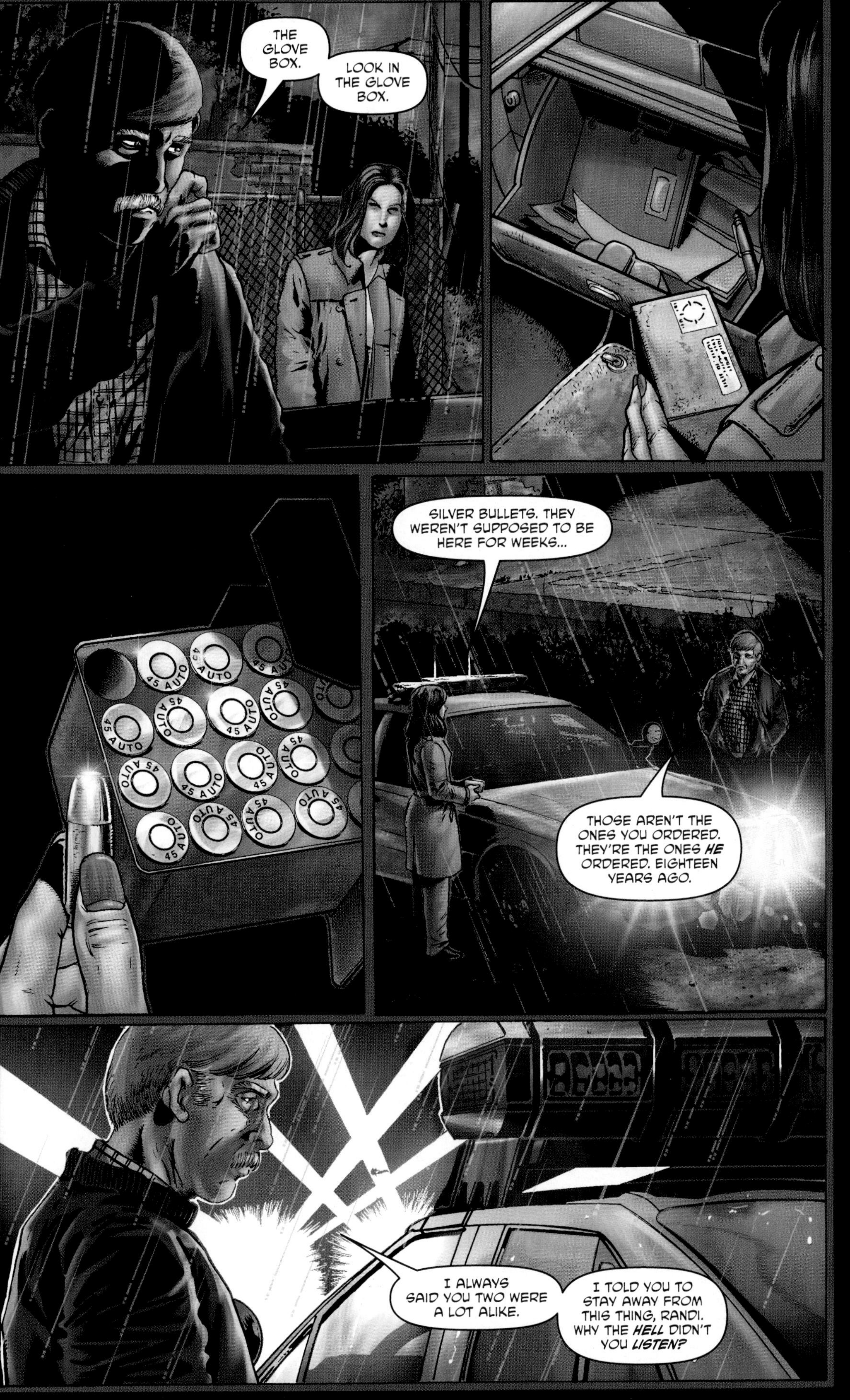
THE GLOVE BOX.
LOOK IN THE GLOVE BOX.
SILVER BULLETS. THEY WEREN'T SUPPOSED TO BE HERE FOR WEEKS...
THOSE AREN'T THE ONES YOU ORDERED. THEY'RE THE ONES *HE* ORDERED. EIGHTEEN YEARS AGO.
I ALWAYS SAID YOU TWO WERE A LOT ALIKE.
I TOLD YOU TO STAY AWAY FROM THIS THING, RANDI. WHY THE *HELL* DIDN'T YOU *LISTEN?*

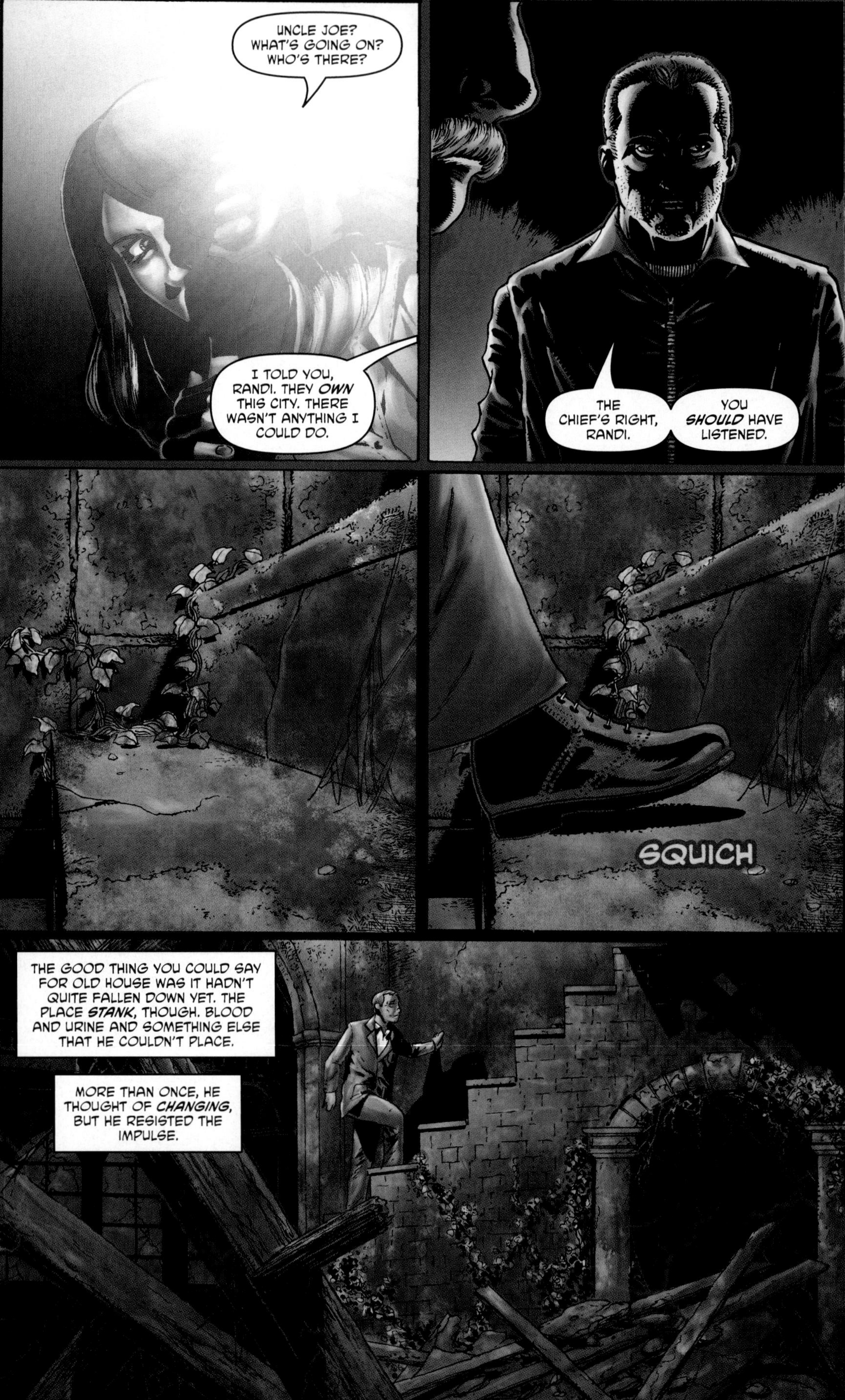
UNCLE JOE? WHAT'S GOING ON? WHO'S THERE?
I TOLD YOU, RANDI. THEY *OWN* THIS CITY. THERE WASN'T ANYTHING I COULD DO.
THE CHIEF'S RIGHT, RANDI.
YOU *SHOULD* HAVE LISTENED.
SQUICH
THE GOOD THING YOU COULD SAY FOR OLD HOUSE WAS IT HADN'T QUITE FALLEN DOWN YET. THE PLACE *STANK*, THOUGH. BLOOD AND URINE AND SOMETHING ELSE THAT HE COULDN'T PLACE.
MORE THAN ONCE, HE THOUGHT OF *CHANGING*, BUT HE RESISTED THE IMPULSE.

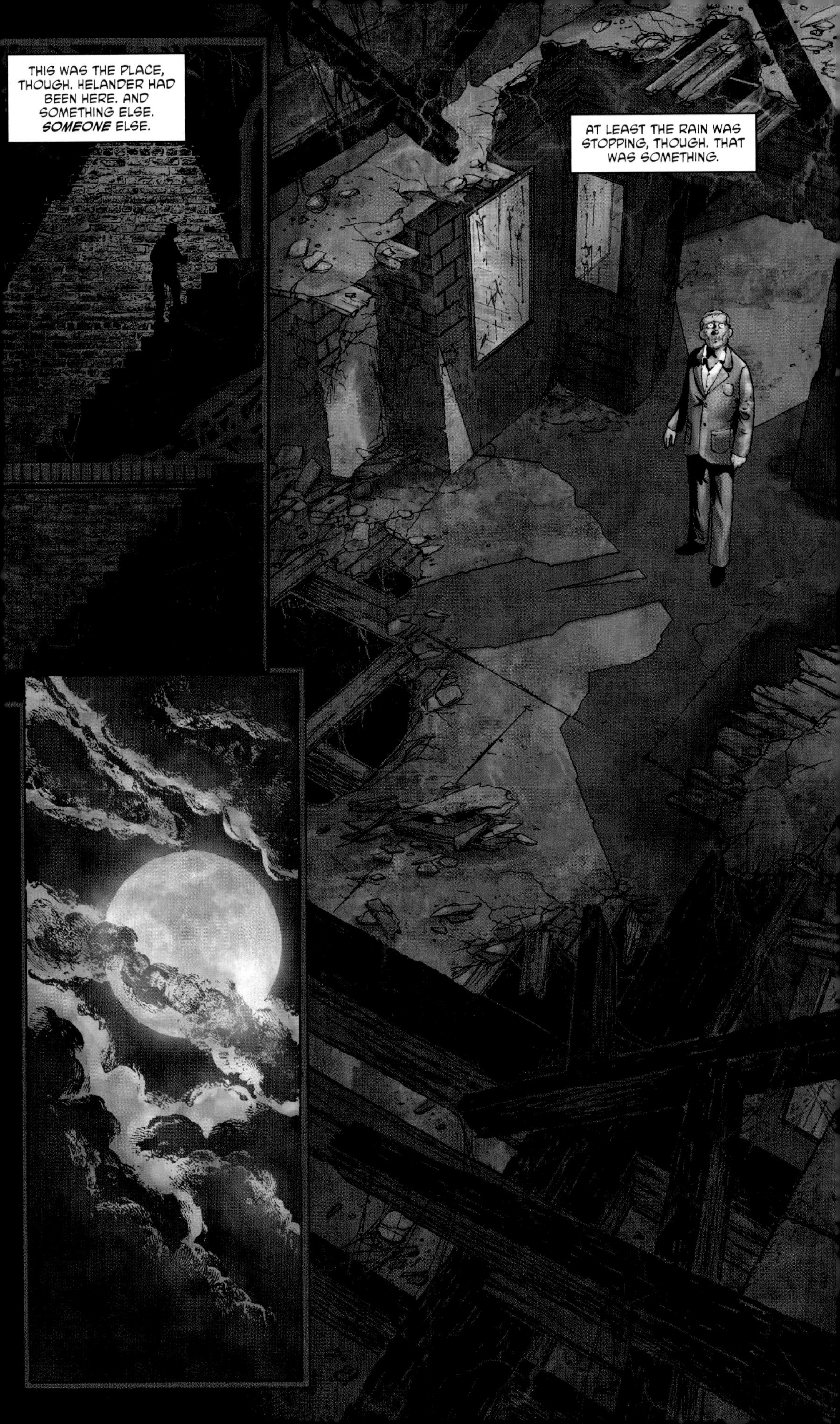
THIS WAS THE PLACE, THOUGH. HELANDER HAD BEEN HERE. AND SOMETHING ELSE. *SOMEONE* ELSE.
AT LEAST THE RAIN WAS STOPPING, THOUGH. THAT WAS SOMETHING.

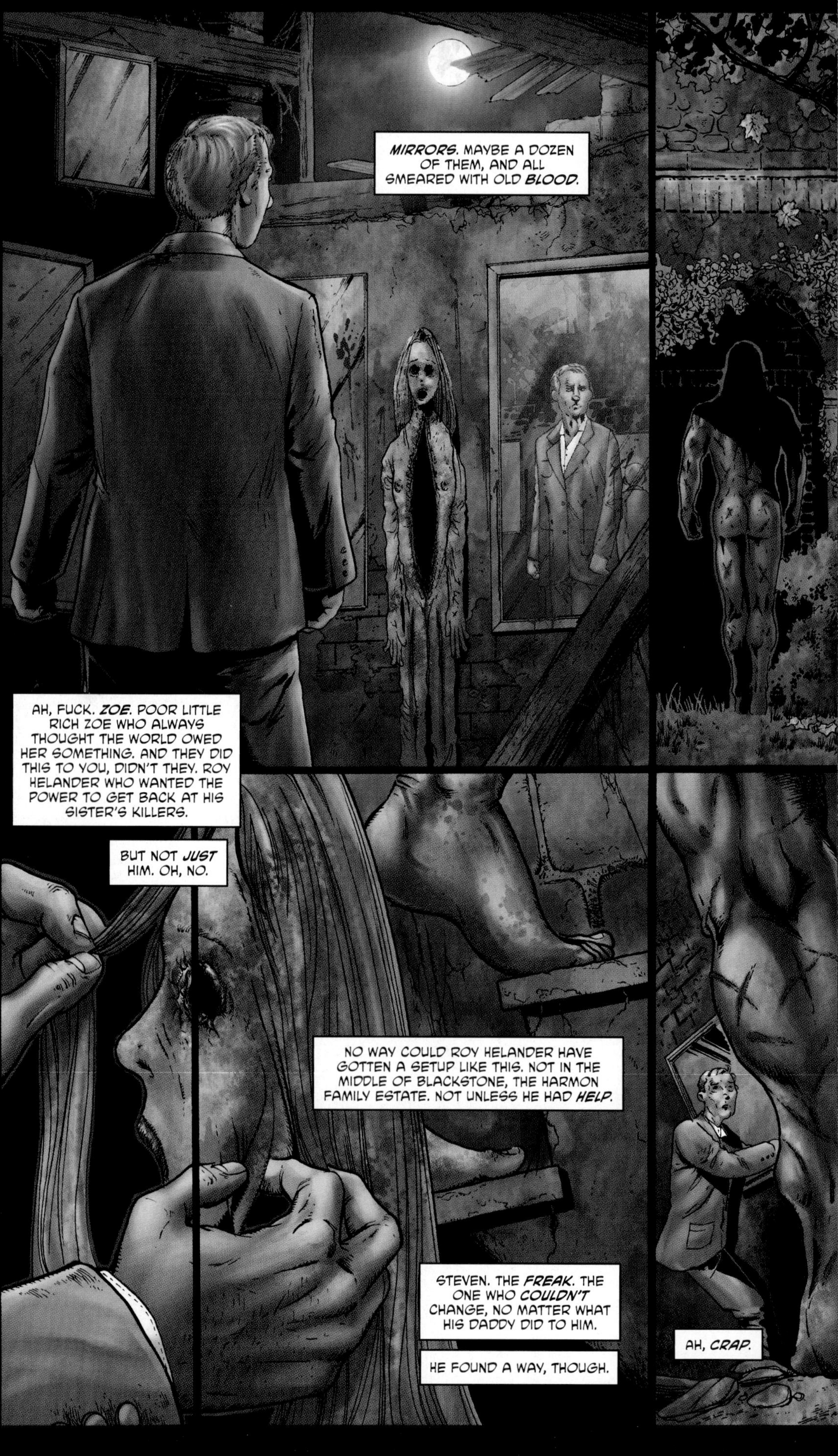
MIRRORS. MAYBE A DOZEN OF THEM, AND ALL SMEARED WITH OLD BLOOD.
AH, FUCK. ZOE. POOR LITTLE RICH ZOE WHO ALWAYS THOUGHT THE WORLD OWED HER SOMETHING. AND THEY DID THIS TO YOU, DIDN'T THEY. ROY HELANDER WHO WANTED THE POWER TO GET BACK AT HIS SISTER'S KILLERS.
BUT NOT JUST HIM. OH, NO.
NO WAY COULD ROY HELANDER HAVE GOTTEN A SETUP LIKE THIS. NOT IN THE MIDDLE OF BLACKSTONE, THE HARMON FAMILY ESTATE. NOT UNLESS HE HAD HELP.
STEVEN. THE FREAK. THE ONE WHO COULDN'T CHANGE, NO MATTER WHAT HIS DADDY DID TO HIM.
HE FOUND A WAY, THOUGH.
AH, CRAP.

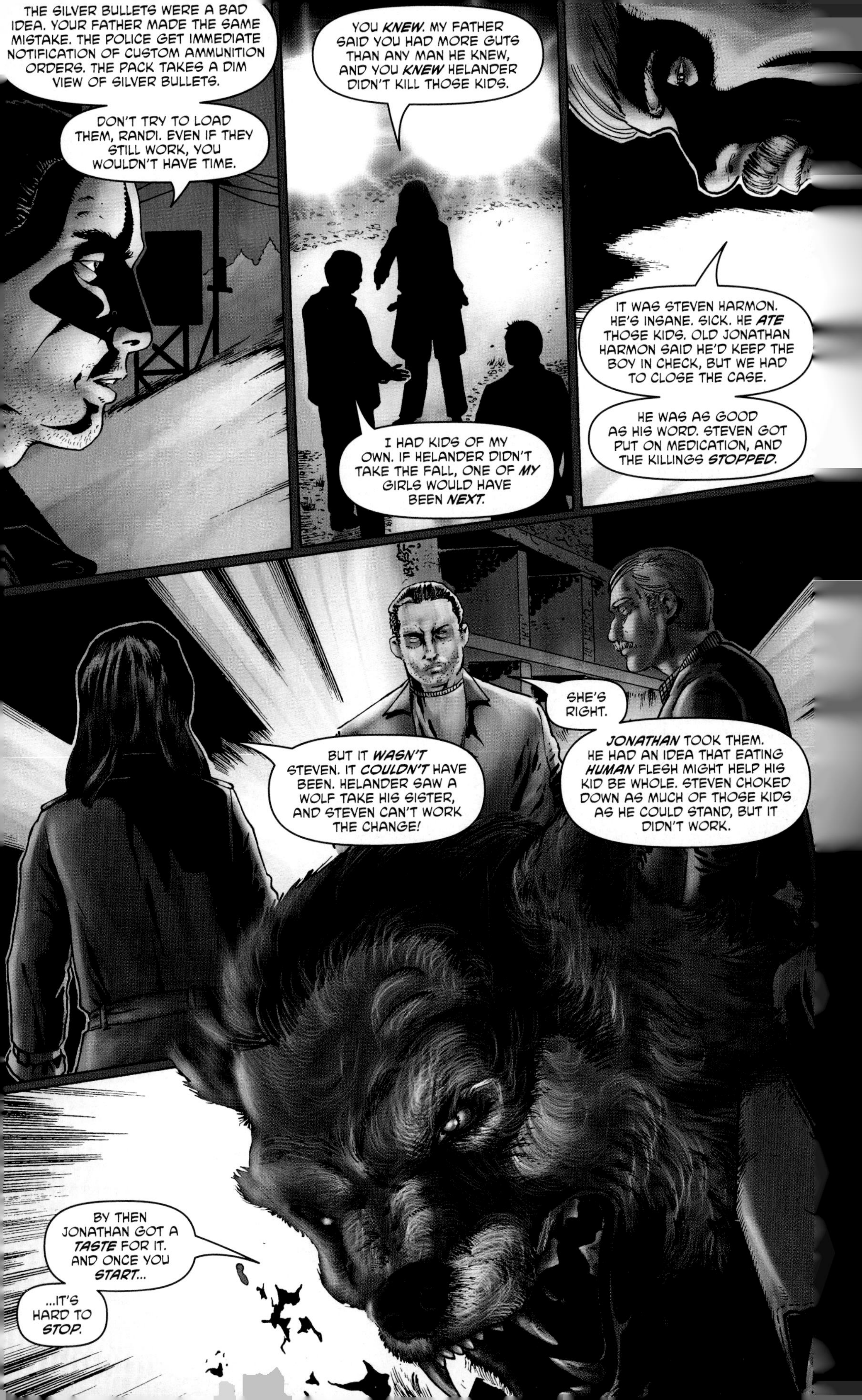
THE SILVER BULLETS WERE A BAD IDEA. YOUR FATHER MADE THE SAME MISTAKE. THE POLICE GET IMMEDIATE NOTIFICATION OF CUSTOM AMMUNITION ORDERS. THE PACK TAKES A DIM VIEW OF SILVER BULLETS.
DON'T TRY TO LOAD THEM, RANDI. EVEN IF THEY STILL WORK, YOU WOULDN'T HAVE TIME.
YOU *KNEW*. MY FATHER SAID YOU HAD MORE GUTS THAN ANY MAN HE KNEW, AND YOU *KNEW* HELANDER DIDN'T KILL THOSE KIDS.
I HAD KIDS OF MY OWN. IF HELANDER DIDN'T TAKE THE FALL, ONE OF *MY* GIRLS WOULD HAVE BEEN *NEXT*.
IT WAS STEVEN HARMON. HE'S INSANE. SICK. HE *ATE* THOSE KIDS. OLD JONATHAN HARMON SAID HE'D KEEP THE BOY IN CHECK, BUT WE HAD TO CLOSE THE CASE.
HE WAS AS GOOD AS HIS WORD. STEVEN GOT PUT ON MEDICATION, AND THE KILLINGS *STOPPED*.
BUT IT *WASN'T* STEVEN. IT *COULDN'T* HAVE BEEN. HELANDER SAW A WOLF TAKE HIS SISTER, AND STEVEN CAN'T WORK THE CHANGE!
SHE'S RIGHT.
JONATHAN TOOK THEM. HE HAD AN IDEA THAT EATING *HUMAN* FLESH MIGHT HELP HIS KID BE WHOLE. STEVEN CHOKED DOWN AS MUCH OF THOSE KIDS AS HE COULD STAND, BUT IT DIDN'T WORK.
BY THEN JONATHAN GOT A *TASTE* FOR IT. AND ONCE YOU *START*...
...IT'S HARD TO *STOP*.

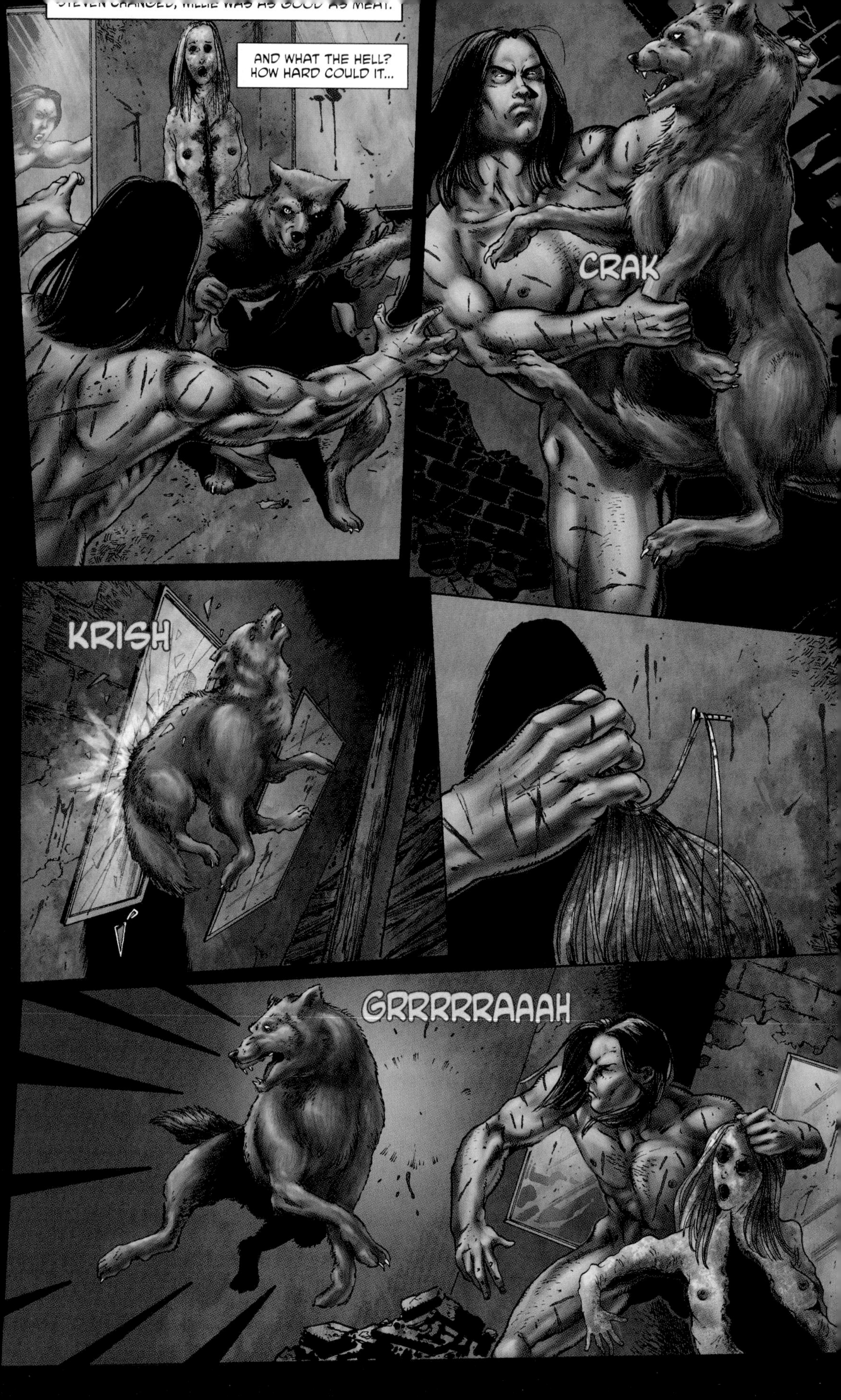
AND WHAT THE HELL? HOW HARD COULD IT...
CRAK
KRISH
GRRRRRAAAH

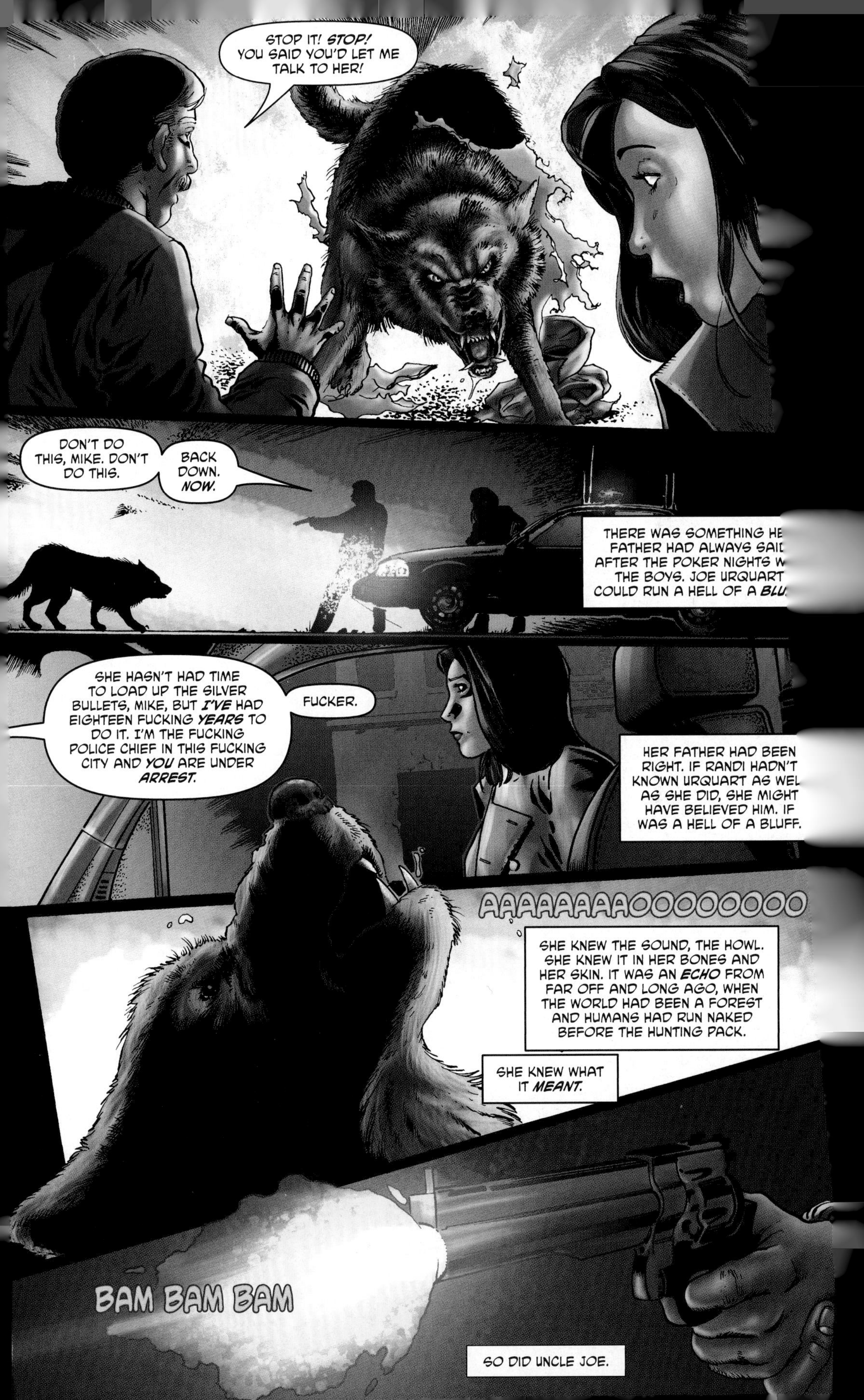

STOP IT! STOP! YOU SAID YOU'D LET ME TALK TO HER!
DON'T DO THIS, MIKE. DON'T DO THIS.
BACK DOWN. NOW.
THERE WAS SOMETHING HE FATHER HAD ALWAYS SAID AFTER THE POKER NIGHTS W THE BOYS. JOE URQUART COULD RUN A HELL OF A BLU
SHE HASN'T HAD TIME TO LOAD UP THE SILVER BULLETS, MIKE, BUT I'VE HAD EIGHTEEN FUCKING YEARS TO DO IT. I'M THE FUCKING POLICE CHIEF IN THIS FUCKING CITY AND YOU ARE UNDER ARREST.
FUCKER.
HER FATHER HAD BEEN RIGHT. IF RANDI HADN'T KNOWN URQUART AS WEL AS SHE DID, SHE MIGHT HAVE BELIEVED HIM. IF WAS A HELL OF A BLUFF.
AAAAAAAAOOOOOOOO
SHE KNEW THE SOUND, THE HOWL. SHE KNEW IT IN HER BONES AND HER SKIN. IT WAS AN ECHO FROM FAR OFF AND LONG AGO, WHEN THE WORLD HAD BEEN A FOREST AND HUMANS HAD RUN NAKED BEFORE THE HUNTING PACK.
SHE KNEW WHAT IT MEANT.
BAM BAM BAM
SO DID UNCLE JOE.

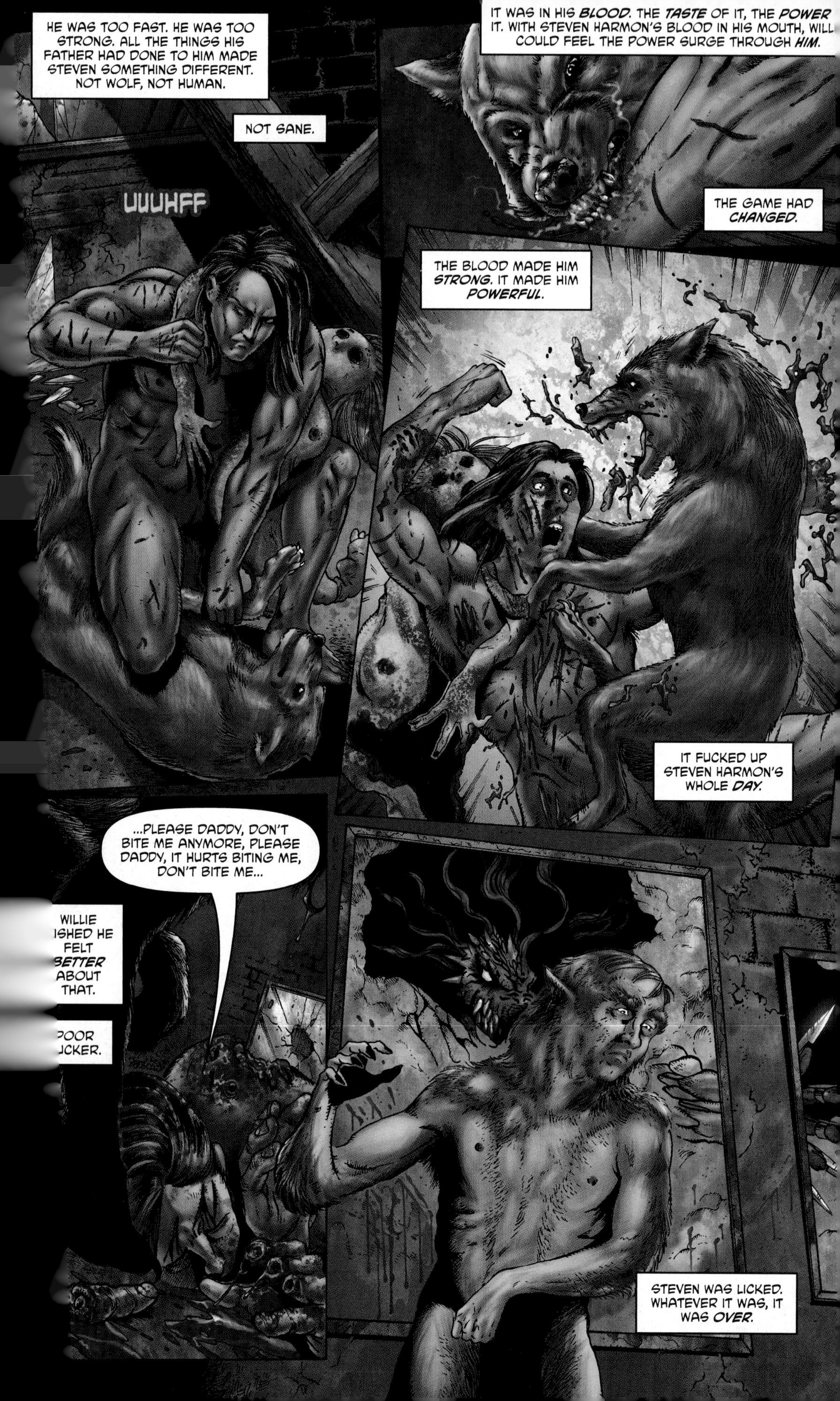
HE WAS TOO FAST. HE WAS TOO STRONG. ALL THE THINGS HIS FATHER HAD DONE TO HIM MADE STEVEN SOMETHING DIFFERENT. NOT WOLF, NOT HUMAN.
NOT SANE.
UUUHFF
IT WAS IN HIS BLOOD. THE TASTE OF IT, THE POWER IT. WITH STEVEN HARMON'S BLOOD IN HIS MOUTH, WILL COULD FEEL THE POWER SURGE THROUGH HIM.
THE GAME HAD CHANGED.
THE BLOOD MADE HIM STRONG. IT MADE HIM POWERFUL.
IT FUCKED UP STEVEN HARMON'S WHOLE DAY.
...PLEASE DADDY, DON'T BITE ME ANYMORE, PLEASE DADDY, IT HURTS BITING ME, DON'T BITE ME...
WILLIE ISHED HE FELT BETTER ABOUT THAT.
POOR UCKER.
STEVEN WAS LICKED. WHATEVER IT WAS, IT WAS OVER.

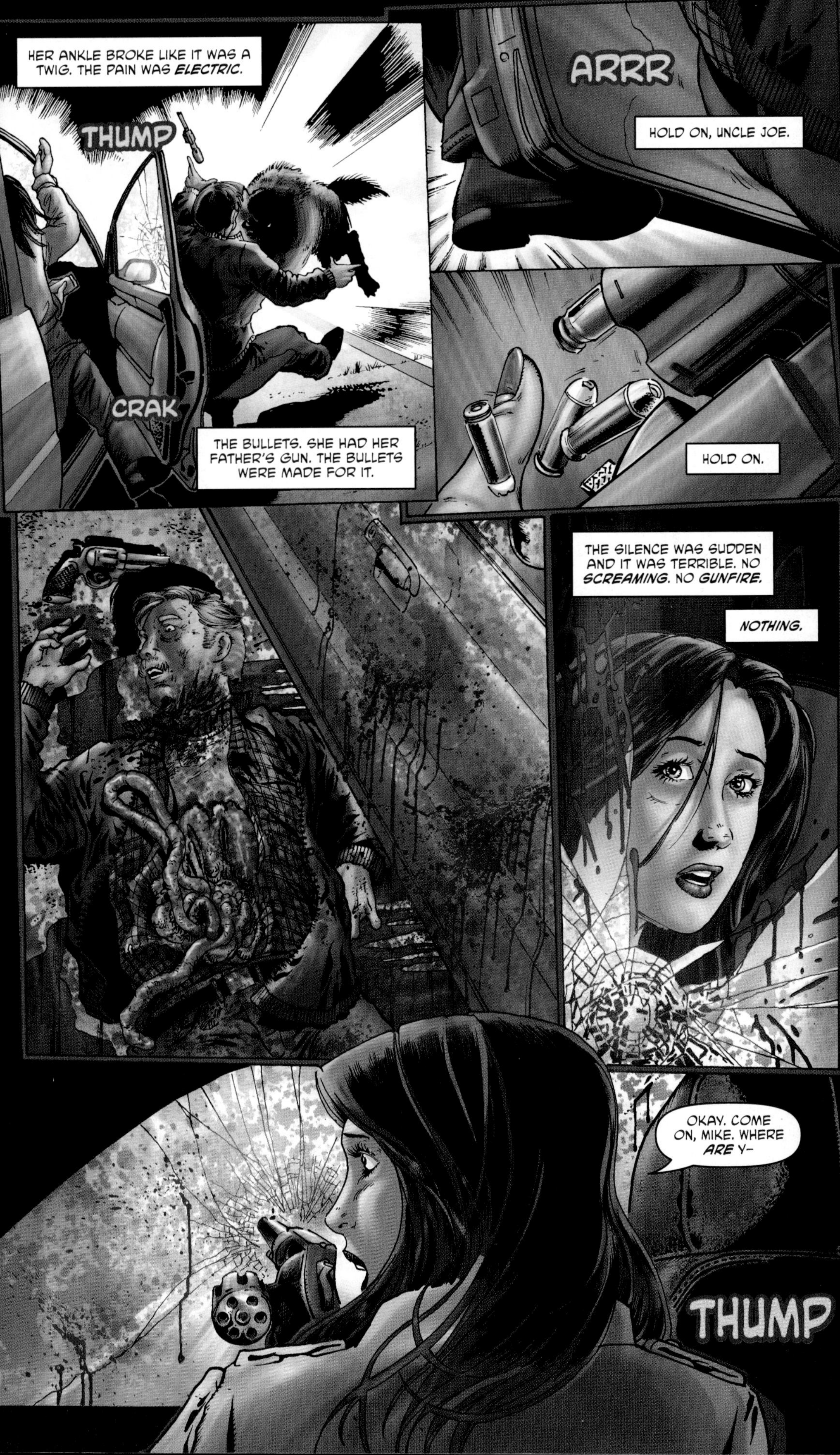
HER ANKLE BROKE LIKE IT WAS A TWIG. THE PAIN WAS *ELECTRIC*.
THUMP
CRAK
THE BULLETS. SHE HAD HER FATHER'S GUN. THE BULLETS WERE MADE FOR IT.
ARRR
HOLD ON, UNCLE JOE.
HOLD ON.
THE SILENCE WAS SUDDEN AND IT WAS TERRIBLE. NO *SCREAMING*. NO *GUNFIRE*.
NOTHING.
OKAY. COME ON, MIKE. WHERE *ARE* Y-
THUMP

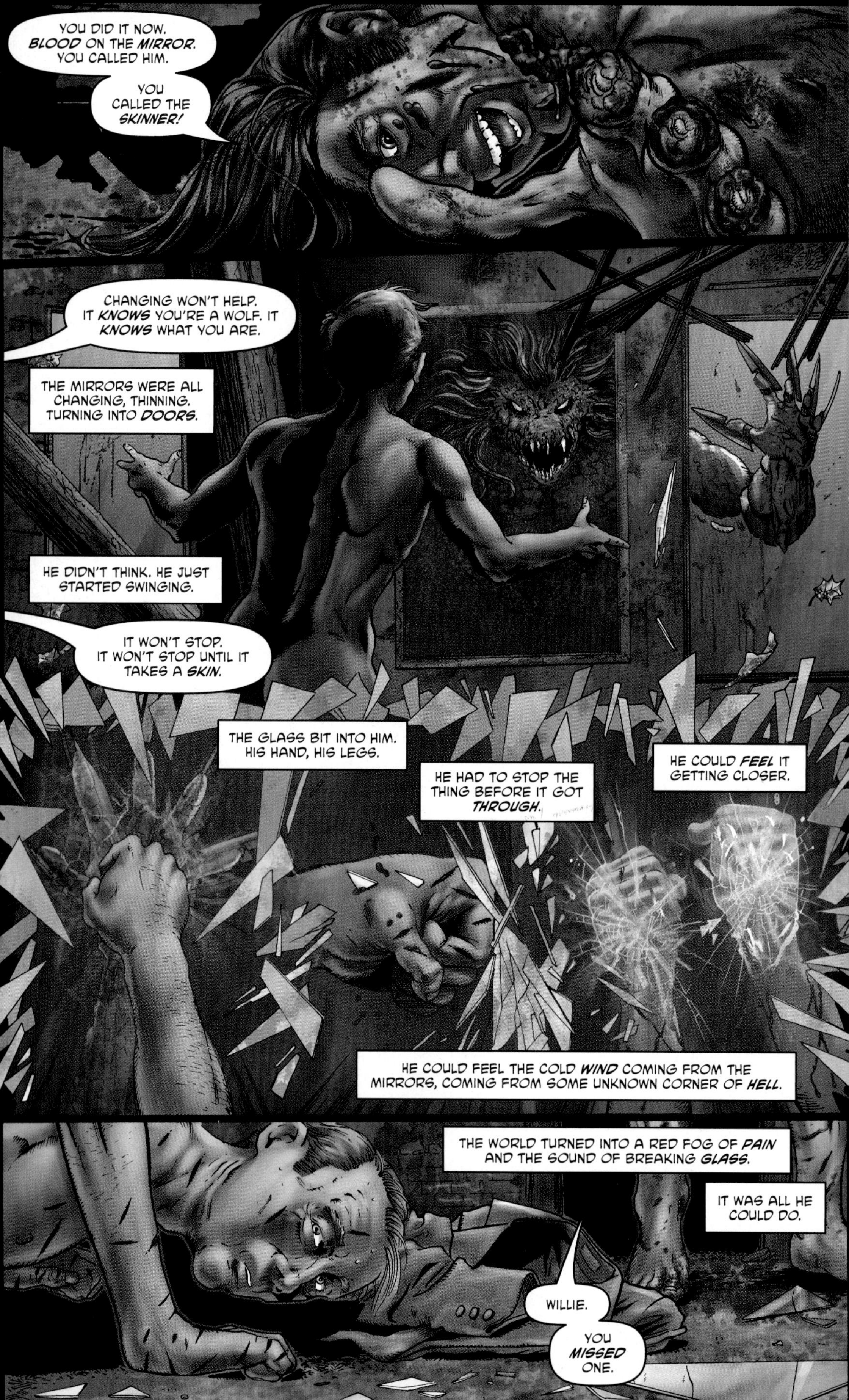
YOU DID IT NOW. BLOOD ON THE MIRROR. YOU CALLED HIM.
YOU CALLED THE SKINNER!
CHANGING WON'T HELP. IT KNOWS YOU'RE A WOLF. IT KNOWS WHAT YOU ARE.
THE MIRRORS WERE ALL CHANGING, THINNING. TURNING INTO DOORS.
HE DIDN'T THINK. HE JUST STARTED SWINGING.
IT WON'T STOP. IT WON'T STOP UNTIL IT TAKES A SKIN.
THE GLASS BIT INTO HIM. HIS HAND, HIS LEGS.
HE HAD TO STOP THE THING BEFORE IT GOT THROUGH.
HE COULD FEEL IT GETTING CLOSER.
HE COULD FEEL THE COLD WIND COMING FROM THE MIRRORS, COMING FROM SOME UNKNOWN CORNER OF HELL.
THE WORLD TURNED INTO A RED FOG OF PAIN AND THE SOUND OF BREAKING GLASS.
IT WAS ALL HE COULD DO.
WILLIE.
YOU MISSED ONE.

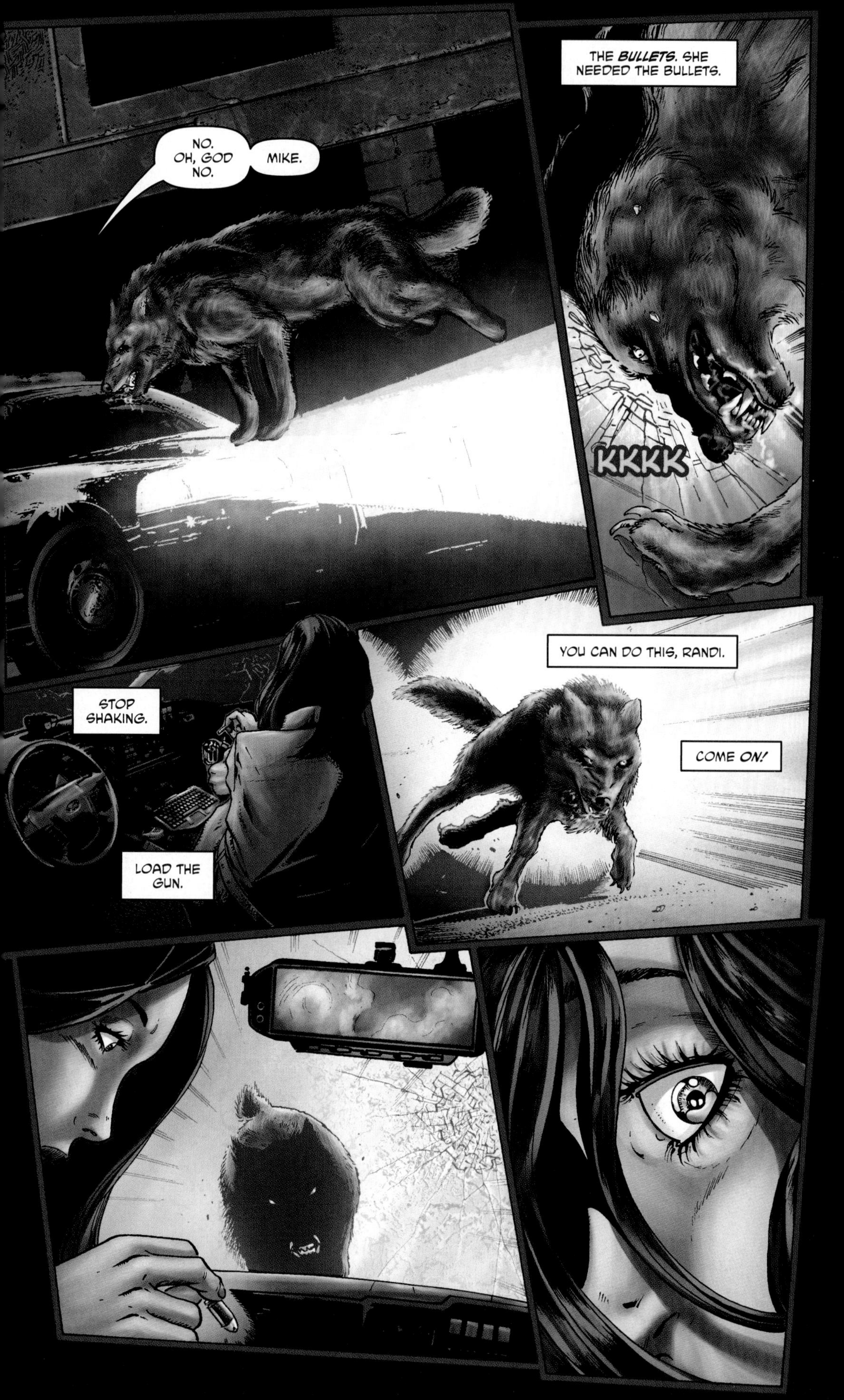
NO. OH, GOD NO.
MIKE.
THE BULLETS. SHE NEEDED THE BULLETS.
KKKK
STOP SHAKING.
LOAD THE GUN.
YOU CAN DO THIS, RANDI.
COME ON!

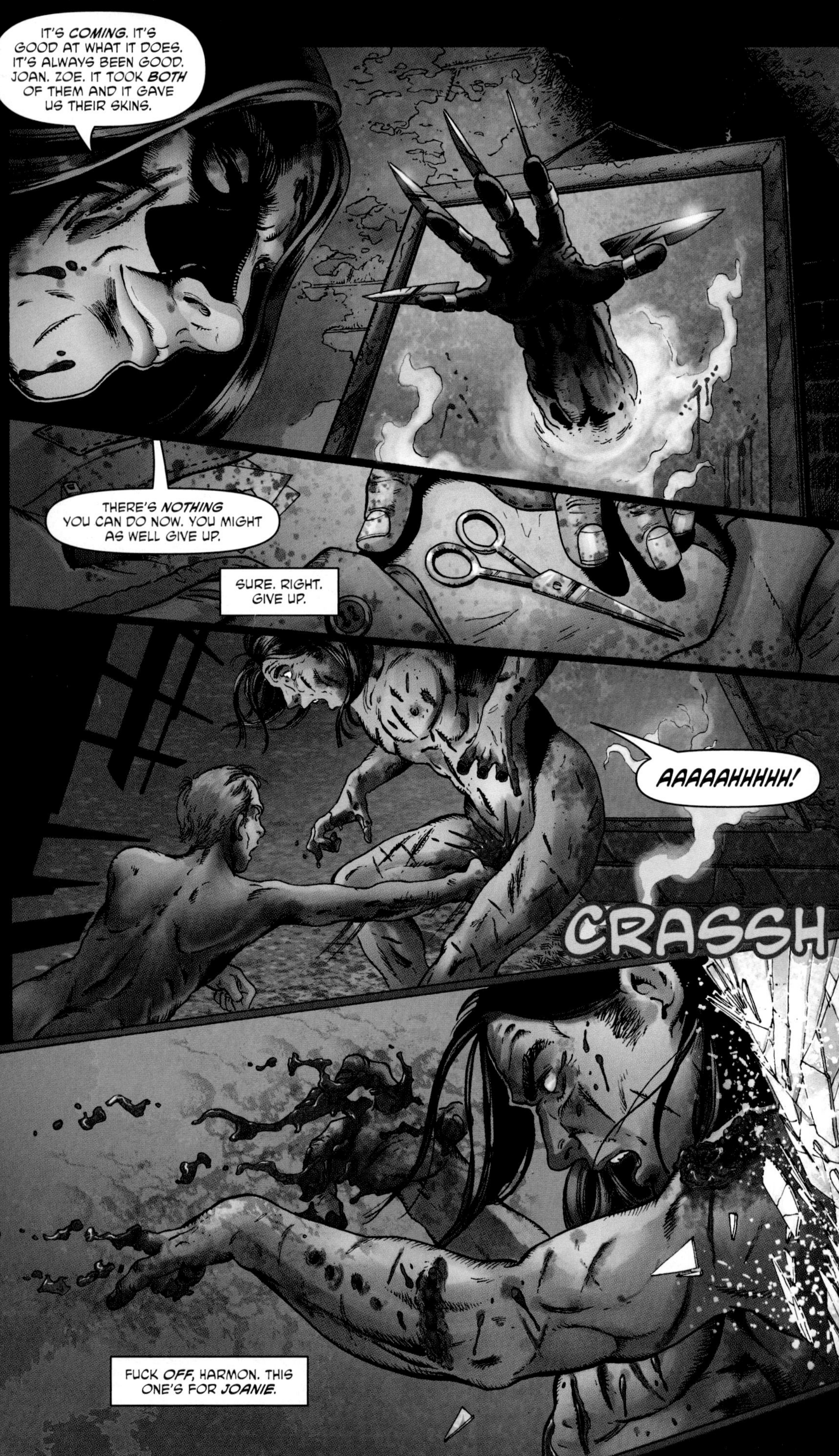
IT'S COMING. IT'S GOOD AT WHAT IT DOES. IT'S ALWAYS BEEN GOOD. JOAN. ZOE. IT TOOK BOTH OF THEM AND IT GAVE US THEIR SKINS.
THERE'S NOTHING YOU CAN DO NOW. YOU MIGHT AS WELL GIVE UP.
SURE. RIGHT. GIVE UP.
AAAAAHHHHH!
CRASSH
FUCK OFF, HARMON. THIS ONE'S FOR JOANIE.

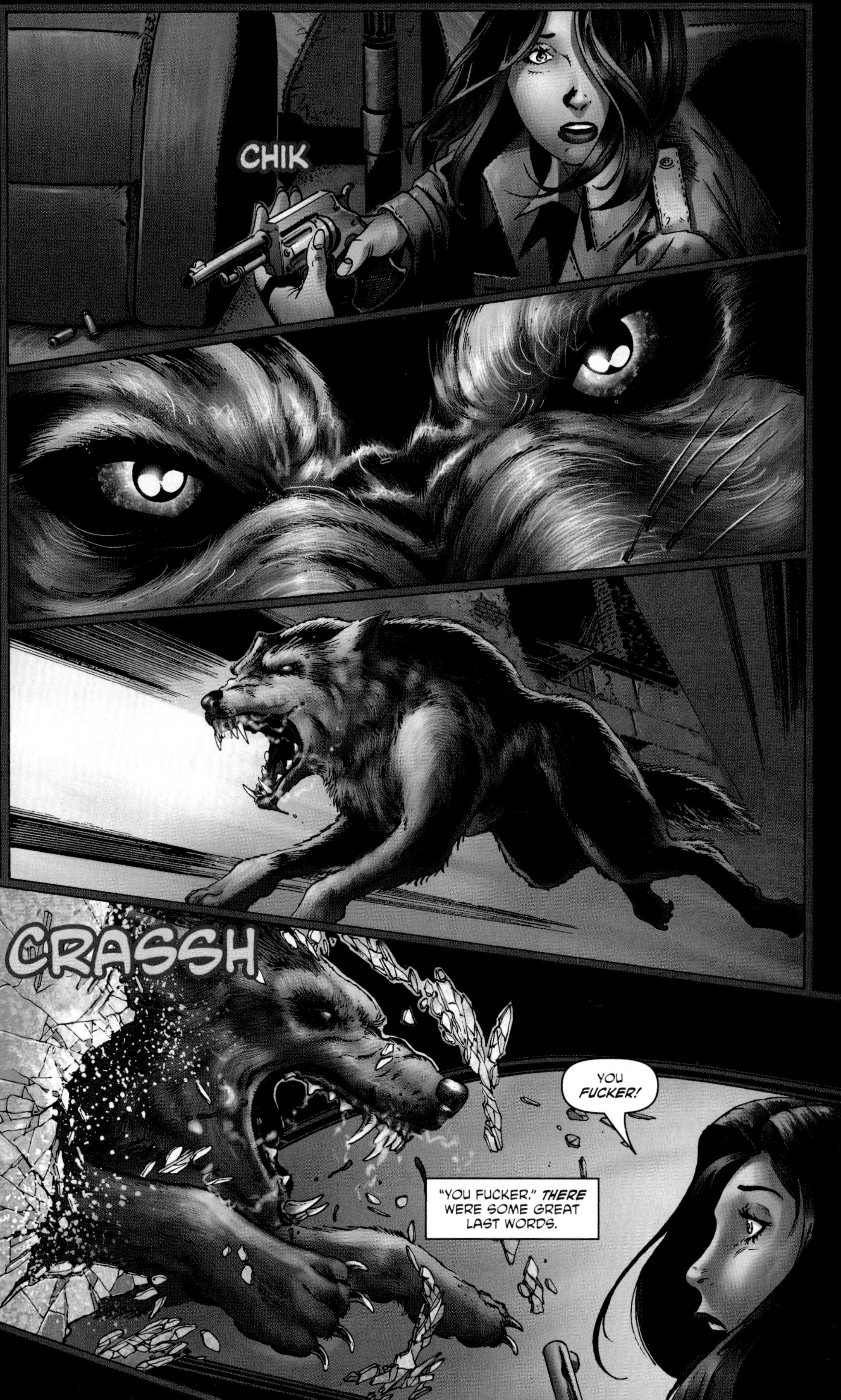
CHIK
CRASSH
YOU FUCKER!
"YOU FUCKER." THERE WERE SOME GREAT LAST WORDS.

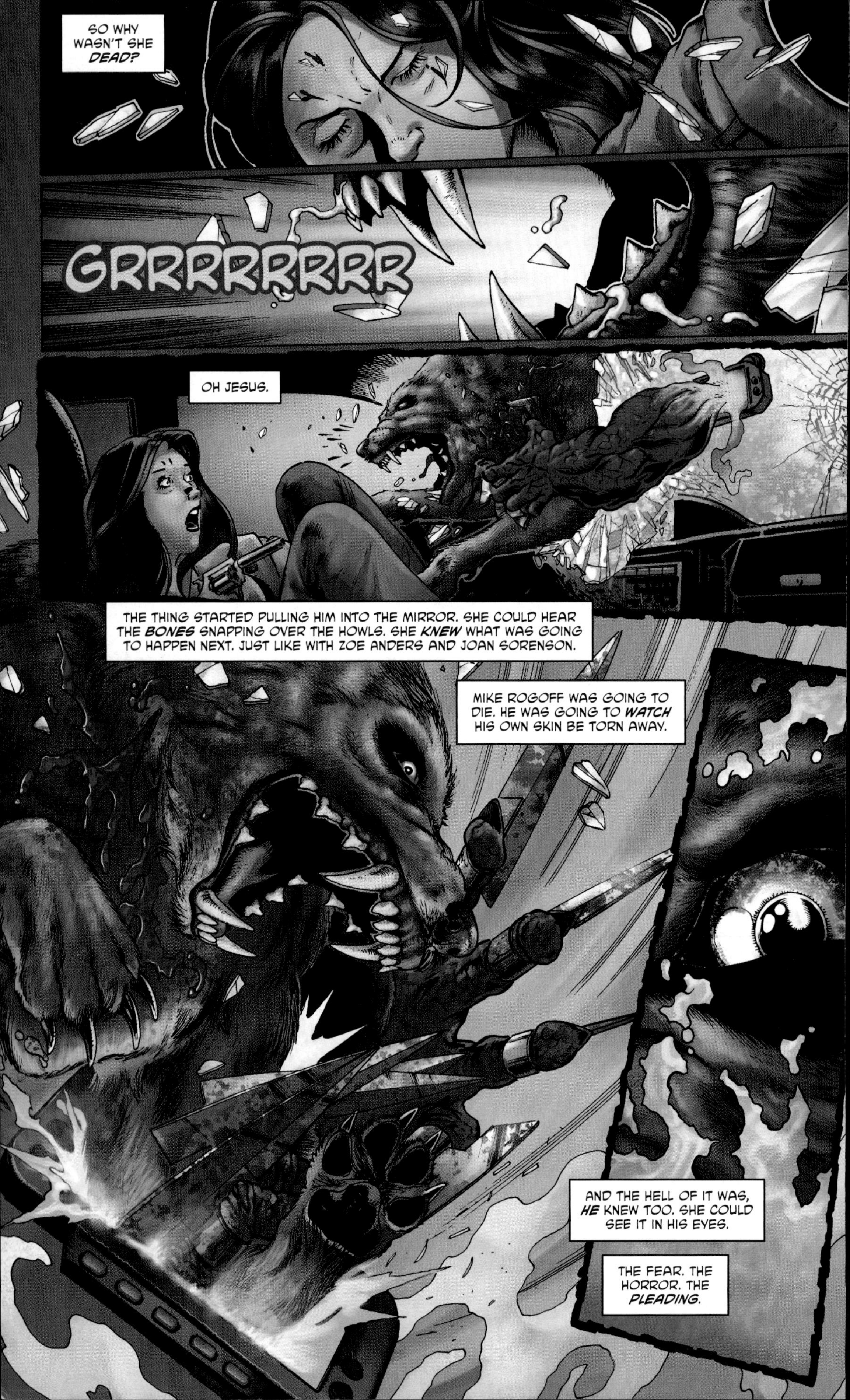
SO WHY WASN'T SHE *DEAD?*
GRRRRRRRR
OH JESUS.
THE THING STARTED PULLING HIM INTO THE MIRROR. SHE COULD HEAR THE *BONES* SNAPPING OVER THE HOWLS. SHE *KNEW* WHAT WAS GOING TO HAPPEN NEXT. JUST LIKE WITH ZOE ANDERS AND JOAN SORENSON.
MIKE ROGOFF WAS GOING TO DIE. HE WAS GOING TO *WATCH* HIS OWN SKIN BE TORN AWAY.
AND THE HELL OF IT WAS, *HE* KNEW TOO. SHE COULD SEE IT IN HIS EYES.
THE FEAR. THE HORROR. THE *PLEADING*.

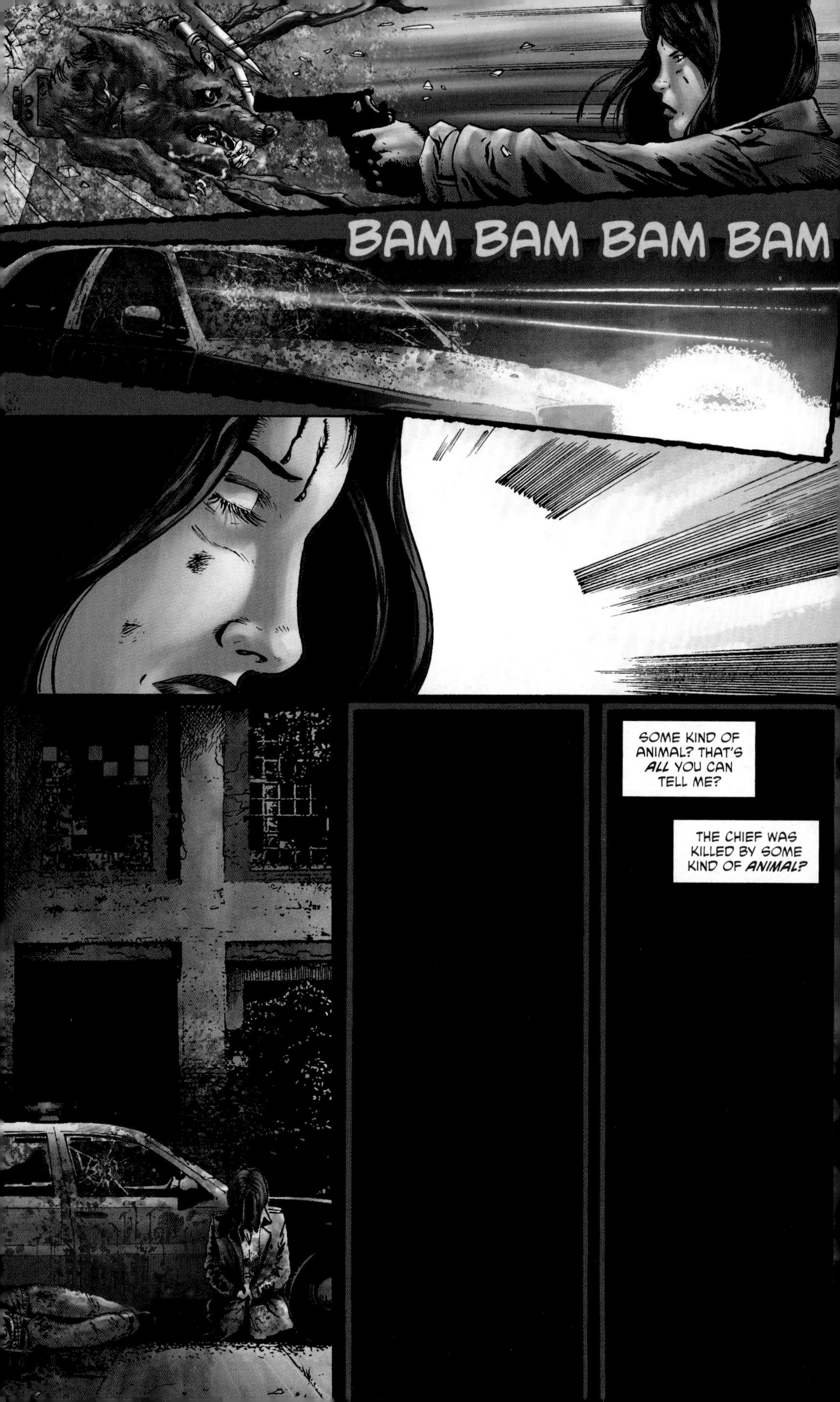
BAM BAM BAM BAM
SOME KIND OF ANIMAL? THAT'S *ALL* YOU CAN TELL ME?
THE CHIEF WAS KILLED BY SOME KIND OF *ANIMAL?*

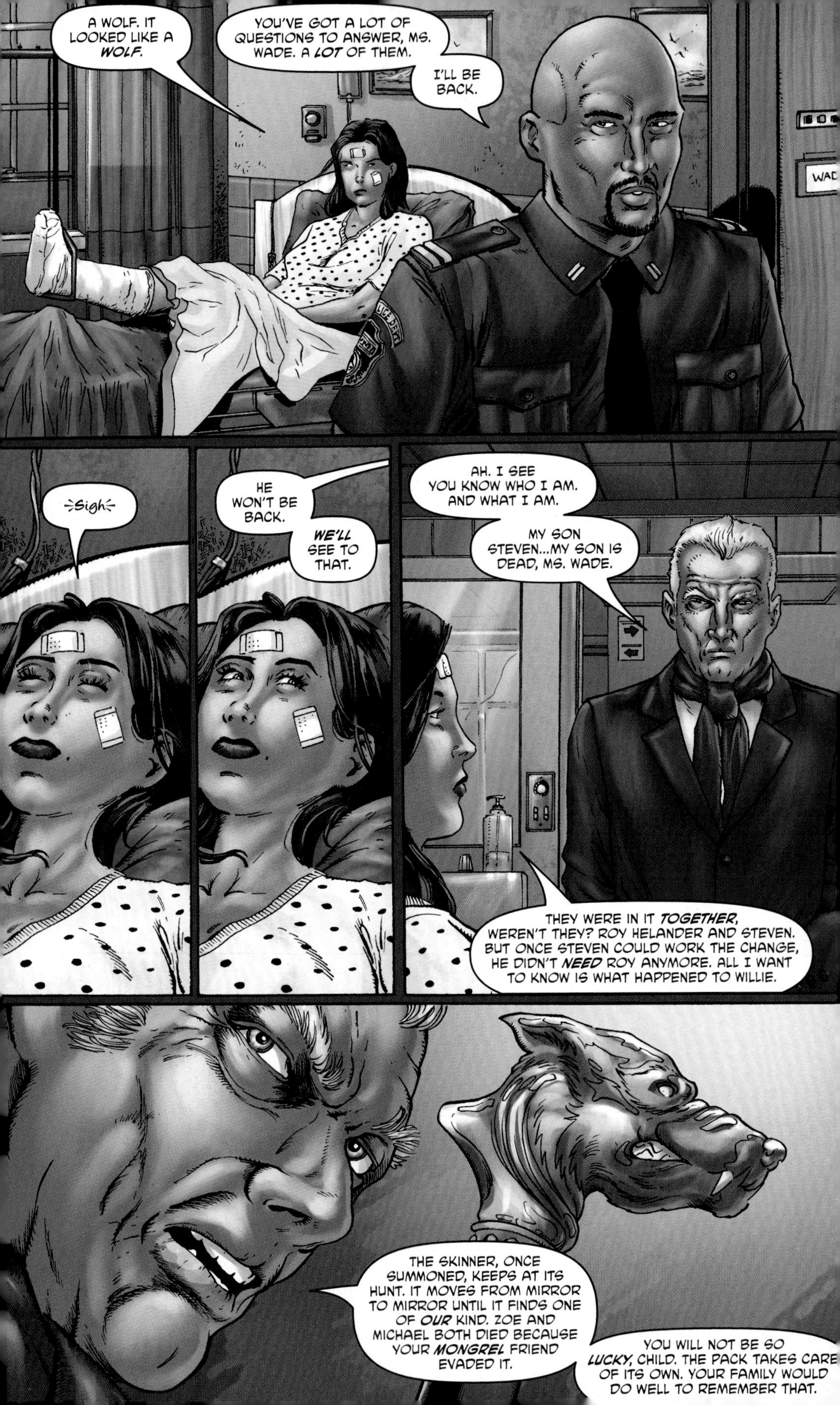
A WOLF. IT LOOKED LIKE A *WOLF*.
YOU'VE GOT A LOT OF QUESTIONS TO ANSWER, MS. WADE. A *LOT* OF THEM.
I'LL BE BACK.
WAD
Sigh
HE WON'T BE BACK.
WE'LL SEE TO THAT.
AH. I SEE YOU KNOW WHO I AM. AND WHAT I AM.
MY SON STEVEN...MY SON IS DEAD, MS. WADE.
THEY WERE IN IT *TOGETHER*, WEREN'T THEY? ROY HELANDER AND STEVEN. BUT ONCE STEVEN COULD WORK THE CHANGE, HE DIDN'T *NEED* ROY ANYMORE. ALL I WANT TO KNOW IS WHAT HAPPENED TO WILLIE.
THE SKINNER, ONCE SUMMONED, KEEPS AT ITS HUNT. IT MOVES FROM MIRROR TO MIRROR UNTIL IT FINDS ONE OF *OUR* KIND. ZOE AND MICHAEL BOTH DIED BECAUSE YOUR *MONGREL* FRIEND EVADED IT.
YOU WILL NOT BE SO *LUCKY*, CHILD. THE PACK TAKES CARE OF ITS OWN. YOUR FAMILY WOULD DO WELL TO REMEMBER THAT.

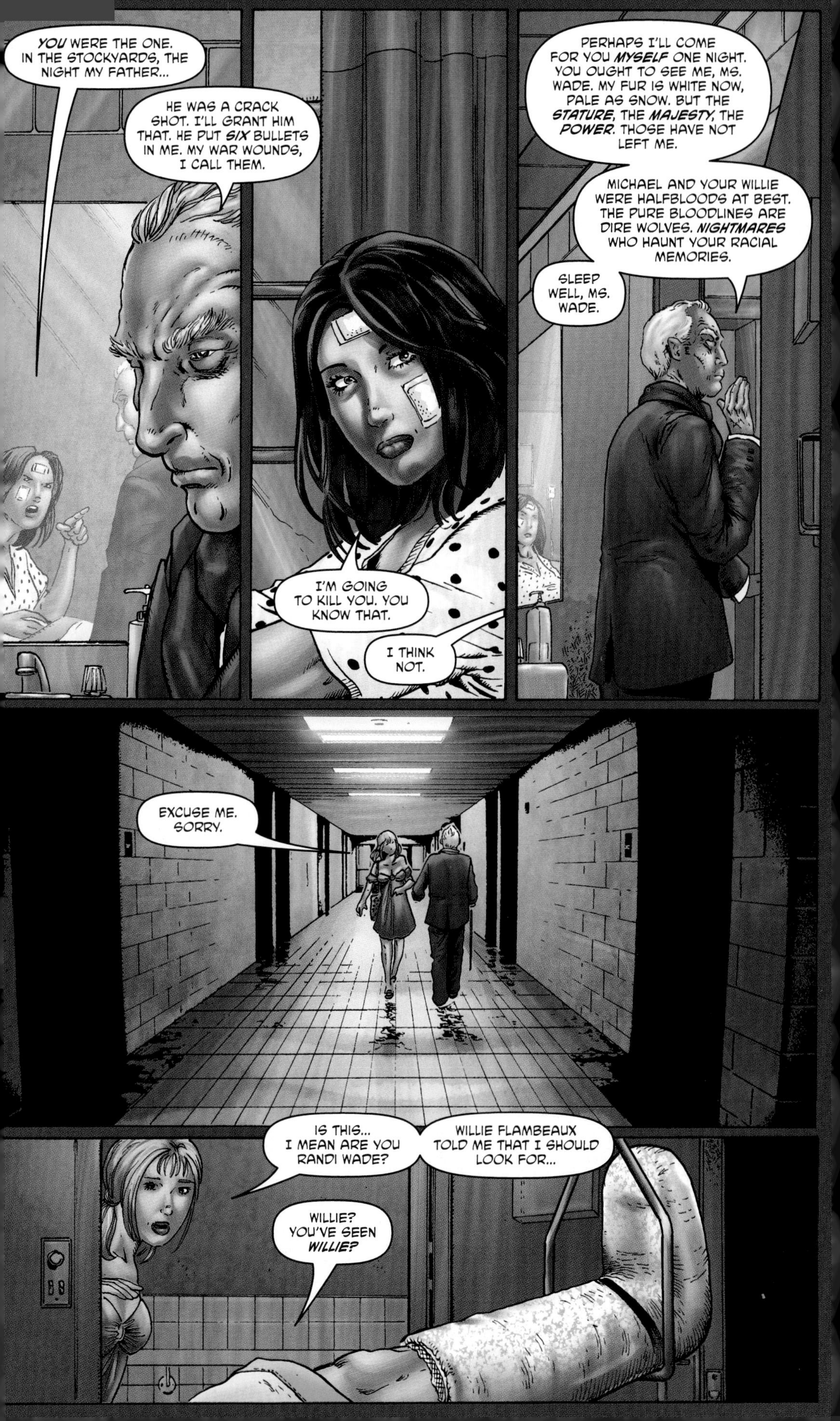

YOU WERE THE ONE. IN THE STOCKYARDS, THE NIGHT MY FATHER...
HE WAS A CRACK SHOT. I'LL GRANT HIM THAT. HE PUT SIX BULLETS IN ME. MY WAR WOUNDS, I CALL THEM.
I'M GOING TO KILL YOU. YOU KNOW THAT.
I THINK NOT.
PERHAPS I'LL COME FOR YOU MYSELF ONE NIGHT. YOU OUGHT TO SEE ME, MS. WADE. MY FUR IS WHITE NOW, PALE AS SNOW. BUT THE STATURE, THE MAJESTY, THE POWER. THOSE HAVE NOT LEFT ME.
MICHAEL AND YOUR WILLIE WERE HALFBLOODS AT BEST. THE PURE BLOODLINES ARE DIRE WOLVES. NIGHTMARES WHO HAUNT YOUR RACIAL MEMORIES.
SLEEP WELL, MS. WADE.
EXCUSE ME. SORRY.
IS THIS... I MEAN ARE YOU RANDI WADE?
WILLIE FLAMBEAUX TOLD ME THAT I SHOULD LOOK FOR...
WILLIE? YOU'VE SEEN WILLIE?

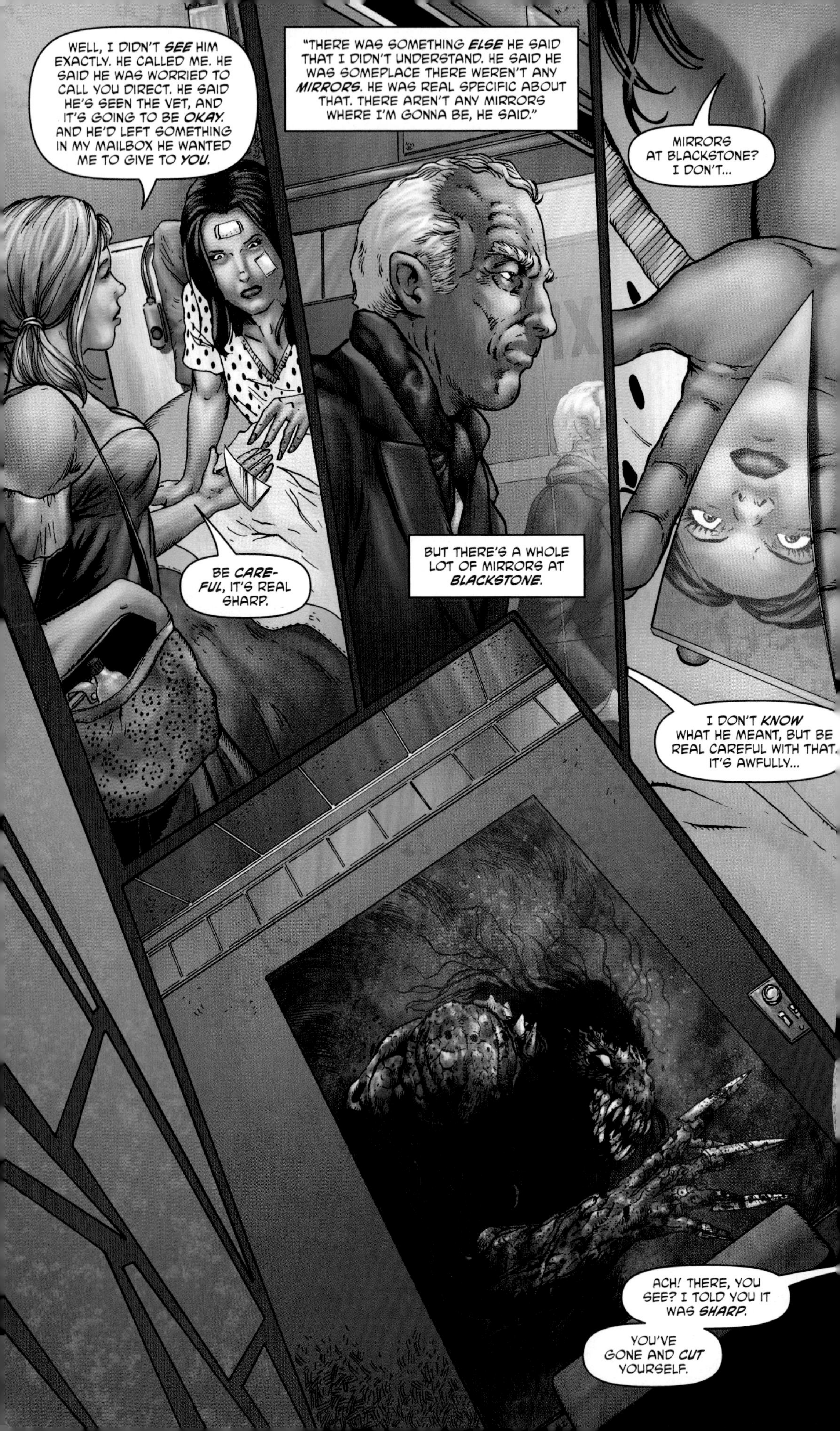

WELL, I DIDN'T SEE HIM EXACTLY. HE CALLED ME. HE SAID HE WAS WORRIED TO CALL YOU DIRECT. HE SAID HE'S SEEN THE VET, AND IT'S GOING TO BE OKAY. AND HE'D LEFT SOMETHING IN MY MAILBOX HE WANTED ME TO GIVE TO YOU.
BE CAREFUL, IT'S REAL SHARP.
"THERE WAS SOMETHING ELSE HE SAID THAT I DIDN'T UNDERSTAND. HE SAID HE WAS SOMEPLACE THERE WEREN'T ANY MIRRORS. HE WAS REAL SPECIFIC ABOUT THAT. THERE AREN'T ANY MIRRORS WHERE I'M GONNA BE, HE SAID."
BUT THERE'S A WHOLE LOT OF MIRRORS AT BLACKSTONE.
MIRRORS AT BLACKSTONE? I DON'T...
I DON'T KNOW WHAT HE MEANT, BUT BE REAL CAREFUL WITH THAT. IT'S AWFULLY...
ACH! THERE, YOU SEE? I TOLD YOU IT WAS SHARP.
YOU'VE GONE AND CUT YOURSELF.

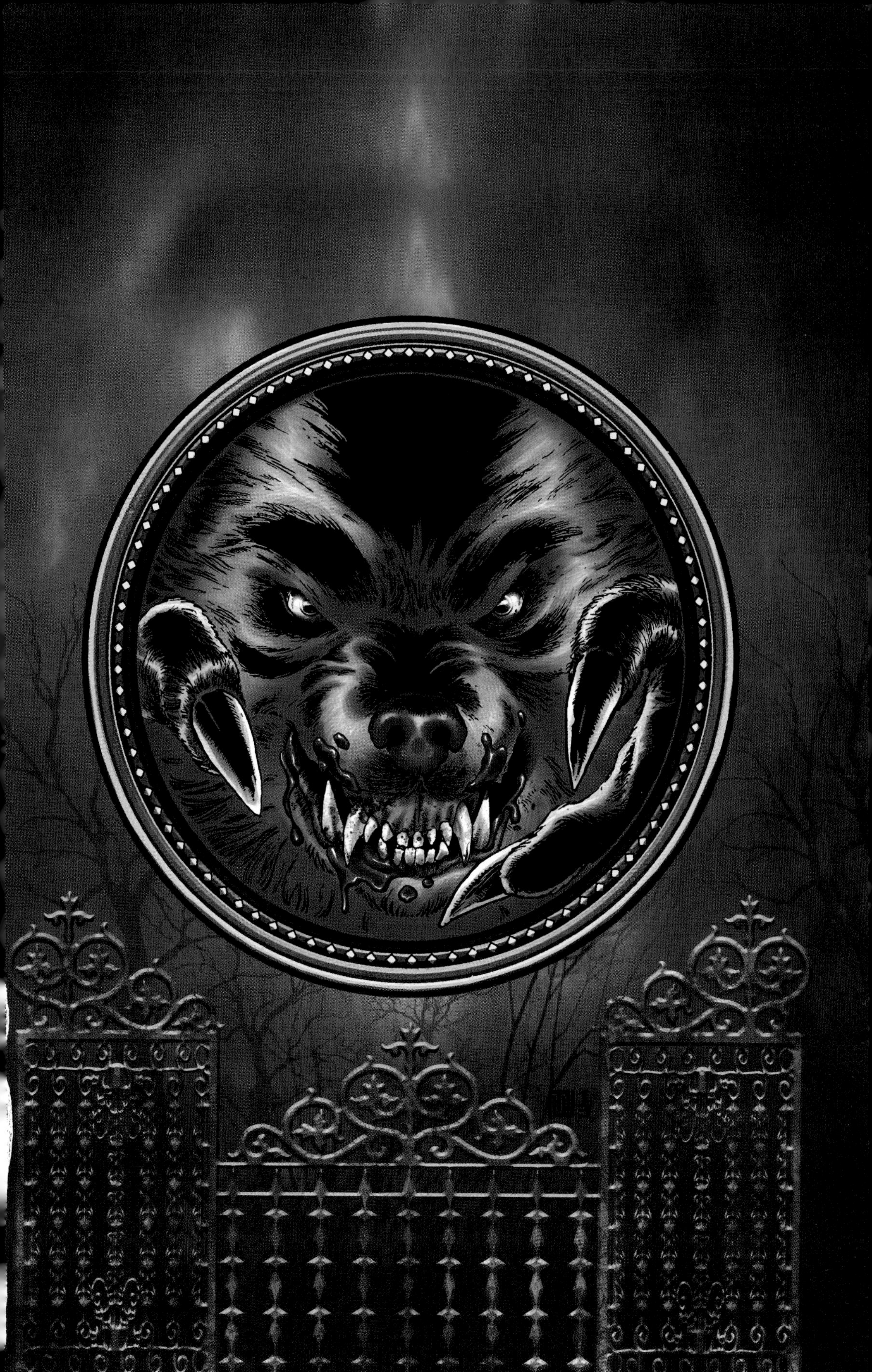

GALLERY

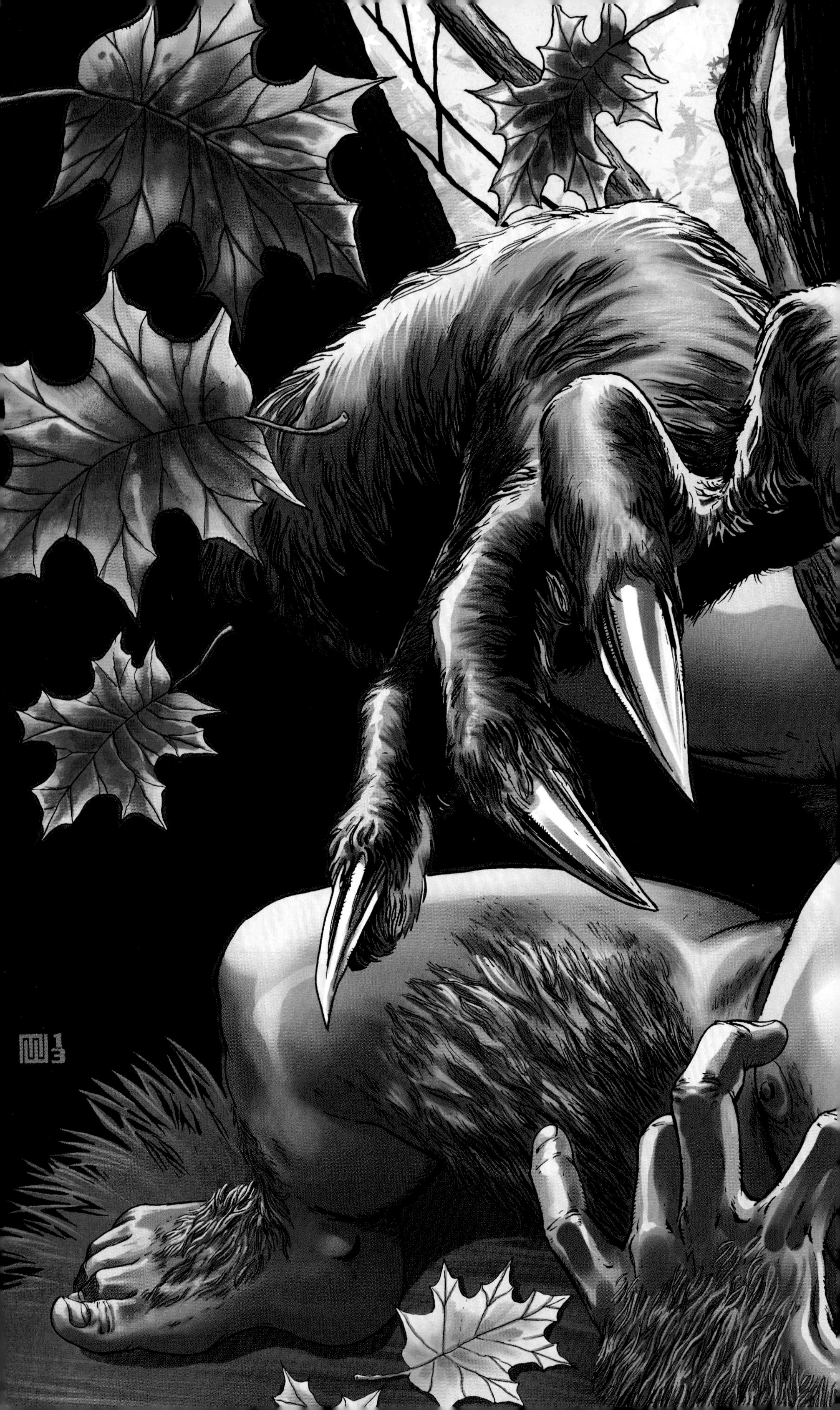

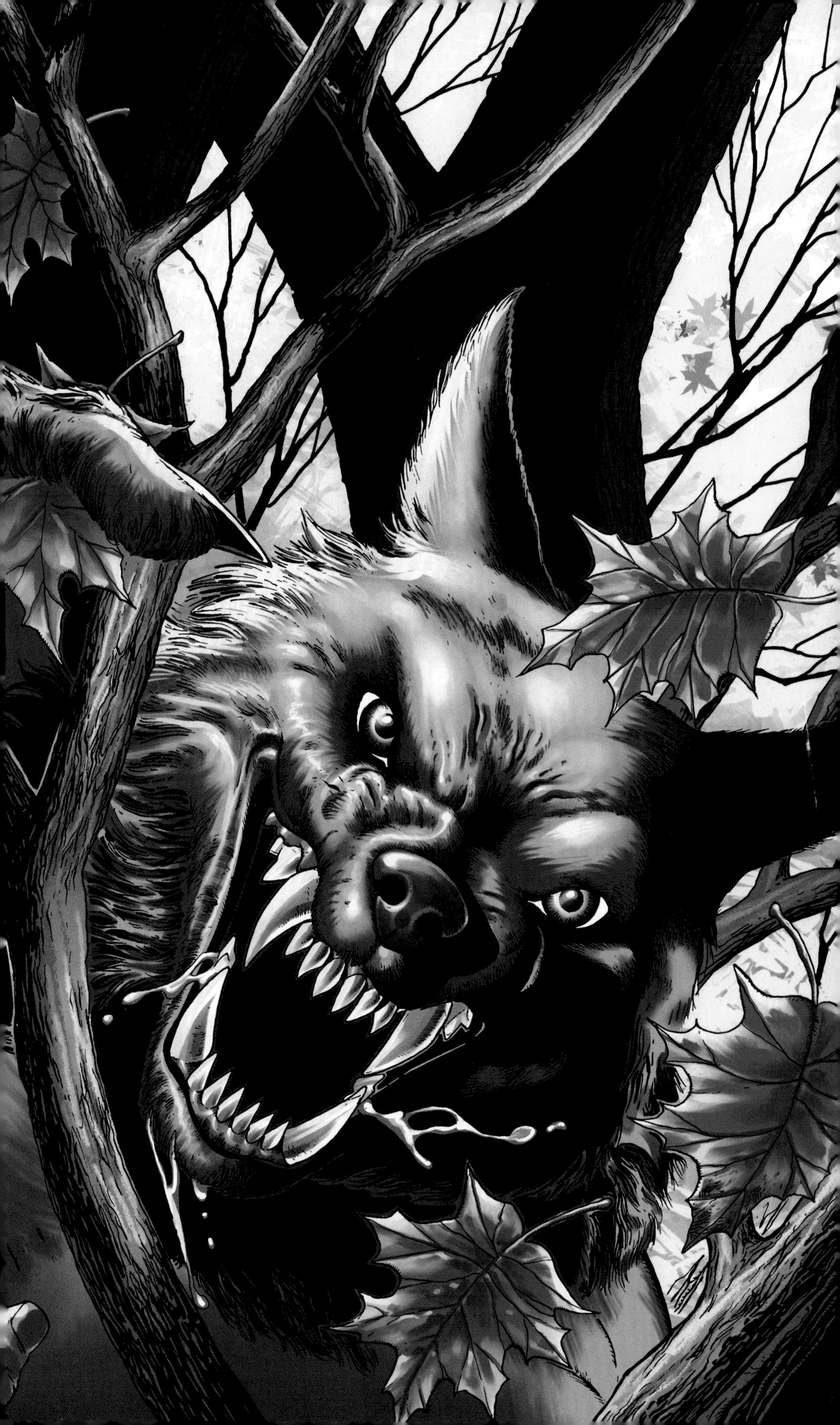

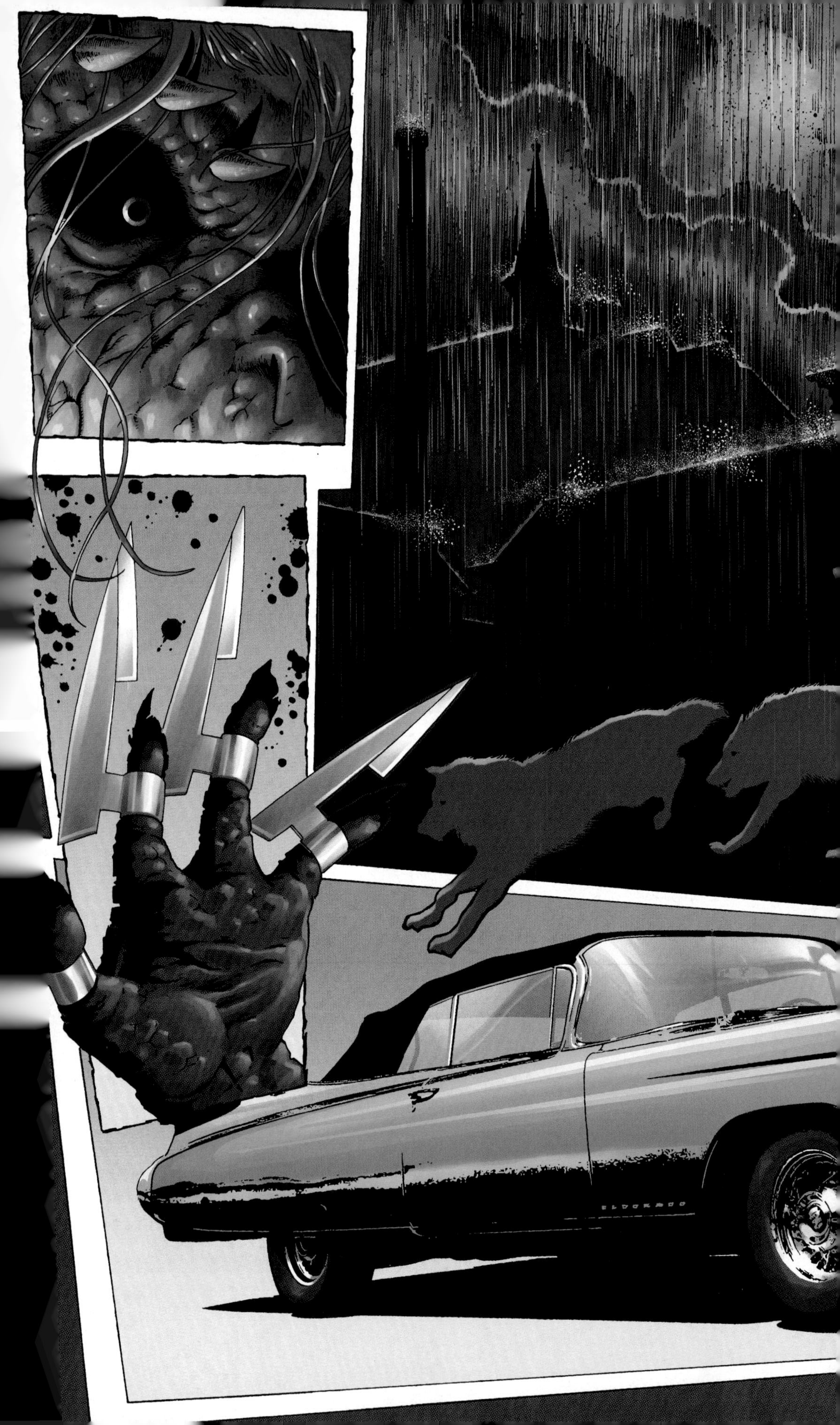

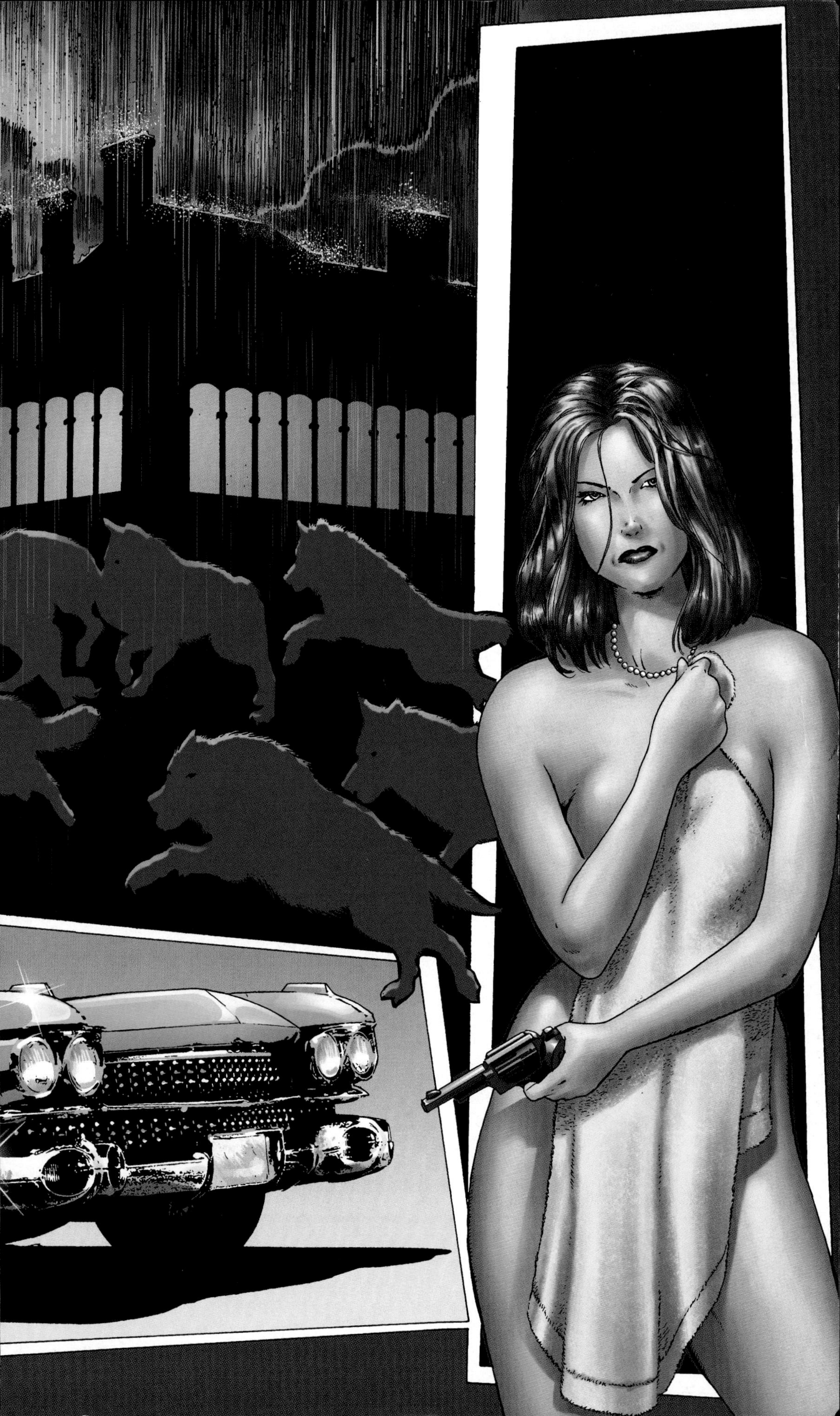

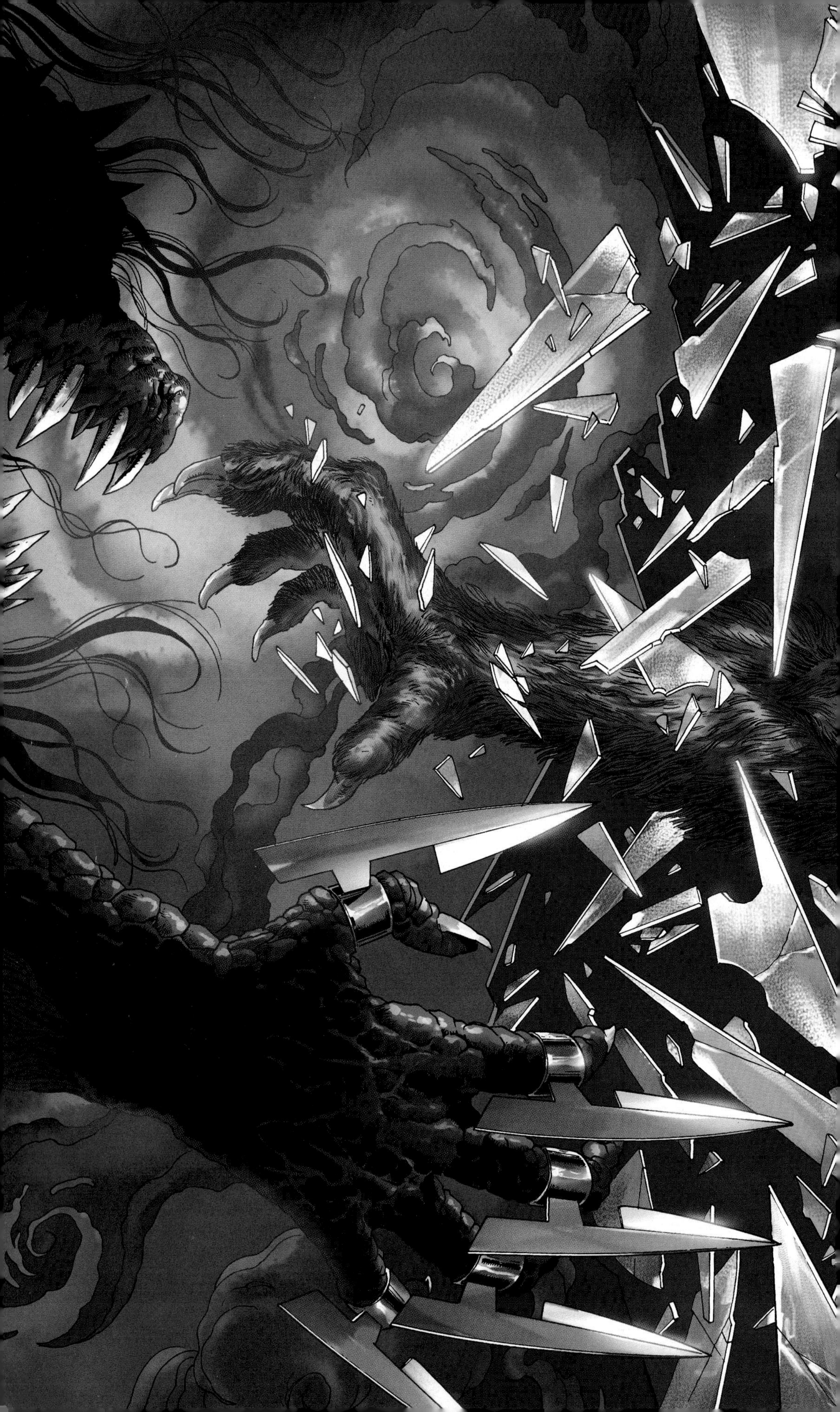

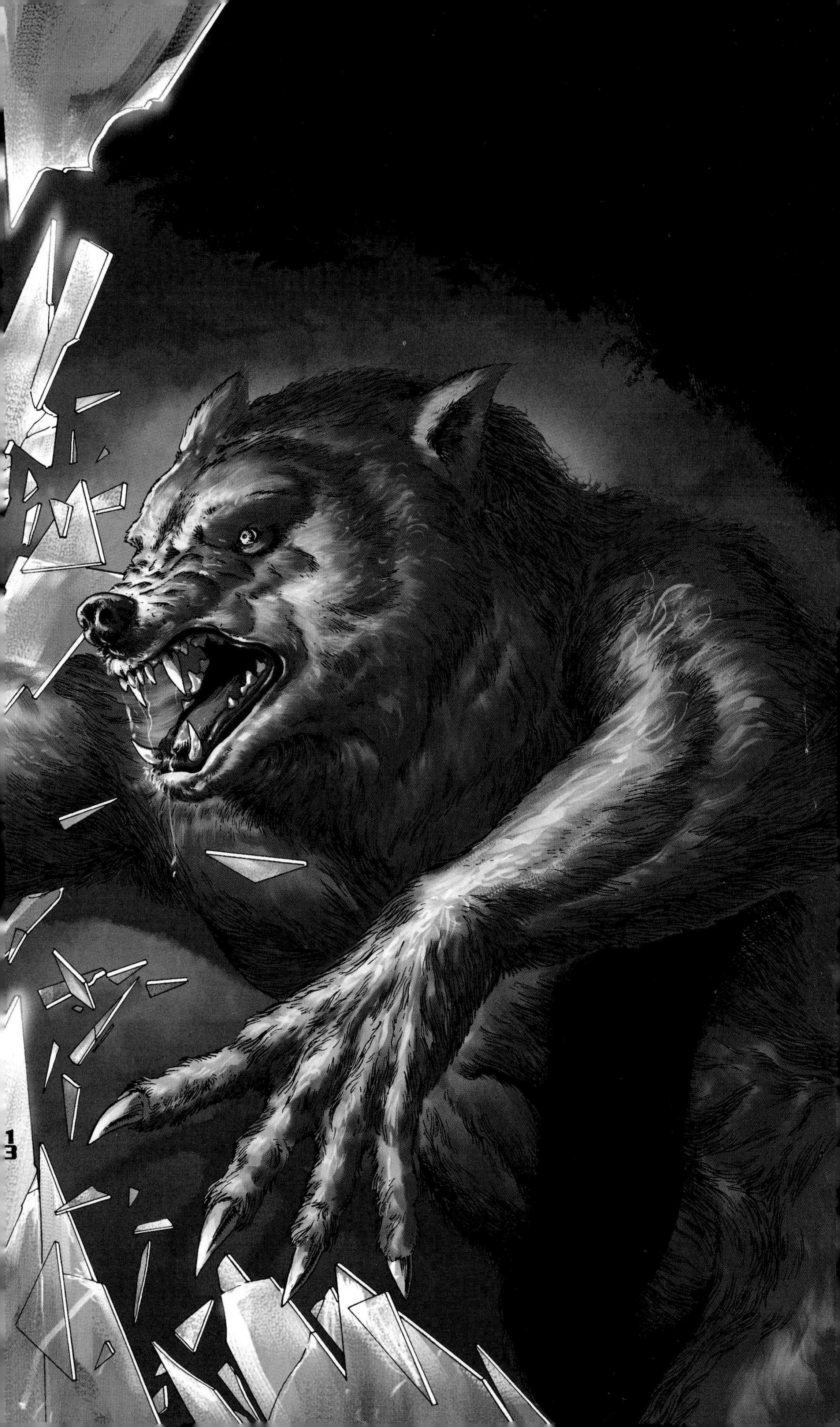

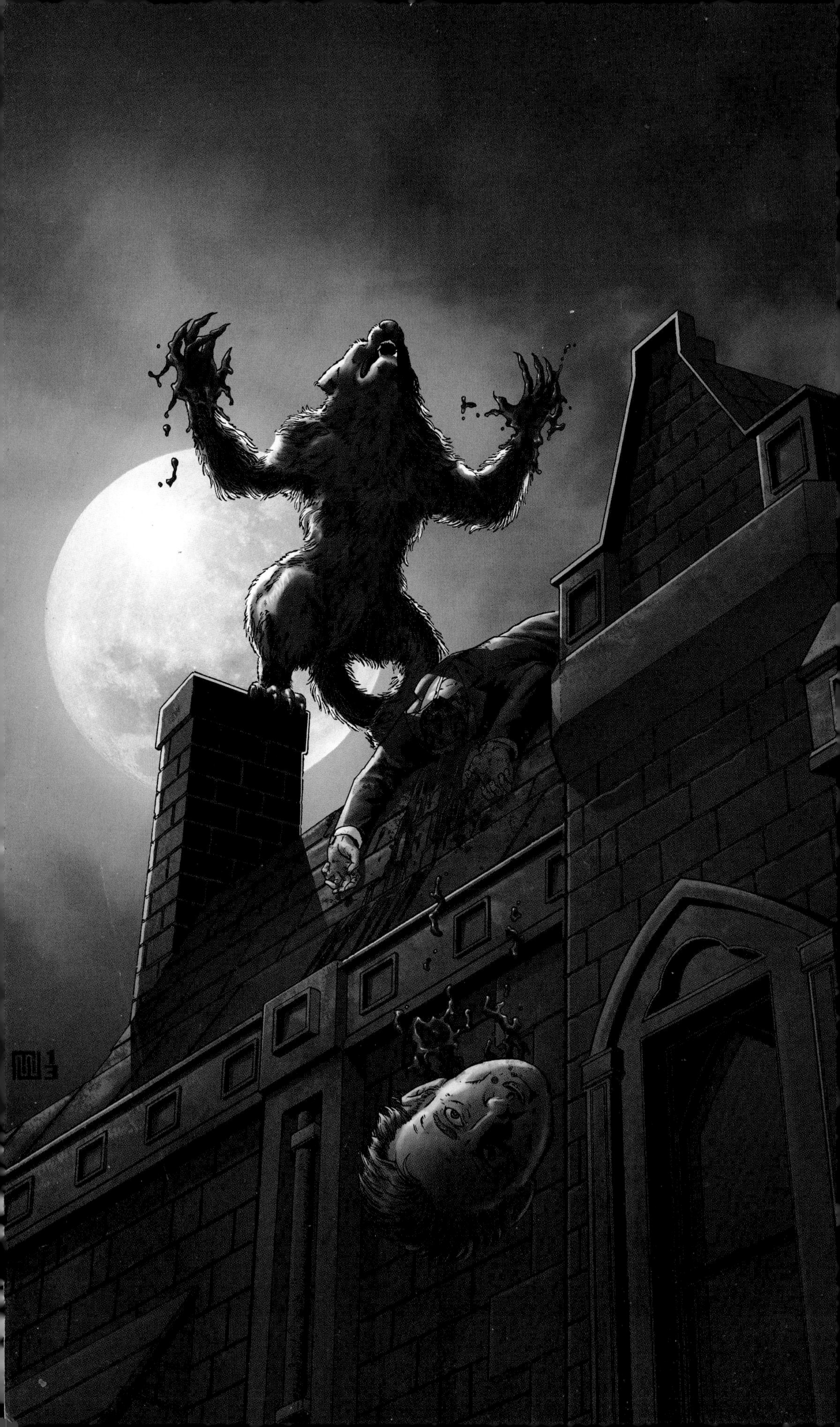